SALES CYBERNETICS

The Psychology of Selling

BY
BRIAN ADAMS

Published by
Melvin Powers
WILSHIRE BOOK COMPANY
12015 Sherman Road
No. Hollywood, California 91605
Telephone: (213) 875-1711 / (818) 983-1105

Library of Congress Catalog Card Number: 85-051180

ISBN 0-87980-412-2

Printed in the United States of America

By the same author: HOW TO SUCCEED.

Foreword

It isn't often that a publisher can honestly say that the book he is introducing is the best one on a particular topic that he has ever read. This is one of those rare occasions. *Sales Cybernetics* is the best book that I've read on the psychology of selling. And I've read a lot of them.

Sales Cybernetics draws its foundation from the "bible" of self-improvement — the classic *Psycho-Cybernetics* by Dr. Maxwell Maltz. Now the powerful principles of self-image psychology are focused by Brian Adams into the scientific techniques of motivational selling. It is my hope that the millions of persons who gained new ways of improving their personalities and erasing negative habit patterns from *Psycho-Cybernetics* will reap the same benefits from this new offering. In short, I hope it will open the way to new riches in your life, personally and financially.

Few things contribute more to an individual's well-being and sense of self-worth than his ability to stand on his own two feet, to achieve independence for himself and the ones he loves. Personal independence is difficult to attain without financial independence. Such independence can only come from your ability to make money. The more you make, the more your self-image will rise. I don't mean this to sound crass or mercenary, but it is undeniably true that one of the greatest joys in life is knowing that you are financially secure. I want you to be worth more by the time you finish reading this book. I want you to be able to make a lot more money; not just a fraction of what you earn at present, but *many times* more.

If you are content drawing an average salary for the rest of your life, accepting the fact that you will only have just enough to "get by," this book is not for you. But if you want your self-image *and* your bank balance to soar, study the time-proven, thoroughly researched methods of *Sales Cybernetics*.

There is only one area in the work force where you stand an excellent chance of making big money. That area is *business*. The great success stories of men like Carnegie, Rockefeller, Ford, and now Iacocca all spring from the field of business.

When I was starting in business, the giant corporations of America seemed overwhelming. There was no way I thought I could achieve the same greatness. But today, I have achieved some of that status for myself. I own a publishing company valued at millions of dollars.

How did I do this? By realizing two all-important things. First, I saw that success in business is primarily related to sales. All the rest is window dressing. The buildings, the staff, the logo, the letterhead, the image, and the advertising are there for only one reason — to sell a product.

Second, I saw that the art of sales is the art of interpersonal relationships. If people believe in you, they will believe in your product. I found that *Sales Cybernetics* explains how to sell both yourself and your product better than anything I've read. It so validated what I personally had learned, and so inspired me, that I was eager to share its secrets with the millions of persons who have bought my other books.

Written by an internationally acclaimed trainer in salesmanship at all levels of business, *Sales Cybernetics* exhaustively covers sound professional advice while putting sales techniques into a new, dynamic framework that works to produce electrifying results. It is action-oriented from the very beginning, a masterful synthesis of 15 proven formulas for getting people to say "yes" to you and your product. This "yes" can translate into untold dollars to anyone who puts the principles to work.

The first two formulas lay the groundwork by using computer programming principles to increase your sales productivity. Effective sales communication comes about through programming persuasive attitudes into your mental computer. An extremely important point is brought out in the discussion of the third formula; namely, that a poor concept of yourself is the biggest contributor to your failure. The chapter devoted to this formula shows you how to raise your self-image and match it with a better reality.

What you believe manifests itself in what you do. This is also true of your customer. If you wish to make a sale, it's important to know the belief system of your client — what motivates him to buy. Mr. Adams presents one of the best analyses of buying motives I have ever seen, and a powerful listing of the traits necessary to being a dynamic seller.

Further formulas tell you how to "get through" to people by making them like you; analyze the changing public tastes and preferences to make certain your product is always in demand; and prospect the market to find new avenues of business.

A truly extraordinary section is the one on how to handle objections through the psychology of harmonious human relationships. Blocks to your making a sale can be eliminated by using such techniques as *capitalizing,* making objections work in your favor, and *indirect denial,* a "yes-but" formula that lets you outflank your prospect's reasons for not buying by diverting his attention to why he *should* buy.

A book such as this is the result not only of many years of the author's experience, but lifetimes of experience of the most successful people in the business world. It is full of practical tips and secrets from leading authorities on how to increase sales. Following this advice can save you years in costly mistakes and help you start making big money. I believe that there is no substitute for experience in the field. This book is not meant to be such a substitute but, rather, a guide to potentiating your experience—making it maximally effective and giving you time to make more sales and more money than you ever dreamed possible.

Sales Cybernetics contains aids to sales of every description, including many illuminating case histories. Read it carefully. Follow precisely the principles laid down and deliberately program yourself to sell until your subconscious mind takes over and makes you an "automatic" supersalesperson.

Brian Adams has written a book to show you how to *help yourself* to make more sales. You will have to exert the effort required to implement the principles. If you do, I can promise that the results will come back manyfold in proportion to the effort needed to produce them. These principles have helped thousands, and I have every confidence that they will now help you. Get ready. You are about to embark on the road to riches.

Melvin Powers
Publisher, Wilshire Book Company

HOW THIS BOOK CAN DEVELOP
YOUR POWER OF PERSUASION

Self power and the ability to *effectively* communicate and motivate are the most sought-after attributes by sales people everywhere. Dynamic image qualities open the doors to wonderful opportunities and help to make your life a (creatively) productive, joyous and outstandingly successful one. The techniques to achieve these ideals are set forth in this book.

SALES CYBERNETICS was prepared in response to a demand by clients, students, training officers and sales executives for a practical, concise book on communication and motivation techniques to meet today's ever-changing sales markets. With these specific requests in mind, I have written this book on the *psychology of selling*.

Scientific salesmanship involves the understanding and often the changing of human behavior patterns. The computer-age salesman must, by necessity, become a practical psychologist, as he is dealing with human emotions—with attitudes and responses: customer urges, desires, needs, fears, frustrations, suspicions, prejudices, habits and moods. The better the understanding of *people* the greater the success in selling, for selling is a *people business*.

This book clearly and dramatically shows you how to identify and understand certain behavior patterns in your own self as well as the 'self' of others. By applying your new-found knowledge you will reap immediate results in your personal dealings with those you live, work and do business with. You will become more tolerant and understanding of the problems of others; you will gather and enjoy a wider circle of friends; you will discover the joy and personal satisfaction of scientific and psychological selling. Your income will rise in leaps and bounds as you join the ranks of professional *master* salesmen.

This book is designed to teach you that your subconscious powers are your secret keys to success in selling. You will learn how to tap the 'infinite source' within you to get the job you want and the increase in income you desire. You will learn how to meet and overcome the frustrations, fears and challenges of life. Each chapter leads you step-by-step, in a very practical way, to the culmination of your life-long dreams.

I have taught these simple truths in the art of communication and human relations to hundreds of sales men and women in Australia, Canada and the United States. In lectures, training sessions and seminars, conferences and conventions, I have watched successful results manifest for students who put into practise the winning formulas now presented in this book.

The scientific communication and motivation principles are not restricted to those in the selling profession. Men and women from every level of society can discover, use and benefit from the mysterious but very real *power of persuasion*: bankers, stenographers, students, medical doctors, actors, models, nurses, teachers, taxi drivers, telephone operators, police officers, personnel managers, housewives, mechanics, politicians. The rewards are:

—Respect, recognition and public acclaim
—New vitality, health and happiness
—New friendships
—Harmonious business relationships
—Greater job opportunities
—Increase in income
—Freedom from self criticism
—A brighter personality
—Self confidence and control
—Greater awareness of the needs of others
—A more affirmative, stronger YOU

SALES CYBERNETICS uses computer programming principles to release your brain's full capacity. It is a dramatic new method to self-motivate greater sales productivity and profitability.

The brain and its nervous system are under the automatic control of your mind. By programming correct attitudes into your (mental) computer, right actions come about.

A computer can guide a missile into outer space and back. A large computer has about 40,000 storage cells. Your brain is a much more complex instrument, it has about *ten billion* storage cells. Yet, chances are, you use but a fraction of its true potential.

Read this book carefully and often. Make a study of it. Put into practise the (mind) computer techniques suggested and you will attract wonderful opportunities for successful living.

From chapter one, we will begin a psychology-oriented program in *effective* sales communication and persuasion.

BRIAN ADAMS

SALES CYBERNETICS FORMULAS

The Author

Brian Adams' career reads like a page from his own book. He is an accomplished actor-writer-director. At the age of twenty-three he owned a chain of newspapers and a radio and television production company in Canada. He is an international lecturer on success and has hosted his own TV programs in Canada, America and Australia.

Born in Australia, he began his career as a copy writer for a Sydney advertising agency. Later he left on a soldier-of-fortune life that took him to many countries in the East, in Europe and to America.

After an absence of 15 years, Brian Adams was brought back to Australia by Sydney's Channel 10 to host their "Tonight" show for a year. Recently he set up BRIAD PRODUCTIONS AUSTRALIA to produce TV and film programs.

As a lecturer, he has conducted numerous seminars on 'salesmanship', the 'self image' and related success topics both in Sydney and abroad. In fact, he is considered one of the top ten motivational speakers in the United States. He has an impressive list of speaking credits which includes companies, men's and women's clubs, chambers of commerce and colleges.

Much of the lecture material is included in this book along with proven success techniques of other successful individuals.

Brian Adams knows the ingredients for health, happiness and prosperity and this book gives YOU the key for the expansion of YOUR life. At present he is working on another title—"Grow Rich with Your Million Dollar Mind".

BOOK ONE

I have often heard the term 'luck' used to explain the success of others. However, I prefer to think of so-called luck as solid preparation and the 'seeing-through' of one's endeavors to a final (successful) conclusion.

LAYING THE FOUNDATIONS FOR A SUCCESSFUL SALES CAREER

Affirmative Ideas in this Chapter

6

1

HOW TO USE THIS BOOK AS A WORKING MANUAL

If you're really serious about enhancing your career in selling, you'll use this book as a working manual, keeping it handy and reading it in the various ways I'm going to suggest. It will become a ready-reference manual, an effective hand book on every facet of professional selling. It is designed to inform, guide and motivate you to bring about personal success in your chosen field.

This book deals with the new science of psychological selling step-by-step. Therefore, do not skim through or skip sections attempting to pick out ideas. Half reading this book will be of little benefit. Read the chapters in sequence. As you study each, you will find the *whole* of the **SALES CYBERNETICS** philosophy unfolding.

It is important that you comprehend the application of the formulas in each chapter before moving on to the next. The cybernetic and psychological techniques are practical and are meant to be applied as you go about your normal activities each day. Behavior is learned; a skill is learned and developed and so too is the art of selling. You can easily *develop* the ability to communicate and motivate. Your development comes with practise and experience. And *results* always match the degree of *effort* put forth. Small effort (study, practise, application) returns small benefits (position, income, creative satisfaction).

Embark upon this program with a definite end result in mind. Select your object of attainment, write it down on a card and place the card within the covers of this book. Know *why* you're reading this book on psychological selling; know *what* you want it to do for you and *when*. Be specific. Unclear desires seldom see the light of day.

High achievement requires that you work at it patiently, persistently and with a sense of purpose. Support your desires with confidence in your ability to get from life the things you want. It will mean repetition of effort, persistent attention to the things that must be done. Once your attention is focused on your desired goals you will find yourself becoming totally involved and dedicated to the success of your life-long dreams and aspirations. And that's the secret of making *Sales Cybernetics* work: *dedicated effort, study and stick-to-itiveness.*

HOW TO IMPROVE YOUR MEMORY AND RETAIN WHAT YOU READ

The key to retaining what you read is discipline of thought movement. Control the movement of your mind. Do not allow random thoughts or unrelated ideas to enter your consciousness and interrupt the flow of ideas emanating from your reading material. Sit comfortably in a room free from the chatter of others. Turn off the radio or television. Avoid daydreaming. *Concentrate* on what you are reading. Distractions cause reading delay and poor comprehension. Put yourself in charge of your thoughts. Become *involved* in the subject matter you are reading. And remember: *ideas sink in slowly.* Superficial learning is not lasting.

Re-read the topic to be learned until key ideas sink in to your subconscious mind. Once the subconscious accepts an idea it retains it.

Memory is a range of processes: impression, recognition, recall. Memory improvement comes to those who are *mentally alert.* To listen intently, to learn, to become impressed with something, is to achieve greater efficiency in the methods of remembering. The most common reasons for 'forgetting' are: disinterest and daydreaming. This can become a hazard in your social life and a disaster in your business dealings.

Don't admit to yourself (or others) that you suffer from so-called 'poor memory'. There's no such malady; there *is* a condition known as *lazy listening.* Far too many people—particularly salesmen—half listen when introduced to others or when taking messages and instructions. It's only to be expected that the name or message given is quickly forgotten or distorted. The cure for lazy listening is to pay attention, concentrate and absorb the things being told to you. Concentration is the key to remembering important dates, places, events, names and ideas connected with the material you are reading. Underscore or circle them with a colored-lead pencil then memorize them.

Apply the five easy-remembering and improved comprehension techniques each time you begin a reading program. Don't squander reading time—*concentrate!* And you will absorb and retain what you read.

---

5 TECHNIQUES FOR IMPROVING COMPREHENSION AND MEMORY

1. *Eliminate distractions—sit comfortably in a quiet area.*
2. *Do not attempt to memorize material when tired or ill.*
3. *Discipline thoughts—concentrate—become involved.*
4. *Do not skim through material—read page-by-page.*
5. *Use 'associations' when storing ideas in your memory vault: paint vivid mental pictures of people—places—things.*

HOW TO USE THE 3-STAGE ANALYSIS TECHNIQUE TO MAKE THIS BOOK PAY OFF

Reading a book of this nature can pay handsome dividends when you know what to look for. The major aim is to discover the author's intent or the *pay-off message.* In the case of this book, it's the problems associated with sales communication and motivation and how to go about solving them. Look for action techniques, analyze them and put them to work.

Read this book in the manner suggested and you'll gain maximum advantage from the common-sense philosophy and principles it presents.

1—SCAN: quickly read through **SALES CYBERNETICS** page-by-page without skipping paragraphs or chapters. The purpose of this quick reading is to grasp the *central theme.* Three questions should be answered at the conclusion of the first reading. They are:

1. What is this book about?
2. Can it assist your specific needs?
3. When, where and how will you put these techniques to work?

The *fast* first reading will help to give you an overall view of your program. It will help you to visualize each part falling into place to make up the *whole.*

2—PREVIEW AND UNDERSCORE: read the book again. This time at a slower reading rate. Search for the author's intent. What is the 'pay-off' message? What special philosophy on the art of communication and motivation is being expounded? Separate facts from opinions. Relate other philosophies and techniques you may have read to those put forth in this book. Again, don't skip over any areas. Reading line-by-line, page-by-page, chapter-by-chapter is the only way to assure complete understanding of the text.

Underscoring is a worthwhile habit to form. It saves hunting through chapters to find specific ideas you want to re-read. Use a colored-lead pencil and score *through* the line or *under* the line of all important passages. A book of this kind is meant to be read repeatedly. Powerful techniques and ideas will impress you; the underscoring procedure will assure the ready-availability of them. It is a good idea to copy underscored ideas on to 3 x 5 cards and carry several cards with you each day as ready-reference guide to sales success.

3—REVIEW: read the book a third time and analyze its message. *Evaluate* the philosophy. Can the ideas and techniques be individualized and personalized to your own specific needs? Look for the possible hooks indicating courses of action that should be taken in your quest for success in selling. Adapt the ideas in each chapter to personal needs and begin applying them immediately.

Purchase a loose-leaf note book and jot down selected thoughts, specific ideas and formulas gathered from **SALES CYBERNETICS**. It's surprising how one idea will trigger off another idea—possibly a better one. The purpose of the three-stage reading technique and use of a note book is to get you firmly engrossed in the cybernetic system of doing things. Self motivation requires total involvement in action systems geared to strengthen your personal commitment to career objectives.

AN INSIGHT INTO THE CREATIVE WORLD OF SELLING

The men who head the list of the top personal tax payers (more often than not) are specialty salesmen. In more than 80 per cent of all American, Canadian and Australian companies, 8 out of 10 executives have been selected from the sales field. In the free world, approximately one-third of the working population is engaged in direct selling. It is a noble profession and one which helps to contribute an immense amount to the economy of the nation it serves.

Selling is a way of life. It teaches responsibility, mental alertness and how to get along with people. There are many rewards for the honest salesman: respect and recognition as a responsible and useful member of society, greater income, better human relationships and a more joyful, creative existence. The more one *gives* to the profession the more is returned in terms of mental, emotional and financial rewards.

I have witnessed amazing changes in the lives of men and women who have attended my Sales Cybernetics training courses. From humble beginnings, many have risen to high ranks of office. They have come from all levels of society: bank clerks, policemen, teachers, taxi drivers, actors, electricians, carpenters, boilermakers, sportsmen, mechanics, accountants, bricklayers, pharmacy assistants, housewives, and university students. These people discovered that their destiny is in their own hands and that by thinking and acting from the stand-point of universal principle, a joyful, productive and financially rewarding career in selling can be achieved.

DEFINING THE ROLE OF THE COMPUTER-AGE SALESMAN

The computer-age motivator is a counselor to his customers and clients. He has a genuine desire to help others to financial success. Therefore, wisdom dictates that he conduct all his negotiations with a sense of fair play. Honesty is the one policy he must never compromise. Trick selling methods, high pressure maneuvers and unethical dealings are not tolerated by ethical company managements. There is no place in the professional ranks for the dishonest man.

As an adviser he must possess specialized knowledge of his company's product (service) so that he can relate this to his customers' needs. An excellent command of the English language, including a good vocabulary is a prerequisite. Words are the salesman's tools of trade which he must use in the best possible way to communicate his sales message.

The study of human behavior patterns—needs, habits, emotions—is the basis of scientific selling and must be undertaken by those desiring to progress beyond the stage of 'order taker'. Self analysis is the key to understanding the motives and actions of others. *Know thyself.* In knowing the 'personal self', it is easier to understand the 'self' of others: *why* they are as they are; *what* motivates them to certain action and *how* they can be motivated toward a definite end result.

---

10 SPECIALIZED ABILITIES OF THE SALES PRO

- ☐ **1.** The art of communication and motivation.
- ☐ **2.** The art of counseling and servicing the needs of clients.
- ☐ **3.** The art of negotiation.
- ☐ **4.** The art of interviewing and gaining market information.
- ☐ **5.** The ability to gather technical and appealing product facts.
- ☐ **6.** The ability to 'read' the thought patterns of others.
- ☐ **7.** The ability to *act* and *react* confidently in all situations.
- ☐ **8.** The ability to solve problems and make right decisions.
- ☐ **9.** The wisdom to think and act affirmatively.
- ☐ **10.** The mental alertness to grasp opportunities quickly.

THE STRINGENT PERSONAL REQUIREMENTS OF THE MASTER SALESMAN

> *'The shortest and surest way to live with honor in the world, is to be in reality what we would appear to be; all human virtues increase and strengthen themselves by the practice and experience of them.'*
>
> SOCRATES

The professional salesman is an individual who has chosen selling as his life-work. He is dedicated to improving his position in this field of endeavor and jealously guards his professional reputation. He is conscientiously honest, reliable and diligent in the application of his duties. He is a sensitive human being, capable of reacting instantaneously and accurately to the many impulses—negative or affirmative—a customer or employer may generate. He is efficient and exacting in the handling of any difficult sales situation concerning his company policy, product or service. He is a person more concerned with *fulfilling needs* than 'selling' things. And he is always aware of his obligations to his clients and customers.

The professional salesman loves to meet people. He is a good mixer, both socially and in business circles. He is a character analyst, able to read the mood patterns and personality traits of those he must do business with.

The essential qualities required of the 'pro' salesman are worthy of deep study and analysis by every individual wishing to enter the selling profession. Personality improvement and strong character development are the two most important steps to be undertaken. They are essential ingredients for success in selling.

It will be noticed that the rating chart listing '20 Personal Attributes' forms a 'state of mind'. An individual's state of mind or attitude, shapes his character and personality and determines his destiny. A slovenly attitude breeds slovenly living conditions. A healthy, affirmative attitude manifests positive living conditions. It is *attitude* that separates the professional salesman from the order taker.

WHEN TO MAKE THAT ALL-IMPORTANT JOB CHANGE

It is a well-reported fact that approximately 40 per cent of the nation's work force are in the wrong jobs or despise the work they are being paid to carry out and secretly yearn for an opportunity to develop and exploit their creative talents in other areas of employment. This percentage, to my way of thinking, is a conservative one. I'd place it much higher. During the past 15 years I've met thousands of men and women while on my world lecture tours and I cannot remember one person admitting total satisfaction with his or her creative development, conditions of employment and standard of living.

Are you in the right job, doing the things you'd like to be doing? Are you exploiting your true potential? Do you carry out your job duties and assignments efficiently? Are you happy in your present job situation? Do you wish—deep down—that someone would wave a magic wand and *change* the conditions of your life? If you answer 'yes' to any one of these questions, then the time to make direct moves to change the course of your life is *right now!*

'Security' is the reason given by many people when asked why they do not seek a new form of employment. Some may choose to call it security. I call it *insecurity*. The man who has confidence in his own capabilities will always support them by taking the necessary chances and challenges when a 'move-up' is desired. If you're not willing to gamble on yourself then you cannot expect to reap self-satisfying rewards in life.

HOW TO GET OUT OF A JOB RUT

Sit quietly and analyze your present situation. Ask yourself the following questions and write down the answers:

1. What do I *really* want to do in life? (What type of sales job?)

2. What can I give in return if I get the job I desire?

3. What financial and other sacrifices must I make to get what I want?

4. What is at stake if I quit my present job?

5. How long can I get by without regular income?

6. What secondary scheme (part time employment) can I become involved in if I do not get what I want quickly?

7. Who can help me in my quest for a better job?

8. Can I count on the support of my wife and family?

9. What special skills or training will I require in the job I seek?

10. What excuses, alibis and fears must I reject before I make a positive move?

The road to success begins with that *first step*. Cease complaining—*do* something about your present poor state of affairs—CHANGE THEM! Do not listen to the opinions of others unless they are experts and qualified to give you advice. It never ceases to amaze me how many people blindly follow the suggestions of grandma, the next door neighbor, friends or anyone asked to put in his two cents worth of advice. *Listen to your own conscience.* Stand on your own two feet. Boldly make decisions and carry them out. If wrong, you'll have yourself to blame—and *only* yourself. You cannot 'grow' in life unless you experience some failures along with successes.

Here's the key to making that all-important job change. Answer and *act* upon these two vital questions:

1. Do you wish to go through the rest of your life doing what you are *now* doing?

2. If not, what are you going to do about it and *when?*

RATING TEST

20 PERSONAL ATTRIBUTES

		YES√	NO√
1.	DEDICATED	☐	☐
2.	IMAGINATIVE	☐	☐
3.	DISCIPLINED	☐	☐
4.	DECISIVE	☐	☐
5.	FORGIVING	☐	☐
6.	GENEROUS	☐	☐
7.	UNSELFISH	☐	☐
8.	TOLERANT	☐	☐
9.	DEPENDABLE	☐	☐
10.	INDUSTRIOUS	☐	☐
11.	SINCERE	☐	☐
12.	TACTFUL	☐	☐
13.	COURTEOUS	☐	☐
14.	RESPONSIBLE	☐	☐
15.	LOYAL	☐	☐
16.	COMPASSIONATE	☐	☐
17.	SELF APPRECIATIVE	☐	☐
18.	PERSONAL INTEGRITY	☐	☐
19.	HIGH IDEALS	☐	☐
20.	COURAGE OF CONVICTIONS	☐	☐

Score: _____

 Place a check-mark alongside each attribute best describing your own personality and character. A score of 20 'yes' points is your foundation for a promising career in selling. Each 'no' answer requires analysis and correction. Personality and character deficiencies are the mark of the failure-type salesman.

HOW TO SELECT AN ACTION COMPANY

Company selection should be closely looked at by those making a job change. The important areas to be analyzed are:

1. Is the company on the 'rise'? What is its growth potential?
2. Is it living up to its policy and fulfilling its purpose?
3. What are the chances of promotion? What is the basis of promotion?
4. What type of employee does it hire?
5. Are executives selected from within the company or hired from other companies?
6. Does the company have a training program?
7. Are there contributing medical and retirement schemes, discounts on goods purchased, a car supplied, adequate commission paid?
8. What is the financial structure of the company?
9. Does the company have adequate market research, advertising facilities and expenditures available?
10. Is there proper and adequate communication between management and staff?

These questions are not as difficult or as embarrassing to find the answers to as one might imagine. Soliciting background information on a potential employer is just as much your right as it is the right of the employer to check your credentials. It's very much like choosing a marriage partner: *both* should be certain of the move before making a commitment.

Begin your company information search at the stock exchange in your city (or stockbroker). A large public company, if listed on the exchange, will have its trading and company structure information available in report form. The cost of this small brochure or booklet is nominal. If the company you are investigating is not listed on the stock exchange, call the company secretary, sales manager or personnel director. Explain that you are interested in submitting an application for employment and would like as much information as possible on their company policy and products or services marketed.

If the company is a manufacturer of products, visit retail stores carrying their lines and chat with the various sales clerks selling them. If possible, use their products and make a list of the *plus-factors* associated with each. These products might include: shaving cream, toothpaste, razor blades, coffee, tea, shoes, shirts, radios, recordings, shoe polish, ice cream, stationery lines, sporting goods, etc.

LARGE COMPANY Vs SMALL

When deciding the size of company to join, keep in mind 'growth' potential. A small company offers its employees the challenge of helping to build that company into a bigger and better concern. As the company grows financially and in stature, its employees share in the success environment they helped to bring about.

THE ADVANTAGES OF WORKING FOR A SMALL COMPANY

- ☐ Closer relationship with management.
- ☐ More rapid advancement.
- ☐ Opportunity to make own decisions and exert more initiative.
- ☐ Less 'pressure' from management.
- ☐ Larger territory available.
- ☐ Possibility of partnership or directorship being offered.
- ☐ Friendly working atmosphere—less hurried.
- ☐ Flexible salary and commission arrangements.

DISADVANTAGES

- ☐ Less likely that company and product image promoted and known.
- ☐ Little or no advertising budget.
- ☐ Fewer special promotions mounted as sales aids.
- ☐ Little or no market research information gathered.
- ☐ Less financial stability if company under-capitalized.
- ☐ Little chance of management promotion if family business.
- ☐ Little or no company training program available.
- ☐ Less job security.
- ☐ Fewer organized sales meetings and problem solving sessions.

THE ADVANTAGES OF WORKING FOR A LARGE COMPANY

- ☐ Advertising budget often quite large.
- ☐ Better company and product image and public acceptance.
- ☐ Support through team efforts of advertising—promotion—sales departments.
- ☐ Greater job security.
- ☐ Greater company financial stability.
- ☐ Continuous market research information available.
- ☐ Regular sales meetings and problem solving sessions.
- ☐ Opportunity to travel.
- ☐ Stable management.
- ☐ More product testing—research and development.
- ☐ Regular training programmes.

DISADVANTAGES

- ☐ Team work essential—less individual freedom.
- ☐ Smaller territory allotment.
- ☐ Less opportunity of communicating with top management.
- ☐ Pressure often exerted to hit sales targets.
- ☐ Relationships tend to be more impersonal.
- ☐ Slower promotion if based on seniority.
- ☐ Usually set salary and commission basis—less pay flexibility.

A large organization offers slightly better job security, advertising, market research and training advantages and the benefit of a pre-sold company and product image. Regular sales meetings and company training programs help to promote a team spirit and they are a motivating force to greater productivity. Perhaps one disadvantage of working for a large company is the difficulty of communicating with senior management. Major decisions are quite often the responsibility of a board of directors and these are men the sales team rarely gets to meet.

The attribute you possess of great value to a company, regardless of its size, is your human potential: your ability to *think* accurately; your ability to *develop* new ideas and concepts; your ability to *produce* more things in a better way. Your ability to perform successfully in a given situation is an open invitation to quality employment in a small *or* large company structure. Your real value is your performance level. The more you can produce for an organization the greater will be your value to it. It's axiomatic that your efforts produce their own rewards.

WHEN TO REJECT A JOB OFFER FROM LARGE OR SMALL COMPANY

The final choice of company selection should be decided *only* after a thorough investigation has been carried out to determine whether your skills, experience and temperament are best suited to the needs of the potential employer. If they aren't, then you'd be wise to reject an offer of employment. A mis-match of skills to requirements could bring an early dismissal.

Pleasant working conditions, cordial staff relationships, high pay, job satisfaction and the like, are important points to consider. But in the final analysis, any lasting relationship with an employer must depend on your ability to fulfill his specific reasons for hiring you. It boils down to: *can you do the job and if so, how well?*

The annual turnover of sales staff (Australia and USA) averages 22 per cent. In some industries the figure races up to an alarming 80 per cent. When greater care is exercised in job matching (abilities to requirements), annual turnover of staff will reduce considerably.

Use the *rating chart* to evaluate advantages and disadvantages associated with small and large organizational structures. As a point of reference, a *small* company is one employing up to 50 employees. A *medium-size* company 50 to 100 employees and a *large* company 100 employees and over.

ANSWERING THE SALES JOB ADVERTISEMENT

Search the classified columns of your city newspaper and mark-off sales positions which appeal to you. Do not apply for positions unless you are certain that you are capable of filling the requirements.

Should the information in an advertisement be insufficient, tele- phone the company (or management consultant) and find out exactly what the job entails before committing yourself to an interview. This saves valuable time for both you and the prospective employer.

Many companies do not write good advertisements detailing the qualifications they seek. A poorly-worded advertisement brings a flood of enquiries from the wrong kinds of people. This results in time-wasting interviews which do little to improve the public image of the company responsible.

A well-worded advertisement should exclude responses from obviously unqualified people. After all, the purpose of placing an advertisement is to recruit highly-suited applicants. A successful advertisement should include:

(a) Age range.
(b) Experience required.
(c) Degree of past success necessary.
(d) Education and other training qualifications needed.
(e) Brief description of duties.
(f) How to apply: phone or write.

MAKING AN APPOINTMENT BY PHONE: applicants requesting an interview are checked as to their telephone technique and how articulately they express themselves during the conversation. Pleasant sounding voice, charm of manner, politeness are *all* noted during the brief phone discussion. Those who pass this initial screening are given an appointment for a first interview screening.

Be sure you have free time available if an interview date and time are granted. (Be prepared to attend an interview on a few hours notice.) Give brief reasons why you feel you are a suitable applicant. Whet the appetite of the phone interviewer just enough to secure a meeting. Don't be brash or demanding. Don't oversell yourself or you'll be given a polite but firm 'goodbye'.

SECURING AN APPOINTMENT BY LETTER: as a general rule, all letters of application should be typed. The exception is when an employer asks you to reply in your own handwriting. He can tell a great deal about you from your wording and neatness of handwriting. The better the letter, the better your chances of being invited for an interview.

Spend time thinking about what you're going to write. A concise, 'punchy', neatly presented letter containing all relevant details indicates your ability to apply the same accuracy to your work. The following suggestions will help you to plan a letter of application:

(a) Outline your letter and refine it before making a final copy.
(b) Keep sentences brief.
(c) Check grammar and spelling.
(d) Present a reason *why* you should be considered.
(e) Give a brief indication of your qualifications.
(f) Request an interview date and time.
(g) Indicate that all details are in a resumé file enclosed with your letter.
(h) Type the final copy and check content before mailing.

SAMPLE APPLICATION LETTER

232 Beaumont Street,
Silver City, 2010 Victoria
Telephone: 323 2320

The Personnel Manager,
George Black Associates (Ltd.),
212 West End Avenue,
Silver City, 2010 Victoria.

Dear Sir:

Selling is a way of life for me. Since my immediate goal is to improve my present sales position, I am answering your advertisement in this morning's Star with the intention of meeting with you to discuss the sales position you are offering.

After making a study of your company and its objectives and policy, I feel quite justified in presenting to you my qualifications. I can more than satisfy your stringent requirements.

My experience in selling was gained in textiles. However, I have used your excellent range of products for many years and I am confident that I could sell them successfully.

I have completed several courses since completing a formal education and these include: public speaking; sales and marketing and speed reading.

I am 26 years of age, married with one child. My state of health is excellent. Further details are included in my resumé which is attached.

I am available for an interview any afternoon of this coming week. I look forward to meeting you at your earliest convenience.

Yours truly,

William Brian.

William Brian.

enc: resumé
 biography
 references
 report

Imagination is the rule, visualization the key to having your letter noticed and then acted upon. Use your imagination to communicate an effective message. Visualize the person who is to receive your letter. Can you see him sifting through dozens of other (application) letters? What is he looking for and what will impress him enough to call you for an interview? What type of letter would impress *you* if you were doing the job for him?

Keep your letter to a few paragraphs—six at the very most. The best letters of application are the shortest, neatest and most to the point. Sometimes two paragraphs are sufficient: one, applying for the position and indicating that details are attached; the second, requesting an interview.

Clever letter writing is like good advertising copy: it communicates ideas to bring a desired response. Your first objective is to motivate the reader to call you for an interview. If the form and content of your letter attracts his *attention,* arouses his *interest,* creates a *desire* to learn more about you, then your interview objective will be met.

HOW TO PREPARE AN EFFECTIVE APPLICATION FILE

An impressive application package giving all possible information on your qualifications and background gives you a head start on other applicants who front to the interview without adequate support material.

Prepare a *master file* from which copies can be made. The package should include:

1. A foolscap manila folder.
2. A single page resumé.
3. A single page biography.
4. A minimum of two references: character and business.
5. A small (passport-size) photograph.
6. A single page report, covering:
    (a) why you want to work for the company.
    (b) how you propose to service its needs.
7. Supporting documents: school credits or degrees earned. Certificates or diplomas awarded for special courses taken.

THE COVER: use a plain manila cover to enclose the various content pages. Type name, address and telephone number on the outside front cover.

THE RESUMÉ: follow the procedure in the 'sample resumé'. Be honest in listing previous positions held, courses taken and degrees earned. It is a simple matter for an employer to check credentials. Under 'previous positions' begin with current or most recent job held. Give *all* details of educational qualifications, experience, general interests, hobbies and sports played. If there is insufficient room on the page, write them on a separate sheet of paper with, 'See note attached' alongside the appropriate heading.

THE BIOGRAPHY: present a brief history of past achievements. Tell of aims and objectives and why you want a career in selling. This is an opportunity to give details of duties performed in previous jobs and indicating *how well* they were performed. Be specific. Be concise. Be accurate.

REFERENCES: two references are minimum: a personal reference from an important individual who has known you for a reasonable length of time and can attest to your character; a business reference from a previous employer indicating your performance record. It is not advisable to enclose too many references. They tend to make a file bulky. But keep them handy in case they are requested.

PICTURE: a passport-size picture is well worth inclusion. It is a reminder to the employer of the image you presented during your initial interview or an indication of your appearance and personality if you are yet to meet. Do not enclose 'backyard' snapshots. Visit a professional photography studio.

REPORT: give reasons why you wish to work for the company. The reasons should satisfy and fulfill the needs of the employer in relation to the position he is offering. Give an account of how you propose to sell his product or service. Do not take more than a page to write your report.

SUPPORTING DOCUMENTS: copies of all important documents supporting your claims to experience and background should be included. They are your professional credentials.

PRESENTATION: engage the services of a public stenographer to type your master file then have photocopies made. Check spelling and sentence construction. Use quality white bond foolscap-size paper. Enclose a business card if available.

MAILING: if the material is to be mailed, place it in a large manila envelope. Do not fold or crease the file. Place a sheet of stiff board inside the envelope to ensure the package arrives in good order. Type your name and address on the back of the envelope and mail 'special delivery'.

APPLICATION FORM: this is supplied by the company or consultant and often filled out prior to the interview. Don't be too hasty when writing your answers. Check misspelled words, poor handwriting which is difficult to read, omission of facts or false information. Take care when listing personal or business references—they will most likely be checked.

21

SAMPLE

RESUMÉ

NAME: .... PHOTO: attached

ADDRESS: .... TELEPHONE: ....

PLACE OF BIRTH: .... DATE OF BIRTH: ....

HEALTH: .... WEIGHT: .... HEIGHT: ....

MARITAL STATUS: (Note if engaged to be married.) ....

EDUCATION: (Name schools and universities attended. Give details of examinations passed and degrees held.) ....

SPECIAL TRAINING: (Special courses completed: technical, trades, business, professional.) ....

HOBBIES: ....

SPORTS: ....

UNION MEMBERSHIPS: ....

CLUB MEMBERSHIPS: ....

ASSOCIATIONS: ....

MILITARY SERVICE: ....

SPECIAL SKILLS: ....

SUMMARY OF OTHER
INFORMATION: ....

PREVIOUS POSITIONS: (List chronologically companies worked for and positions held. Detail special features of duties performed. Begin with current or most recent job.)

BIOGRAPHY: attached ....

REFERENCES: attached ....

NOTE: If information listed under one heading cannot be completed because of lack of space, do not carry it over to another page, but begin the next page with the new heading and particulars. Write, 'See note attached' alongside the appropriate heading on the Resumé Page.

BIOGRAPHY

JOHN Q. SMITH

SALES REPRESENTATIVE

BACKGROUND: More than 5 years intensive sales experience and significant achievement in developing a minor territory into the number one sales position for my company. Winner of two 'Best Sales' awards (1972-1973). Associate member of the Sales And Marketing Club.

EXPERIENCE: Two years with a manufacturer of vending machines. Began as a sales trainee and given a territory 6 months later. Two hundred new customers were signed in 18 months due to an effective prospecting method I devised. Left this position after being offered a sales job with more scope and challenge.

Three years with company marketing fire-fighting equipment. Began as junior salesman in team of 20. Promoted in one year to third position on the team due to new business brought in and high percentage of sales made in excess of target figures.

Quite often assist the sales manager at sales meetings and training sessions. My duties include speaking engagements to clubs and organizations.

I have always had a great interest in people and make friends easily. This helps considerably in my present position as many of my sales presentations are to groups.

I am furthering my career by attending a commercial sales training program which I expect to complete in June. I have an extensive library of books in the human relations, psychology and sales fields. Being an avid reader, I subscribe to several business journals and to a magazine devoted to international affairs.

My ambition is to develop my skills in communication and motivation and use them to reach the position of sales manager and eventually marketing director with a progressive company.

23

PLANNING THE INTERVIEW

Job interviews can be a nightmare for the uninitiated job seeker. The reason is *hidden fear*. And this negative emotion destroys the applicant's chance to project the major quality the prospective employer seeks in a sales representative: *confident personality*.

Fear can be controlled by carefully preparing *all* areas leading up to the interview. Knowing what you are going to say and how you will answer questions helps to eliminate the fear of performing poorly.

Make a list of possible questions you feel will be asked. Write down suitable answers. Play through the interview in your mind. Know *why* you are seeking this particular job with this company and what you hope to achieve for it. How will you go about your tasks? What salary do you require? Is your application file in readiness?

Solid preparation will support your claim to 'professionalism' in selling. It will help also, to remove the fear of failure at the designated time of the interview.

When planning answers to possible questions think in terms of 'specifics'—direct statements that enhance your position. Avoid small talk or being sidetracked by the interviewer. If the interview bogs down and you feel you can move it along, throw in a question or two of your own to lead the conversation back to important issues. A clever salesman will always take control of an interview if he sees that it is heading in the wrong direction.

Think of a pleasant or 'unique' opening remark to make when you are introduced to your interviewer. This helps to 'break-the-ice' and puts both of you in a friendly frame of mind. Opening remarks should seem spontaneous and natural. Your opening words should not sound contrived. They must fit your personality and speech style. Eliminate hackneyed expressions such as: 'Good morning, I'm here in response to your advertisement.' Be original—*THINK!*

ELIMINATING INTERVIEW NERVES

Natural tensions arising from 'fear of failing' strike just about everyone on that all-important day of the interview. Calming the nerves is no easy task, but it must be done if a successful meeting is to come about.

Affirmative thinking is the rule. Control your thoughts. Do not dwell on things negative. What you fear you attract. What you sincerely desire and believe in, you draw to you.

Unwind physically by taking a brisk walk prior to the interview. Take deep breaths as you walk and you'll find the 'butterflies' being smothered. Visualize a pleasant interview. See yourself shaking hands with the interviewer as he congratulates you on being selected for the job. If your mouth feels dry place a pinch of salt on the end of your tongue before entering the interviewer's office.

24

Write the following affirmation on a small card and carry it with you. Read the card while waiting for your interview.

3×5 CARD   CONFIDENCE BOOSTER

My qualities, skills and potentialities are in evidence and my prospective employer quickly responds to them by offering me the position I seek . . .

I know I am worthy and capable of high achievement in my chosen field of selling. I have everything to gain by being totally relaxed and confident. Success is mine. And mine *now*.

SELF CONFIDENCE—YOUR GREATEST INTERVIEW ALLY

Job selection is a two-way street. The employer seeks a particular calibre of person to fit his company's needs. The job applicant, a specific type of position and company to satisfy his creative and financial requirements. One party is *buying* services, the other *selling* them. If the match is beneficial to buyer *and* seller it puts them on equal ground.

Never attend a job interview 'hat-in-hand'. A shy, timid individual is virtually ignored. If you're presenting yourself as a salesman you can't afford to be ignored. You've got to project a dynamic self image. Don't confuse this with conceit. Self confidence elevates your personality and gains for you the respect of others. An overbearing, brash and conceited attitude is the worst enemy you could have.

During the all-important ninety seconds of *impression creation*, exude a personal power that puts you on the same plane (or higher) as your interviewer, no matter what title he may carry. The initial impact must be an apparent *distinctive personality*.

Whatever your aims in life, their success depends on your ability to 'control' people. Your self power is but a tool for accomplishing your aims—in this instance to secure the right job. An affirmative awareness of your *true* value will bring the desired confidence and control you seek and allow you to sell yourself effectively.

If you possess the qualifications expected of a sales professional then you have every right to meet the prospective employer on his level. You must not present yourself apologetically. When you talk or act apologetically others see you as lacking backbone. You must make people conscious of you in an affirmative way. Present yourself as a strong, self-assured, decisive, genuine and friendly individual.

25

LIKELY INTERVIEW QUESTIONS

- What do you know about our product (service) and company?
- Why do you want to be a salesman?
- Why do you wish to work for this company?
- What experience and background do you have in selling?
- What is your educational background?
- What sports do you play?
- What are your hobbies?
- Do you get along well with others?
- What salary are you expecting?
- What special training have you undertaken?
- Do you own your own home or are you renting or boarding?
- What is the state of your wardrobe?
- Do you own an automobile and if so what make and year model?
- What was the title of the last book you read?
- Do you belong to any community organizations?
- Do you hold union memberships?
- What clubs do you hold memberships in?
- Do you consider yourself a good salesman and if so why?
- What magazines and newspapers are on your regular reading list?
- Would you be prepared to undertake further training in this field?
- Do you find it easy to make your own decisions on major matters?
- Do you work best under supervision or alone?
- Are you under consideration for employment by any other company?
- What is your condition of health?
- Why are you leaving your present job?
- Are you an interesting conversationalist?
- What are your goals in life?
- Do you have any personal or family problems worrying you?
- Are you willing to travel to other states?
- When are you available to start?
- What kind of satisfaction do you seek from your new position?
- What are your major assets and weaknesses?
- Which of your past achievements are you proudest of?
- What's more important to you in a job—salary or opportunity?
- Tell me about your present job. Are you successful in it? If so, why are you leaving?
- Do you have other information that would be helpful?

GIVE YOUR APPEARANCE A FINAL CHECK BEFORE MEETING YOUR FUTURE BOSS

Your appearance creates the first impression—good or bad. Neatness and cleanliness are the two important factors in creating a favorable first impression. Be well groomed. Wear well-cut, conservative clothes. Make certain that your suit is well pressed, shirt and tie clean and tidy and shoes highly polished. Slip into a restroom in the building where the interview is to be held. Wash hands, straighten tie, comb hair into place, wipe scuff marks from shoes and check your overall appearance.

First impressions are often the most *important* impressions at job interviews. The way you dress could be a deciding factor. Your interviewer judges you from the moment you enter his office. Before you utter one word you have been assessed—primarily by your appearance. In person-to-person interviews, first quick impressions influence that most critical decision—to hire or *not* to hire.

Remember: impressions *really* matter—make the *first* one count.

DRESS AND GROOMING CHECK-LIST

☐ SUIT—well pressed, pocket flaps out, coat buttoned.
☐ SHIRT—all buttons in place, clean and tidy.
☐ TIE—conservative, clean, knot in place.
☐ SHOES—highly polished and in good repair.
☐ HAIR—clean, combed into place, reasonable length.
☐ FACE—scrubbed, clean shaven.
☐ HANDS—clean, free from perspiration.
☐ NAILS—clean, trimmed, shaped.
☐ TEETH—clean, free of food particles. (Breath free of alcohol or food odors.)

HANDLING THE JOB INTERVIEW

For the first time you are face-to-face with your prospective employer. The time has come to boldly step forward and create a powerful and thoroughly likeable self image.

As you meet your interviewer, introduce yourself in a clear, well-modulated, firm tone of voice. Smile, hold eye contact and silently project the thought: 'I like this man. He is my friend.' Take the initiative and give a firm handshake, drawing his hand slightly toward you. Don't sit or smoke until invited to do so. Use the interviewer's name frequently throughout the conversation. Don't slouch, fidget or mumble. Do not be nervous about asking for an indication of your prospects for getting the job.

Present your application file at the appropriate time. Do not overstay your welcome. Thank the interviewer for his time and ask when you will be advised of his decision.

USE THE SOFT-SELL TO MOTIVATE ACCEPTANCE

Overselling should be avoided. While projected enthusiasm can be contagious, it can also frighten some people. By all means be enthusiastic about your desire to expand your life but don't scare the interviewer by over-estimating your worth or making false claims as to your experience.

A management consultant friend suggests: 'Think through every question likely to arise. Then provide *acceptable* answers without hesitation to show you've anticipated and planned for the occasion. Present your ideas and reasons for wanting to work for the company in logical sequence. Don't say 'I know I can do the job'—state *why* and *how* you will do it.'

At the conclusion of the interview, sum up the more salient points —the *anticipated advantages* of your services to the company. Be careful to avoid an air of superiority when making your summation. This could influence the interviewer to decide against you because of your conceited attitude.

By putting yourself in the interviewer's shoes, by imagining how *you* would react were the positions reversed, you will be able to do a much better job of presenting your ideas and personality.

HOW TO HANDLE THE QUESTION RELATING TO EXPERIENCE

A word about that age-old question asked by interviewers: 'What selling experience do you have?' For the 'beginning' salesman this question usually rings the death bell.

There *is* a logical answer and it's this: 'Mr. Interviewer, I've had no direct experience selling your product. But I have had 25 years* experience dealing with people. As you are well aware, selling is a "people" business. And in this respect, I consider myself to be highly qualified. After all, communicating ideas and motivating people to accept them is the principal function of the sales representative. Gaining product knowledge is my responsibility and I will fulfill it immediately if I am employed. I am confident that I will be adept at presenting your product within two or three days, Mr. Interviewer. This is the experience I can bring to your organization and I believe it is the experience you are *really* seeking.'

Many potentially good salesmen have been lost because sales managers or personnel directors have insisted on 'selling experience'. Perhaps a better question to ask would be: 'Can you communicate ideas and get along well with people?' I'd prefer to hire a salesman who can sell ideas and get along with people than one who can't, even though the latter may have been in the selling field for 20 years or more.

* Refers to the actual age of the applicant.

INTERVIEW AIDS

- Anticipate Interview Questions And Prepare Answers
- Plan Wardrobe The Day Prior To Appointment—Dress Conservatively
- Be Well Groomed—Your Projected Image Is Important
- Go To The Interview Alone
- Smile—Be Friendly
- Take The Initiative And Shake Hands With The Interviewer
- Don't Sit Until Asked To Do So
- Don't Smoke Unless Invited To Do So
- Don't Place Briefcase Or Packages On Interviewer's Desk
- Do Carry All Necessary Papers In A Neat File
- Do Answer All Questions Honestly
- Carry The Conversation—Sell Yourself
- Don't Be Brash Or Rude—Exude Charm—Politeness
- Check Your Posture—Don't Slouch Or Slump Down In Chair
- Maintain Eye Contact Throughout The Interview
- Stress Your Motivation To Sell
- Don't Mention Personal Problems Or Be Negative In Any Way
- Don't Run Down Previous Employers
- Give Valid Reasons For Leaving Your Last Job
- Don't Say You Have Applied For Other Jobs
- Sit Easily And Comfortably And Keep Still
- Don't Scratch Or Use Your Hands Nervously
- Use The Interviewer's Name Frequently
- Be Confident But Not Lacking In Humility
- Place A Proper Value On Your Abilities
- Ask Questions—Sensible Ones
- Communicate Your Ideas Effectively And Clearly—Don't Mumble
- Stress Your Ability To Deal With Others On A Psychological Basis
- Leave A Professionally Packaged Background File For The Interviewer
- Don't Overstay Your Welcome
- Thank The Interviewer For His Time
- Be Prepared To Take Psychological Tests

MAKE AN ASSESSMENT BEFORE YOUR FINAL MOVE

Don't be too anxious to sign-on until you've had an opportunity of assessing the position offered and the company offering it. You cannot make the best use of your talents unless you are absolutely happy in your work. Salary and commission arrangements should meet your immediate and future needs. You must feel confident in your ability to carry out the work requirements without alibis or apologies. Be aware of advancement possibilities. What position of importance are you likely to hold in the company five years hence? What growth potential does the company have? Does the company conduct its business ethically? When you have satisfactory answers to these questions *then* make your final decision.

29

ENLISTING THE AID OF A MANAGEMENT CONSULTANT

Consultants act on behalf of both employer and job applicant. An employer wishing to avoid the time-consuming process of advertising and interviewing applicants sometimes engages a professional consultant to carry out these tasks for him.

If the consultant doesn't have suitable people already on his books to fill the position he will advertise for them. Interested applicants will be requested to reply in writing stating qualifications or to phone for an appointment.

From all applicants' letters received, about one third are selected to attend a first interview. From this group three or four will be put on a 'short-list'. Company forms and psychological tests will then be completed in readiness for a meeting with the employer.

Most management consultants work in specialist areas: business, professional, technical. If you feel there would be an advantage in having a consultant act on your behalf, seek a company specializing in sales recruitment. The classified section of the telephone directory is the best source of enquiry.

Consultants work on a fee basis and this varies from country to country. In the US, the applicant usually pays the fee. In Australia, it is the employer who pays. A phone call will bring the desired information on fees and special requirements.

THE VALUE OF PSYCHOLOGICAL TESTS FOR SALESMEN

Psychologists are quick to point out that there are certain limitations associated with testing. They are geared to *assist* in the selection process not to *make* the selection. Dangers are likely to arise when untrained personnel officers or sales managers seize on tests and their results as infallible guides to staff selection or promotion. The tests themselves are coming under close scrutiny and doubts are being voiced about their effectiveness in screening job applicants.

Critics of psychological and personality tests maintain that Winston Churchill, Charles De Gaulle, Napoleon and other great leaders would have failed psychological tests because of their stubbornness, inconsistency and other personality problems. What success then can we expect from the use of tests for sales, marketing and management personnel?

Canada's largest retail chain, Eaton's, uses intelligence and aptitude tests for management selection but only on selected occasions. The company isn't particularly impressed with personality tests.

Ford Motor Company uses aptitude tests on lower echelon employees but not for managerial prospects.

Bell Telephone is reported to favor the personal interview as the best hiring method. The company questions the validity of certain tests.

My own opinion of psychological tests is that they do give indication of the personality strengths and weaknesses a sales candidate may have, but they do not always show *true* potential. Used in conjunction with a personal interview, they are useful in *describing* a candidate rather than predicting his success or failure. For this reason my own company frequently uses them with success.

Two tests for sales applicants worthy of mention are:

1. Sales Comprehension Test.
2. Personality Capacity Analysis Test

SALES COMPREHENSION TEST: comprising 30 questions related to selling situations. Each question is followed by four possible answers. One answer is selected as the best possible solution to the problem.

PERSONALITY CAPACITY ANALYSIS TEST: 100 questions revealing personality and character traits indicating whether a person is making the best use of native intelligence, ability and aptitude. The results show where improvement is desirable. Useful information is revealed about social relationships, an individual's health and career progress satisfaction.

Until recently, many companies gave psychological tests to everyone being considered for employment. The trend is now toward selective testing used as an adjunct to skilful interviewing.

SALES SALARIES

The straight salary method is by far the largest single method of payment. Salary with incentive bonus rates next, then salary and commission and finally straight commission.

A greater proportion of high salary earners are in the 'salary plus commission' category. This indicates that a salesman on a straight salary is not as well motivated as his counterpart on commission.

The size of organization or its sales volume has little effect on salaries, for salesmen. There are just as many big money earners working for small companies as there are for larger ones. A small company, to some extent, is more flexible in salary and commission negotiations than its larger brother, which may set a uniform pay scale for its sales team.

It would be pointless to set down a comprehensive list of pay scales in this book. Salaries vary from company to company, from year to year and from country to country. The amount of salary, commission and other inducements is negotiable according to the experience and special skills of the applicant. Expense accounts and fringe benefits must be taken into consideration. Fringe benefits are sometimes more desirable than a higher salary, particularly in the face of high income taxes. Fringe benefits include: extra paid vacation time, free hospitalization, medical and life insurance, stock options, superannuation, profit sharing schemes, etc.

It is not uncommon for a good sales representative to earn $35,000 per year or more. Some super salesmen earn more than the presidents of their companies—$100,000 per year and higher. Straight commission salesmen are the top income winners.

The amount of money earned as a salesman largely depends on what kind of selling is undertaken, educational background, personality, experience and track record as a seller. The region in which the representative works also plays an important role in the salary structure. Higher incomes can be earned in highly industrialized and economically sound states than in less progressive ones. Certain industries pay high starting salaries. Most of these are in the technical fields employing engineering and science graduates.

A WORD ON EDUCATION AND SPECIAL TRAINING

It has already been indicated that higher salaries are paid by certain industries to well educated salesmen. Most companies are willing to pay more to applicants with college or university training and a great deal more for university-educated engineering or science graduates. Some companies require a university degree for sales positions. Within the next twenty years this could be a prerequisite for sales employment.

Sales aspirants lacking a higher education should make every attempt to increase their knowledge in the behavioral sciences, advertising, accountancy, business practices, marketing and any specialized area where personal development is required. Community colleges, technical schools and universities offer adult night courses for relatively small fees. Attending adult night classes is time well spent.

Company training programs, where the sales employee is indoctrinated in all aspects of company policy and product, are increasing. Private sales training colleges are a good investment. Executives of local firms teach many of these courses. They are aimed at the sales trainee and salesmen wishing to take a refresher course in modern selling techniques. Some companies offer to pay all or part of tuition fees for those willing to spend time on study.

With the technological revolution, new sales and marketing techniques are inevitable. For the modern-trend (psychological) salesman, the challenge will be in his ability to keep up with changes within his profession—changes that dramatically affect his selling expertise. The answer is in training and a higher level of education.

SAMPLE

(MANAGEMENT CONSULTANT) APPLICATION FORM

DATE ....

NAME (Print) ....
Surname   *First*   *Middle*

PRESENT ADDRESS .... *For how long?* ....
PREVIOUS ADDRESS .... *For how long?* ....
Home Phone .... *Bus. Phone* .... *Married?* .... *Dependents* ....
Date of Birth .... *Place of Birth* .... *Age* ....
Where were you brought up? .... *Date arrived in this country* ....
Last School or University Attended .... *Standard* ....
Technical Courses Attended ....
Any other Courses ....

Personal) 1. *Name* .... *Address* .... *Phone* ....
References) 2. *Name* .... *Address* .... *Phone* ....
Your Bank .... *Branch* .... *Savings/Trading* ....
How long have you been driving? ....
Make & Model of your Car ....
Is it available for you to use in business? ....
Why are you applying for this position? ....

LAST OR PRESENT POSITION

Company .... *City* .... *From* .... 19 .... *to* .... 19 ....
Industry .... *Products Handled* ....
Nature of Work at start .... *Starting Salary* ....
Nature of Work at leaving .... *Salary at Leaving* ....
Superior .... *Title* .... *How was he to work with?* ....

PREVIOUS POSITIONS

	Name of Firm	*Product*	*Position Held*	*From*	*To*	*Salary*
1.						
2.						
3.						

(OFFICE USE ONLY) Comment .... *Rating* ....

33

SUMMARY OF IDEAS TO GET YOUR SALES CAREER IN TOP GEAR

1. If you're serious about enhancing your career, use this book as a working manual and diligently apply the principles given.

2. The key to better memory is to discipline the movement of your mind. Do not allow your thoughts to wander when reading or listening. Concentrate . . . distractions cause reading delay and poor comprehension.

3. The role of the computer-age sales professional is not an easy one to play. There are many skills to perfect— character and personality attributes to develop. Above all, there must be a genuine desire to 'serve' the needs of others.

4. Analyze your motives for wanting a change of job. If you are in a rut, then find out why and what you can do about it. Take action to put your life in order. Success in any enterprise demands that *you* take the *first* step.

5. Before deciding on a particular company or line of selling, make a careful analysis of the experience, qualifications and personality type needed. You must *match* your abilities to the requirements of the company desiring to hire you.

6. Prepare a neat, comprehensive personal file to sell yourself to a prospective employer. Include all supporting documents: references, diplomas, certificates, etc.

7. Interviews can be a nightmare; to make the interview work in your favor, PLAN every aspect of it prior to your meeting. Solid preparation will support your claim to 'professionalism' in selling.

8. Do not attend an interview 'hat-in-hand'. You have assets to sell. Place a true value on them and boldly present your case. You have nothing to fear but fear itself.

9. First impressions are all-important. Check dress and grooming. Wear conservative clothes. Dress-up your personality— SMILE!

10. Psychological tests indicate areas that need development. Submit to them if asked to do so by a company or management consultant.

HOW TO PERSONALIZE
THE SCIENCE OF
CYBERNETICS

Affirmative Ideas in this Chapter

36

2

GOING BEYOND THE 'CLOSED SYSTEM' OF SALES INDOCTRINATION

A few years ago, while evaluating the progress of students in my 'effective salesmanship' classes, I became concerned with the results, which varied more dramatically than I felt should, particularly since the method of instruction was a comprehensive one.

My first theory—that uneven educational levels including the ability to learn and apply new information was the cause—proved to be wrong. Some poorly educated students progressed far beyond others with excellent academic qualifications.

My second anaylsis of the problem brought the answer *and* the solution. I discovered that students were working at two levels: those who (successfully) programmed information into a healthy and relatively trouble-free mind and those who tried (but failed) to channel it through an emotionally-disturbed, failure-oriented consciousness.

The remedy was clear: establish each student's problem area at the time of enrolment. Then train him to 'think' and control his emotional responses before stuffing his ears with technical data his cluttered mind surely would reject.

I was, at the time, teaching another personal development course to business men and women on the laws of mind. The program included inward perception and contemplation of divine realities and philosophic disciplines to develop security, power and wisdom. Being metaphysical in origin, the age-old principles bring outstanding success when applied correctly and conscientiously.

The techniques use the mechanisms of the subconscious mind to change negative habit patterns and replace them with the great eternal truths and principles of life. The result is an harmonious interaction between the conscious and subconscious levels of the mind bringing emotional and physical freedom.

So successful have been these techniques for students from various social levels that I decided to incorporate some of them in an entirely new and rather unorthodox sales program, which carries the same title as this book. The results have been most gratifying: a more self-controlled, self-motivated and emotionally stable sales student has now emerged.

Teaching salesmen a standard method of selling, including the internationally accepted *AIDA* formula, is essential. But setting down adequate self concepts, affirmative thinking habits and emotional responses, must, to my way of thinking, be given first priority— particularly if lasting results are desired.

This book encompasses the aforementioned teaching philosophy; thus, it surpasses the usual 'closed system' of teaching salesmen a regulated set of rules—regardless of their emotional capacity to receive and handle them.

In these early chapters, I have set down a method for stabilizing the emotions—putting the 'self' in order—before attempting to instil in the mind of the reader technical and psychological techniques of computer-age selling.

CYBERNETICS EXPLAINED

The ICBM and the Poseidon MIRV missile systems, the computer, the automatic pilot and other complex electronic calculating machines are the results of physicists and mathematicians studying the science of Cybernetics.

Man has studied the human brain, copied its function and put it in a machine. This *mechanical* brain responds automatically to signals, performing accurate calculations in a split second. The computer sciences are now helping man to better understand and appreciate his personal 'in-built' *mental* computer.

The word cybernetics comes from the Greek *kybernetes,* meaning *helmsman.* The actual science of Cybernetics is a study of the work- ings of electronic calculating machines and the human nervous system in an attempt to explain the functions of the human brain. It is the 'steering' of facts or processes to a successful conclusion or planned end result.

The brain and nervous system are under the automatic control of the mind. The brain is *not* the mind. The mind *uses* the brain as its instrument. Just as a computer or missile can be programmed, your brain can be programmed to *automatically* increase skills and per- formance.

Simply stated, Cybernetics is a guidance system that responds to signals. The success or failure of the system depends on the signals it receives. Faulty programming causes the system to miss its target or fail. Accurate programming allows the system to function correctly and thus succeed in its mission.

THE PRINCIPLE OF MIND CYBERNETICS

The pattern of your thoughts, feelings and beliefs decides your success or failure in life. Attitudes, mental habits, concepts, beliefs, when programmed into the central nervous system produce corresponding actions. What you think about yourself you ultimately become. *Like attracts like.* Healthy attitudes produce healthy conditions, negative attitudes produce negative conditions.

The brain and nervous system comprise a computer-like mechanism and faithfully act on signals received. This statement is worth repeating and remembering:

> *The brain and nervous system work like a computer and faithfully act on 'signals' received: faulty signals produce failure conditions. Accurate programming produces success conditions.*

Every individual who aspires to professionalism in selling must grasp the importance of developing strong mental attitudes: healthy, vigorous, harmonious, joyful, affirmative thoughts, feelings and beliefs. Weak thoughts produce timidity, low self esteem and lack of self control. Gather your thoughts, strengthen them, discipline them to bring about positive action. And this is the principle of *Mind Cybernetics*—programming into your mental computer successful attitudes, habits and concepts to reap successful living conditions.

> *The greatest events of an age*
> *are its best thoughts. Thought*
> *finds its way into action.*
>
> BOVEE.

APPLYING THE SCIENCE OF POSITIVE PROGRAMMING

In recognizing the analogy between the brain and the computer, we now take the Cybernetics theory—programming data to bring automatic success responses—and apply it to personal desires and goals.

Just as the computer can be programmed to bring desired results, you too, can program your 'mental computer' to (automatically) increase sales, enhance personality, develop self confidence, perfect skills or purchase a new car, house, boat, trip around the world, etc. Remember, we're talking about *automatic control,* which means once you've given the orders and your subconscious processes them, your brain responds automatically and you begin to reap the 'end result' of your directives.

Now we take a step that makes successful results a mathematical certainty. It entails *positive programming:* feeding the right data into the subconscious mind so that it is indelibly impressed on the memory cells. Negative thoughts, feelings, beliefs, habit patterns, baseless fears, misconceptions, low self esteem, inadequate personality traits must be grounded once and for all. The *inner* self must change first before *outer* responses change. Building automatic *success habits* into your life through positive programming, will remove the possibility of (automatic) failure.

AN EXAMPLE OF POSITIVE PROGRAMMING

- I know what I want to do in life. My goals are planned.
- I know what I want to be. My desires are realistic.
- I know how to accomplish my desires. My actions are affirmative.
- I am thankful for my abilities which I develop at every opportunity.
- I am at peace with myself. My mind is free from fear and worry.
- I am at peace with the world. I love my fellow man and exude goodwill.
- I am in perfect health. I am alive with the energy of life.
- I am in control of every situation. Nothing disturbs me.
- I exude self confidence and strength of purpose.
- I stand behind my personal convictions.
- I am honest, trustworthy, reliable and conscientious.
- I am conscious of the needs of others and unselfish in my attitudes.
- I am friendly and helpful and offer my advice freely.
- I am calm, quiet and serene. Harmony and balance surround my life.
- I am an excellent salesman, respected by my employer, clients and friends.
- I am a success.

Don't be shy. Make your needs and desires known. Be proud of them. The more positive programming you do the more positive results you will experience. Attitudes become habits; if your attitude habits are negative, you're on a failure path. By holding to negative attitudes and creating images of failure in your imagination, you set negative vibrations in motion—attracting failure circumstances.

REVERSE WRONG PROGRAMMING HABITS AND BEGIN TO SUCCEED IMMEDIATELY

Reverse present thoughts and thought habits if they are negative and program into your mental computer affirmative ideas, feelings, beliefs and desires. Develop the habit of thinking in terms of *specific affirmatives:* exact times, places, dates, people, things, goals, etc. Don't be vague about your desires. *Think, talk* and *act,* in terms of specifics. The more times you program specific affirmative ideas into your mental computer the less *time* there will be for negative concepts to take charge of your mind and reduce your sales effectiveness.

The pattern of your habitual thinking determines your destiny: a success pattern is your passport to opportunity; a negative pattern brings forth after its own kind. You cannot grow an apple tree if you plant a lettuce seed—you must produce a lettuce. If you sow negative ideas you cannot expect to attract successful conditions and events in your life. Each produces after its own kind. This is a basic tenet of natural law.

The cosmic laws* or principles of life are with man to guide him safely and successfully through his earthly existence. Laws operate through everything to bring balance and harmony. The law of mind is the law of belief. What you believe you attract. Sow an affirmative belief and you will reap an affirmative action. When you 'think', the laws of *attraction* and *cause and effect* go to work to influence the outcome of your thought habits. (Every salesman would do well to make a serious study of the cosmic laws.)

Thought is the invisible power of which you are very much aware. What you think tends to manifest itself in very quick order. If you produce a series of negative thoughts you must be prepared to reap the consequences of your 'thought' decision. The wise thing to do is to *reverse* negative thought habits and substitute affirmative concepts from which you can extract a glorious and successful life.

POSITIVE PROGRAMMING CHANGED THE COURSE OF EDDIE'S LIFE

Eddie hadn't been a cracker-jack salesman. He'd lost his last two sales jobs because of 'poor performance'. When I met him he was washing dishes in a restaurant in Los Angeles.

'I bought your success book,' he said, as he cleared away the dirty dishes. 'Reading it has sure made *me* positive—positive I'm a failure!' That was the first thing I discovered about Eddie Jarrett, his sense of humor.

'You look as though you do a successful job of washing dishes,' I quipped. 'Sure,' he said. 'But who ever heard of a successful salesman washing dishes?' He had a point. But I wasn't to be topped. 'Who ever heard of a successful salesman with a negative attitude?'

Eddie was interested. In fact *so* interested he stopped collecting dirty dishes and sat down beside me. He lost that job too. The manager said dishwashers belonged in the kitchen, not in the dining room fraternizing with guests. So, he fired him. I didn't bother going to his aid. Eddie didn't belong in that job anyway. And the quicker he got out of it the faster he'd be back on the road selling.

I talked to Eddie for an hour or more. He had a wonderful sense of humor. He never used it as a selling aid he said, because he felt clients would think of him as a joker. That was his first programming

---

* See *How To Succeed* (chapter 6) by Brian Adams.

mistake and I told him so. 'People like to laugh. It makes them feel good,' I said.

I gave him a set of affirmative programming ideas and told him to put them on cards and to use the technique of repeating them each night prior to sleep. I impressed upon him the importance of reversing negative programming thoughts and thought habits and supplanting only specific affirmatives. He was instructed to forget past job losses and concentrate on what he wanted to happen now and in the future.

I never expected to hear from Eddie Jarrett again. I put the incident from my mind. A year later, while lecturing in Los Angeles, I received a surprise telephone call from him at my hotel. He invited me to lunch—at the same restaurant. I must say, I barely recognized him. A 300 dollar suit does wonders for a man. So does a *changed attitude*. Success has arrived for Eddie Jarrett. He is now sales manager of a large manufacturing concern in Los Angeles. His employer thinks a lot of him, too. He pays Eddie an annual salary of $50,000. Not bad for an ex-dishwasher.

'Positive programming, for sure. *That* did it!' And he added: 'A year ago I was positive I was a failure. Now look at me. I'm positive I'm positive!' Eddie got the last word. I couldn't think of anything to top that.

> *You have 'within' the power to become the*
> *GREATEST SALESMAN ON EARTH. What you 'think'*
> *you become. Think of yourself as a $50,000 a*
> *year salesman (or higher) and that is what you*
> *can become. BELIEVE in your ability to succeed*
> *and hold to your self belief and you will win.*

PERSONALIZING THE SCIENCE OF SALES CYBERNETICS

Sales Cybernetics is automatic control that achieves the goal it sets out to achieve—like Eddie Jarrett and his determination to succeed in selling. Sales Cybernetics is aimed at a specific target— winning the sale—and the right moves are taken before the sale begins. If, in the planning, sights are set accurately, the target will be hit—the sale will be completed successfully. That's Sales Cybernetics working properly. If the target is missed—the sale lost—then that's Sales Cybernetics working negatively. And the cause is faulty programming.

One of the benefits of the positive programming technique is that the 'end result' of your daily efforts springs from the preparation you do. Just as the mighty oak begins as a seed in the tiny acorn, your success in life begins as a series of thoughts, feelings, beliefs and plans in your mind. *Think and plan the 'right things' at the beginning and the end result takes care of itself.*

Plot your course of action. *What* are you selling and to whom are you selling it? Does the product or service match the need of the customer? If it does, find the benefits to motivate the client to your product or service and he'll buy automatically. In essence, you haven't sold him anything. He's bought what he wants, needs and can use.

Phoney objections, alibis, excuses, are things of the past when you work cybernetically and psychologically. Scientific selling leaves no room for customer 'cop-outs'—nor should it. You are carrying out a mutually beneficial transaction. No gimmicks, no pressure, no dishonesty, just a fair exchange which promotes complete satisfaction and goodwill.

The *key* to selling cybernetically, is to set your aim accurately before you attempt to hit the target. Never begin a sales presentation unprepared. Know the full facts of the situation, including knowledge of your customer's needs and all there is to know about the product you wish to sell him. To put it simply: *do your homework.* The more you plan, the greater your chance of clinching the sale. Cybernetics apart, the technique is one of *common sense.*

Take the principle of Cybernetics to your heart. Personalize it so that it becomes a way of life—a way of thinking correctly and acting successfully. Feed into your mental computer specific ideas you want to see materialize. Don't waste time and energy worrying, fretting, fearing or in any way negating any aspect of yourself or life.

COMMAND RIGHT ACTION

Recognize your inner treasure house: mind, brain, nervous system. Put them to work in a positive way. Victory, achievement and prosperity are yours when you tap the power of your mind. All the riches of life are *within* the mind. They begin as thoughts, feelings and beliefs awaiting your command. A negative command fed through your mental computer brings a negative situation. An affirmative command draws from the invisible storehouse of your mind *success* in the thing you really want in life.

IF YOU WANT YOUR MENTAL COMPUTER TO PERFORM MIRACLES DESIGN AN ACCURATE PROGRAM

The attitudes and habits designed and fed through an electronic computer often bring desired results. Sometimes they don't. This is no fault of the computer. It's the fault of the programmer. He must redesign his program and feed it through again. A computer functions only as well as the program it receives. A poorly designed program, produces a failure response.

Your mind works in exactly the same manner as any electronic computer system. If you feed negative thoughts and thought habits into your mind day after day, it's only reasonable to expect negative responses or failure conditions. When negative circumstances and conditions arise in your life, don't blame your mind. Blame the patterns of thought you are feeding into your mind. Change your thoughts and you change your destiny.

Don't back away from practising the habit of positive programming. Certainly it's easier to let thoughts fall where they may (which is usually on the debit side of the ledger) instead of disciplining the mind to construct affirmative thought patterns. Face up to the task of constructing your thinking habits along affirmative lines. Take on the challenge of thinking respor ·bly and accurately. It's a simple adjustment of attitude: *cease* thinking of yourself as an individual governed by chance and *start* thinking of yourself as a person who controls his own destiny. Get firm control of your life. Learn to 'think'; program thoughts you know will return 'good' to you.

It doesn't take a lot of effort to reprogram thoughts and thought habits. It *does* take a personal motive, a strong *desire* to make sure you stick-with-it. Desire to make the *most* of your life. Design an 'accurate' program and persist with it until success arrives.

ACCURATE THINKING IS THE MARK OF THE CHAMPION SALESMAN

The champion salesman thinks from the standpoint of what *is* possible not what isn't. He removes himself from mental bondage by releasing negative concepts and substituting a flow of clear, logical, honest, uplifting thoughts. He programs the idea of 'big sales' into his subconscious and reaps 'big' earnings. He instils the belief, 'I am worthy' and his actions are always consistent with this belief. The professional salesman organizes his thoughts into winning patterns, producing a consciousness which is then success oriented.

POSITIVE AFFIRMATIONS WORK WONDERS FOR INSURANCE SALESMAN

An insurance salesman I know programs a series of 'accurate thoughts' into his subconscious prior to calling on clients. Here are three (of many) he uses:

(1) 'I am now attracting the right clients who need the services I have to offer.'

(2) 'My accurate pattern of thoughts work in my favor to instil confidence in my approach and presentation. I am in complete charge of this sale.'

(3) 'This client is my friend. He looks to me for guidance. This trust I truly appreciate. I return the compliment by giving my utmost attention to his needs. The transaction will be a fair and mutually beneficial one.'

His persistent use of these ideas and promises has attracted to him a great number of loyal clients. New leads come to him seemingly from out-of-the-blue. A quick analysis of his success indicates the *law of attraction* working in his favor. It might also be called the law of *reciprocal relationship*. This salesman *gives* something good and he *receives* something good. Accurate thinking *positively* produces tangible results.

44

AFFIRMATIVE SPECIFICS REMOVES THE GUESSWORK FROM SUCCESS

Take a close look at your own desires. Analyze them and throw out those that aren't practical. Produce a 'short list' of sensible, practical *wants* and attach to each, solid, accurate belief in your ability to achieve them. Your goals might include: winning new clients, closing sales, increasing commissions, improving skills, moving into a management position, taking an overseas trip, starting your own business. Whatever they are, synchronize them with the automatic responses— *I can, I will*—and your dreams and aspirations will take shape. Remember: to think accurately is to think in terms of specifics— *affirmative specifics*. Know *what* you want and *how* you intend to get it. You must be 'accurate' in your aim or you'll miss your target— and that's failure cybernetics.

PRODUCE MENTAL DATA CARDS AND FEED THEM THROUGH YOUR PERSONAL COMPUTER

Make a list of requests (goals) and write them on 3 x 5 cards. Transfer this list onto *mental* data cards. Run the cards through your mind computer one at a time. Hold on each desire for at least 90 seconds. Throw it up on the screen of your mind and silently affirm:

> *This is my earnest desire. I am worthy of its rewards. I believe I am capable of accomplishing this goal and I know it will come to pass in good order. I give my thanks in advance of receiving it.*

Repeat this process each night prior to dropping-off to sleep. Your continuous positive programming will take hold and your in-built guidance system will find its mark in each case.

THE DYNAMICS OF SELF-SUGGESTION

Programming mental data cards is another term for *self-suggestion*. The method, when applied conscientiously and repeatedly, produces far-reaching effects for the practitioner. The technique of *repetitive, positive statement* and suggestion of positive ideas to the subconscious mind develops an affirmative consciousness. And this is the essential 'state of mind' required to attract successful living conditions.

The power of affirmative self-suggestion can be applied to produce health, happiness, peace of mind, joy, harmony and financial and creative satisfaction. Your *performance* as a salesman for example, is identical to the *concept* you hold of yourself *as* a salesman. The ideas you program into your subconscious about yourself return to enhance your image or detract from it. *You become the thing you contemplate.*

Success and failure are no mere accidents of chance. They occur according to *mind conditioning*. Once desires are fed into your mental computer and accepted, they work automatically as part of the Creative Principle. Deep impressions made in your subconscious mind by repetitive thinking or auto-suggestion, are compulsive—they take hold. When *conviction* (or belief) supports your desires, they are made manifest in your experience.

HOW TO MATERIALIZE THE POWER AND WEALTH WITHIN YOU

The human computer is much more complex than any mechanical brain made by man. But, like the electronic brain, the human brain functions as a success *or* failure oriented mechanism depending upon the goals it receives and the accuracy of the information supplied.

If you feed data into your mental computer to the effect that you are unworthy, incapable, lacking in talent and inferior to others, this information is processed and acted upon. According to the law of reciprocal relationship, you then develop a negative and inadequate personality and character.

If you want to be an energetic, enthusiastic, personable, respected, skilful and successful sales personality, *aim* at these targets and program for them accordingly. Think in terms of 'end results' and then program belief in your ability to produce successful end results. *Belief in victory is often a battle won.*

The brain and nervous system are designed to react automatically and impersonally to information received. No favorites are played. No time is spent considering or wondering whether the information is worthy or unworthy, just an immediate and impersonal reaction. The human computer places no importance on the values of success or failure. It does exactly what it's told—no more, no less. It does not argue controversially.

Be accurate with data programmed into your mind. Eliminate all negative concepts from your consciousness. No easy task to accomplish. But certainly worth the effort—if success in life is your aim.

All spiritual, mental and material benefits of the universe are the gifts of Divine Intelligence. The greatest gift of all is your mind. By studying the laws of mental action, you will draw from the infinite storehouse within you, all you need to live harmoniously, gloriously and beneficially.

You were born to succeed. And you *will* experience successful conditions and circumstances by applying the principles of life and properly using (programming) your God-given mind.

SUMMARY OF IDEAS TO HELP YOU PERSONALIZE
THE SCIENCE OF CYBERNETICS

1. Before attempting to absorb technical data on selling, put your 'inner life' in order. Your mind must be free from emotional disturbance. Feelings of frustration and anxiety restrict your learning ability. Do not allow people, places or things to affect you. The situation is not as important as your *reaction* to it.

2. The ICBM and the computer are patterned after the workings of your brain and nervous system. The brain and nervous system are under the automatic control of your mind. The mind uses the brain as its instrument. Just as the computer can be programmed to bring a desired result, your mental computer can be programmed to increase skills and performance.

3. Cybernetics comes from the Greek *kybernetes* and means *helmsman*. You 'steer' your life along the path you wish it to take by controlling your thoughts and thought habits.

4. The pattern of your thoughts, feelings and beliefs decides your success or failure in life. Like attracts like. Success thoughts produce success conditions.

5. Write down the goals you wish to materialize in your life. Positive programming means to program only those thoughts which you *know* will bring success. *Believe* in your ability to succeed.

6. Reverse negative habit patterns and substitute *specific affirmatives*. Don't allow negative concepts to slip into your consciousness and reduce your effectiveness.

7. Study the cosmic laws of life. Every salesman should be aware of them and work *with* them.

8. Accurate thinking is the mark of the champion salesman. Release a flow of clear, logical, honest, uplifting thoughts and you will free yourself from the bondage of negative thought habits and failure conditions and circumstances.

9. Produce mental data cards and play them onto the screen of your mind prior to sleep. Include your life-long desires, dreams and aspirations.

10. The greatest gift given to you is your mind. By studying the laws of mind you will open up new vistas and flood your life with magnificent riches.

HOW TO PROJECT
DYNAMIC IMPRESSIONS
THAT WIN SALES

❖

Affirmative Ideas in this Chapter

- Success In Selling Hinges On Your Personality
- Getting To Know The REAL You
- Visual Impact—The First 90 Seconds You Are On Trial
- Monitor The Image Values You Project
- How To Create Dynamic Impressions
- DYNAMIC IMPRESSION 1: Dress And Grooming
- Your Clothes Tell A Lot About Your Personality
- A Word About Clothes Care
- Accessories Selection
- Good Grooming
- 5 Points To Improve Your Dress Sense
- DYNAMIC IMPRESSION 2: General Manner
- Increase Your Height—Stand Tall
- How To Develop Good Posture And Enhance Your Visual Image
- Your Walk Indicates Your State of Mind
- How To Energize Your Life And Avoid That Run-Down Feeling
- Discover Personal Energy Rhythms
- 10 Reasons For That Run-Down Feeling
- How To Stay Alive Longer And Look Younger
- Condition Yourself Against The Worry Habit
- How To Remove The Hang-Dog Look
- Hang-Dog Look Killed Sales For George The Terrible
- 10 Steps To Stem Anxiety And Worry
- If You Want To Look Great And Enjoy Better Health Exercise
- If You Want To Count Your Commissions Longer Watch What You Eat
- A Suitable Diet For Salesmen To Increase Energy And Zest
- Salesman's Planned Meals Program
- DYNAMIC IMPRESSION 3: Speech Pattern
- Correction of Speech Problems
- Your Speaking Voice Contributes To Your Individuality
- Developing A Resonant And Well-Supported Tone
- 5 Techniques For Developing A Resonant Voice
- Words Are Tools of Trade For The Salesman
- Increasing Your Word Power
- That Special 'Something' People Look For In A Salesman
- Build A Daily Word Program
- 12 Most Persuasive Words In Selling
- Vocabulary Expander
- DYNAMIC IMPRESSION 4: Attitude And Personality
- Attitude Analysis Chart
- Your Inner Beliefs About Yourself Must Be Updated
- What Is Personality?
- The Two Personality Types: Adequate Personality—Inadequate Personality
- Sell Your True Personality
- How Negative Personality Develops
- Eliminate The Detractors
- Personality Composite Chart
- Summary of Ideas To Help You Create Dynamic Impressions

3

SUCCESS IN SELLING HINGES ON YOUR PERSONALITY

The unhappy, failure-type person cannot hope to become an effective salesman. An individual aspiring to professionalism in selling must acknowledge the importance personality plays in communication and motivation.

The failure personality type will always find a way to fail even if opportunity is placed before him. An inadequate concept of the self is the biggest single contributor to man's failure. Discovery of the *true* self and a value placed on this self is the road to success. You always act and perform like the sort of person you *imagine* yourself to be. Poor thoughts, feelings and beliefs about the self return poor performance. Your personality can be enhanced and put to work to return creative and financial rewards.

GETTING TO KNOW THE REAL YOU

In this chapter we will take a look at human personality and how it can be developed to create an *affirmative impact*. There are many parts that go to make up the 'whole' man and these will be examined to help you to develop your own *personality plus* image.

Did you ever ask yourself, 'Who am I?' If so, you have asked one of the *big* questions of life. It is significant for you to know and understand that life can have a *meaning* to you only in relationship to yourself.

There is more to you than flesh and bone—you are *much* more than a physical body—*more* than you *seem* to be. Consciousness or that thing which you *really* are, is the gift Life has made to you. It is your treasure, your source of solace and inspiration.

There are hidden powers, undeveloped talents which you can (and should) bring to the surface and use to create the type of person you earnestly desire to be. You can mold and fashion a personality (image) that is dynamic, creative, charming and respected. *YOU* hold the key to building a greater more admirable *YOU*.

Your first efforts in the direction of image development must be given to *attitude*—thinking and feeling—and your *acting* or actions stemming from your thoughts. There must not be any forcing or strain in your program of personality development. You must not attempt to become anything other than *yourself*.

Imitation gives you a mask to wear which hides your true self. It compels you to be someone and something you aren't. Your aim is not to change the basic self of you but to change the *estimation* you hold of yourself as a human being. You will soon discover that attractive thoughts about yourself produce an attractive personality. Your physical self mirrors your 'inner' self: thoughts, feelings and beliefs. There is much more to you as a person than you have perhaps imagined. And this *new you* is for you to discover and project. Your success in selling depends on it.

VISUAL IMPACT—THE FIRST 90 SECONDS YOU ARE ON TRIAL

Each customer you meet for the first time sits in judgement and forms an opinion of you. He sees you as a package of personality traits, attitudes and visual form: dress, grooming, posture, manner, etc. Your reception depends on the decision the customer makes on the image you project. *The sale begins with your personality*.

Your first job is to sell yourself (personality package). Once this has been achieved (successfully) the way is clear for you to present your product or service. You set a steady bead on the target (sale) and confidently move ahead to completion and fulfillment.

There is a degree of suspicion on the part of a buyer each time he meets a new salesman. He doesn't know what to expect. A sales representative with a totally open personality—honest, courteous, friendly, helpful—has no trouble winning the confidence of the buyer; he drops his 'guard' and gives attention to the salesman's introduction and presentation. A negative personality—surly, cold, unfriendly, disinterested—puts the buyer on the defensive and the salesman has a difficult time winning the confidence and attention of his client.

It is said that a sale is won or lost during the first 90 seconds of a salesman's introduction. The impression given—positive or negative—is the reason for this. When positive *visual impact* is lacking, the salesman is out-of-step with the prospective buyer and this negative vibration places the salesman at a decided disadvantage.

Poor visual impact accounts for a major percentage of difficult sales or loss of sales by representatives unaware of the importance of projecting dynamic self image values. Enhance your visual package by: SMILING — RADIATING CHARM — PROJECTING ENTHUSIASM — BEING COURTEOUS AND CONSIDERATE.

MONITOR THE IMAGE VALUES YOU PROJECT

It is your first duty as a sales representative to 'get along' with people. Therefore, opinions held by others regarding your projected self image values should be monitored regularly and changed if necessary.

This does not mean that you should consciously *try* to make a good impression or 'act out' a personality role. To do so would be to invite inhibition—a self-conscious awareness creating a surface or false personality.

When you are introduced to another for the first time, the attention he gives you is determined by how he sees you and the importance he places on you. In judging you, the other person never places a higher value on your abilities than the value you have set on yourself. Others are able to 'sense' your true worth and this opinion is supported by your attitudes and actions.

The person with true humility is aware of his personal skills and assets and he values them and projects them confidently. This honest self appraisal produces an adequate self image without fear of conceit rearing its ugly head.

You are saying, 'I have the capacity of greatness and right action within me and I am determined to live up to my full capacity in all that I do.' You do not fight yourself. You get along with yourself. You see yourself as a worthy, responsible, creative and honest individual who has a role to fulfill in life and a duty to perform. You decide to:

1. Get along with yourself and others.

2. Get along with your world.

3. Get along with life.

HOW TO CREATE DYNAMIC IMPRESSIONS

Successful first impressions are created by raising the standard of four aspects of the 'self'. These aspects are:

1. DRESS AND GROOMING.

2. GENERAL MANNER: posture—walk—handshake—energy —health.

3. SPEECH PATTERN AND VOCABULARY.

4. ATTITUDE AND PERSONALITY.

Ninety seconds is not very long to establish impact in the four areas listed. But this is all the time it takes for your customer to come to a decision about you. His mental computer associates your plus and minus personality factors with those of other people he knows— particularly other salesmen. Thus, if the manner in which you walk, talk, dress and react are linked to the memory he has of others who have done him an injustice, he places you in a category marked 'negative'.

To overcome this negative association, an individualistic personality must be developed and projected that sets you apart from the 'typical' salesman image and creates an immediate affirmative impact in the minds of those you meet and do business with.

Success in the career that you desire *and* deserve will depend to a large degree, on the image impressions you create and project. Make yourself a striking personality. A person of *real* personal power that is instantly recognized by others.

DYNAMIC IMPRESSION 1: DRESS AND GROOMING

Good clothes are a salesman's best friend. A man who wears stylish, well-cut clothes is more likely to be an effective leader than his more conservative, unkempt counterpart. Success in selling depends so much on the impression created. As the initial impression is a visual one, clothes and how they are worn, come under close scrutiny.

With today's fashion trend concentrating on a youthful look, 'trendy' clothes do make men look more individual than former conservative and uniform grey flannels. Style, cut and color are being given more attention than in the past and this has taken the drabness out of clothing worn by modern-day businessmen.

YOUR CLOTHES TELL A LOT ABOUT YOUR PERSONALITY

Clothes reflect a man's personality and character. Dull colors and conservative cut usually indicate a shy, conservative-thinking type. Dirty, unpressed, shabby, old-fashioned clothes indicate a slovenly mind. The sure mark of a leader is his dress sense and grooming habits. The leader is aware that he must set examples for those working under him. Leadership potential is often measured by a man's physical look in addition to his social disposition and skills. A leader must *look* like a leader as well as *act* like one.

An Australian psychologist, Gavin Sinclair, lecturer in psychology at the University of New South Wales, maintains that a man who wears 'dashing clothes' is more likely to be an effective leader than his more conservative counterpart. A case of 'clothes make the man.'

Film and television stars are trendy dressers. Ever-conscious of projecting a first-rate image to their fans, clothes and grooming (for the most part) are first considerations when appearing in public. Looks are all-important to the showman to create the 'right' impression. A salesman is no less a showman (in that he's dealing with the public) than the theatrical personality.

Consideration should be given to the style of clothes to be worn. The television type is at home in a trend-setting suit, brightly patterned shirt and tie, but not so the salesman calling on conservative business people. Modern, well-cut clothes, yes! Outlandish, attention-drawing gear, no! *Dress to suit the situation.* Be comfortable without feeling self conscious. The question to be asked is: 'Is it in good taste?' Your purpose is to create a dignified, dynamic first impression. Forward-looking clothes, neatly worn and well-cut, will help to create this picture.

A WORD ABOUT CLOTHES CARE

Nothing is more important to the maintenance of a man's wardrobe (and his appearance) than suit rotation. A salesman requires at least four good suits for business and should wear them in strict rotation to make the best use of his wardrobe.

The life of every suit is more than trebled when worn on a rotation basis. The man who has only two suits will find he will have to replace them within 12 months. But the man who rotates four suits and has them cleaned and pressed as the need arises, will have the privilege of becoming tired of them before they are worn out.

Keep clothes in good order by purchasing rounded plastic hangers. They are specially-shaped aids to hold the 'shoulder line' of quality garments. Place your suit on a hanger immediately it is taken off. When entering a car or sitting for long periods, remove your jacket and place it on a hanger. This avoids creasing the back panel.

ACCESSORIES SELECTION

A dozen good shirts will ensure that you have a clean one to wear each day and a fresh one for evening appointments or socializing.

A *shirt* with wrinkled collar and frayed cuffs creates a poor impression. Spend a reasonable amount of money on a good wardrobe. When you wear well-cut, clean clothes it produces a feeling of confidence and helps to bolster your enthusiasm for meeting people.

Ties require rotation if they are to retain their shape. Quality silk ties enhance an expensive suit and shirt. Match color tones and select modern patterns and tie widths. Too-bright tie colorings tend to draw attention to you and can be distracting.

Shoes are another item worthy of spending extra money on. Quality, leather shoes need to be selected for comfort as much as for looks. Salesmen do a lot of walking and well-fitting shoes are a must. Keep shoes highly polished. Carry a shoe polishing kit in the glove compartment of your car and polish shoes when scuffing occurs.

A word about *socks*. Buy long socks in plain colors of black or brown. They help to give support to the calf muscles. In addition, they feel better than short socks and they certainly look better.

GOOD GROOMING

Good grooming is essential when dealing with the general public. Hair must be of a reasonable length, clean and combed into place. Nails should be well manicured and kept clean and shaped. Shower twice each day. Use a body deodorant and an after-shave lotion.

Aristotle Onassis, talking on the secrets of success, suggests that business executives keep a tan, even if it means using a lamp. 'To most people, a tan in winter means only that you have been where the sun is and in that respect, sun is money,' says Greece's top motivator.

5 POINTS TO IMPROVE YOUR DRESS SENSE

A salesman is in the person-to-person business of selling. A business where good impressions are essential to success. And the way a salesman looks—his dress sense—can be the most important factor in creating good visual impact. Clients and prospects judge the salesman the moment he enters their premises. Before one word is spoken an assessment has been made which can influence that crucial decision: to purchase or not to purchase. Follow the points given to enhance your visual image. (See diagram on Page 57).

1. Button suit jacket when meeting or speaking to others. Close the center button on a 3-button jacket, the top button on a 2-button coat. Keep pocket flaps out. Jacket collar should fit snugly across the back shoulder. Make sure jacket lining is pre-shrunk, if not it can pull the jacket out of shape after cleaning. Jacket length should cover trouser seat and reach about thumb length. Jacket should fit smoothly across chest without pulling at buttons.

2. Trousers must fit without bagging. Keep a knife-edge crease by steam pressing. Length should brush shoe tops. Seams should be neatly sewn. Careless stitching causes pucker.

3. Shirt collar higher at back (1¾ inches up). Points are longer and wider to sit comfortably under lapels. Cuffs should protrude at least half an inch below coat sleeves. Shirts should be coordinated with suits in terms of colors and patterns.

4. Coordinate shirt, tie and pocket square. Width of tie and knot size in accordance with current fashion trend. Patterned ties should match the bold colors of striped or solid shirts. Ties and shirts must look *right* together.

5. Shoes for business require current fashion without gaudy effects. Do not wear suede or patent leathers for business. Match color and style, to suits. Keep shoes highly polished and in good state of repair. Shoe trees are a good investment.

HOW TO DEVELOP GOOD POSTURE AND ENHANCE YOUR VISUAL IMAGE

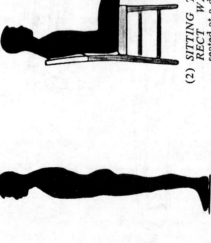

(1) *STANDING THE CORRECT WAY:* the body weight should be evenly distributed between the ball and the fore part of the foot. Standing 'tall' with the lower abdomen flattened and shoulders down and back, promotes a feeling of well-being. The silhouette (above) is the correct way to stand.

(2) *SITTING THE CORRECT WAY:* when seated at a desk the hips should be back far enough in the chair to allow the thighs to support the body weight. Feet should be placed flat on the floor while the lower part of the back is supported by the chair back. A good chair also gives support to the upper back. Don't allow the head or neck to droop when sitting.

(3) *POOR POSTURE:* silhouette (above) depicts the wrong way to stand. While poor posture is often the end result of fatigue, it is also the *cause* of fatigue in many salesmen. A poorly-postured, sickly, drawn-looking salesman cannot command the attention of others in a dynamic way. Don't allow the body line to get out of balance with the line of gravity. You should have a feeling of relaxation.

(4) *POOR SITTING POSITION:* make yourself look as good as you can when sitting. Don't drop down into a chair, sprawling your legs out and allowing the spine to curve. Most back pains and ailments come from poor sitting positions. There is strain on the back and abdominal muscles and a general tiredness sets in.

DYNAMIC IMPRESSION 2: GENERAL MANNER

You don't have to utter a word for other people to know what you are like. The way you walk, stand, sit, greet others says all. Mannerisms are the personality and character give-away. Whatever you do with your hands, feet, arms, head, eyes, is monitored by others and assessed as to the 'type' of person you are.

How do you sit in a prospective employer's office? Is your back straight in the chair or do you slouch, stretch out your legs in an ungainly fashion? Do you nervously clasp and unclasp your hands, scratch your face, keep changing your position? Your character comes through with every mannerism.

Do you lean or prop yourself up against walls, sit on the edge of your client's desk, stand with one leg bent at the knee and hands behind your back? The way you position yourself can tell a lot. The characteristics mentioned indicate mental laziness. Don't indicate anything other than a strong, capable, enthusiastic and mentally alert sales professional. Check your *physical manners* at all times.

INCREASE YOUR HEIGHT—STAND TALL

Good posture is a personal attribute that contributes toward a salesman's social and economic success. It can also be a vital factor in maintaining good health.

A good posture creates visual impact—*affirmative impact*. Even the best-made clothes can look ill-fitting on a poorly-postured body. Hold the shoulders back, lift the chest and chin. This gives an attractive body line and enhances the cut and fall of clothes.

In good posture, the body is held in such a way that there is a minimum of strain on muscles, bones and ligaments. An easy balance is maintained without tension or fatigue arising. Check your posture in a mirror. If any part of the body sags out from the center line (as in the poor-posture chart) then the chest should be lifted upward and the lower abdomen flattened. The buttocks should be tucked in at the back with lower back curve evenly positioned.

YOUR WALK INDICATES YOUR STATE OF MIND

Correct walking—brisk, energetic movement—gives an immediate impression of mental alertness. Correct walking can help too, in good posture. The weight should be carried along the center and outer side of the foot with the feet being used in a parallel position so that the toes point straight ahead. You should feel 'tall' with the top of the head pulling upwards from the soles of the feet.

Don't slouch, lope along, droop the shoulders, drag the feet or in any way give the impression that you are tired or disinterested in your job or life in general. Your approach, walk, handshake, greetings, are indicators of your attitude toward your job.

When meeting a client, walk toward him in a brisk manner, hold eye contact, smile and extend a warm greeting. *Remember:* he is watching you and making judgments. If you desire to earn high commissions, then *look, talk* and *act* in a friendly, thoroughly professional manner.

HOW TO ENERGIZE YOUR LIFE AND AVOID THAT RUN-DOWN FEELING

Some salesmen feel tired at 9 a.m. and are on their 'last legs' by 5 p.m. Excessive feelings of tiredness destroy your ability to present an energetic front, play havoc with your appearance and take away your enjoyment in life.

Environmental conditions may be part of the cause of excessive tiredness. Emotional stress is the major reason. A salesman besieged by personal problems can be tired all week long, regardless of his physical work-load.

No individual can work efficiently while under the strain of anxiety, frustration, fear and worry. Physical well-being stems from mental well-being. Worry and fear attract tension, nervous dyspepsia, heart disease and other ailments. The psychological drive to succeed should be the feature of every salesman's philosophy, but this drive should not become an obsession which drives the salesman to an early grave.

Medical experts believe that many of the diseases at 40 years of age and over are diseases which began at an earlier age because of mental stress. A salesman can be physically fit but in poor health: depressed, bored with life, lonely, overworked, emotionally insecure.

DISCOVER PERSONAL ENERGY RHYTHMS

Discover your own personal energy rhythms. Your body has preferences for work pace—high activity and rest periods. Pinpoint your strong and weak periods and work *with* instead of against them. Discover the jobs you dislike doing and find a new approach to their accomplishment. Don't push yourself beyond your physical and mental limit. Stop what you are doing and change your assignment and work pace. Call on friends who have an outgoing personality. Fall into their effervescent mood patterns. Think of yourself as a human dynamo with energy to spare. Get out of your negative, tired, listless state and recharge your run-down mental batteries with super-charged, affirmative thoughts, ideas and feelings.

---

10 REASONS FOR THAT RUN-DOWN FEELING

1. Sitting for long periods in cramped office chair or car seat.
2. Ill-fitting clothes.
3. Poor state of health due to imbalanced diet.
4. Unable to make decisions and cope with problems.
5. Working for long periods without rest breaks.
6. Insufficient sleep.
7. Too much sleep.
8. Boring, routine work.
9. Poor job performance through fear of failure.
10. No outside interests, sports or hobbies.

HOW TO STAY ALIVE LONGER AND LOOK YOUNGER

If you're going to become a big money earner, you'd better stay alive long enough to enjoy it. Getting tense and worried at every little set-back will do more to shorten your life span than anything I know. The remedy is to control your thought processes. Become *master* of your thought, not slave to it.

A distinguished psychologist I know, told me that 80 per cent of the people are sick because of maladjusted minds. 'People can't cope with problems. Tensions arise and they buckle-under. Fear, frustration and anxiety affect the whole body processes and those so affected start to break down chemically. The result is mental and physical collapse,' he said.

Scientists who specialize in the study of aging (gerontologists) are now convinced that people age too quickly because they are under pressure which produces tenseness and fatigue. Those who cannot control personal problems age quickly and die sooner than those who are relaxed, poised and emotionally stable.

Job pressure accounts for about 80 per cent of tension and worry experienced by salesmen and particularly sales managers. If the work load is too much, tension builds up. As the hours tick by, muscles begin to tighten and the busy executive finds that he cannot function efficiently because of jangled nerves, tiredness, lack of energy and mental depression.

It's a case of runaway emotions. Get firm control of your thoughts. Apply common sense when tension, worry and fatigue begin to build up. Stop whatever you are doing and give your mind and body a rest. Think about something pleasant: a tranquil farm setting; a tropical island in the sun; a cool mountain stream. Get your mind away from the tension-producing situation and onto a relief-giving mental Shangri-La. Cease annoying yourself with petty problems that affirmative reasoning can cure. There is no situation you aren't capable of handling, therefore, give your problem-solving ability a boost of confidence and eliminate worry.

CONDITION YOURSELF AGAINST THE WORRY HABIT

Of all the personal problems confronting salesmen the 'worry habit' must rank as number one. A salesman must be able to see through the outer confusion of life to the 'inner center' of peace and contentment. There is no *sure* success for the chronic worrier.

Relax—move to your deep inner thoughts of wisdom to free negative ideas and emotions. Uncontrolled thoughts and feelings are the enemies of the salesman and he is bound to them until he conditions his mind to repel them. Right thought produces right action. Condition your mind to accept ideas of harmony, balance, perfection instead of tension, confusion, and worry.

Never let your mental guard down. Strengthen your attitudes and the dynamic power within will respond to your call. The negative thought, the destructive emotion and the purposeless action will be dissolved in the twinkling of an eye. It is a matter of practise makes perfect. Repeated effort in this direction will pay-off in your personal and business dealings.

HOW TO REMOVE THE HANG-DOG LOOK

It is impossible to create a dynamic first impression if your mind is clouded with anxiety and worry. Tension affects the eyes, the mouth and your posture. You take on a 'hang-dog' look that detracts from your general appearance. If you allow problems and responsibilities to exhaust you, then zest and enthusiasm are lost.

Your worst-imagined troubles seldom occur. Stop worrying about what *might* happen. You will never be confronted with a situation you are not capable of handling. So stop upsetting and robbing yourself of sales opportunities, friendships, happiness and health. Worry takes years from your life, brings wrinkles to your brow and sours your personality.

Your health is a direct reflection of your thinking habits. Think and speak constructively at all times. Eliminate little negatives: 'I'm tired.'—'Business is slow.'—'The buyer doesn't like me.'—'I can't get along with the salesmanager.' Everything you (positively) think, feel, say and do contributes to your well-being. Cast from your mind all negative ideas. You'll stay alive longer and look younger while you succeed in your career.

HANG-DOG LOOK KILLED SALES FOR GEORGE THE TERRIBLE

His boss called him 'George the terrible'. He had a sorrowful look that made clients feel sorry for him—but not sorry enough to increase his sales figures.

George was sent to one of my sales classes in Sydney. When I saw him I wanted to pat him. He reminded me of a forlorn looking Basset hound.

'What's your trouble, George?', I asked him. 'Everything,' he said. 'First of all, I can't get along with people. They bug me. I fight with my wife, argue with my kids, row with my sales manager and get disgusted with my customers. I can't help worrying about things,' he said.

I instructed George to cast out of his mind all preconceived ideas about past relationships with others and begin to think of people in terms of, 'my friends who want to see me a success.' Each time an argument cropped up he was to reverse his attitude and smile.

During the 9 weeks George trained at the Sydney college his fellow students (as an exercise) attempted to bait him into an argument. At first, George reacted negatively. But eventually, he learned to control his reactions to the 'attitudes' of others. George stopped getting upset. He refused to worry about negative situations. He began to see things in a new light. The world isn't such a 'bad place' and people are 'okay', is George's *new* philosophy. And when trouble looms, George just *smiles*.

'Now, he's known as "Smiley" the customer's friend. Hang-dog look gone, attitude changed, thoughts uplifted, George's new image is a winner—and his sales figures prove it,' was the happy comment of George's sales manager when I next saw him.

---

10 STEPS TO STEM ANXIETY AND WORRY

1. **ALWAYS THINK OBJECTIVELY:** rid the mind of preconceived ideas and prejudices. Don't be an irrational thinker.
2. **ADAPT EASILY TO CIRCUMSTANCE:** don't force yourself into problem situations or attempt to 'buck the system' because of pride.
3. **FACE FACTS:** see things as they really are not as you *think* they are.
4. **DON'T BE DEPENDENT ON OTHERS:** make your own decisions and lean on your own ability. Be a leader, not a follower. When you rely on others you place a 'power' in their hands and are often disappointed at their non-performance.
5. **DON'T FEAR FAILURE:** what you believe you attract. Have utter confidence in your ability to succeed.
6. **VISUALIZE WHOLENESS:** see perfection in every part of your body. Relax your body and allow the healing energy of your subconscious mind to restore health and vitality.
7. **KEEP YOUR ACTIONS CONTROLLED:** don't allow your reactions to situations to take charge of your life. It isn't the situation that counts, it's your reaction to it. *Keep your cool.*
8. **COUNT YOUR BLESSINGS:** you have a lot to be thankful for: miracle powers of your mind; talents and skills; ability to do good for others; ability to experience, love, joy, happiness.
9. **KNOW WHAT YOU WANT TO DO AND TO BE:** organize your life and plan your future. Give yourself a sense of security.
10. **GIVE THANKS IN ADVANCE FOR YOUR FUTURE SUCCESS:** it's only a matter of time before your aims and objectives become a reality. Give thanks in advance and know that success is yours—*now*.

IF YOU WANT TO LOOK GREAT AND ENJOY BETTER HEALTH—EXERCISE

Regular exercise keeps the body in trim, tones up flabby muscles, helps to prevent heart disease, colds and 'flu and increases your life span. Exercise reduces tension and strain and brings relaxation to tired muscles.

To relax means to cause a condition of tension to become *lax*. A person who is tense can find relaxation in vigorous physical exercise. Fast walking, jogging, swimming, tennis, doing push-ups, riding a bicycle will bring relief and improve the general state of health.

Overweight salesmen lack drive and vitality and present an unfavorable physical image. Exercise combined with a sensible diet and freedom from worry and tension all help to lose excessive pounds of flab.

IF YOU WANT TO COUNT YOUR COMMISSIONS LONGER WATCH WHAT YOU EAT

Stomachs abused with inferior and indigestible foods cause chemical imbalance. Cut down on fats, sugars and starches. If you're over-weight, do something to reduce it—diet! Excessive weight puts an added burden on your heart and legs and means more work for the lungs and digestive system. A heart surrounded by fat finds it difficult to pump. It has been calculated that for *30 pound overweight* there are 25 miles of extra veins through which blood must be pumped.

An increase in weight occurs when more food is eaten than is required each day—particularly the wrong type of food. Balance your diet. Don't starve your body of vital health-giving nutrients. Include milk (small amount), meat, cheese, eggs, fish, fruit, vegetables, whole-meal bread in your diet to maintain a feeling of well-being both physically and mentally.

An abused, undernourished, harassed body, cannot house a brain capable of top performance. A brain must be well nourished to function efficiently. A healthy body produces extra *energy* in times of stress and helps you to 'cope' with challenging situations. A healthy mind and body keeps you looking young. You'll feel better and improve your life span. Your mind will be in peak running order stimulating optimum thinking and reasoning.

If you must smoke cigarettes and drink alcohol (and it's recom-mended that you don't) then do it in moderation. Smoking and drink-ing to excess are dangerous to your health—and your job.

Dr. J. De Witt Fox, head of the Neurologic Center in Los Angeles, writes in his excellent book* *Why Not Smoke?:* 'That cigarette you hold in your hand is as powerful as dynamite, as toxic as arsenic, as addicting as morphine, as death-dealing as cancer, which it pro-duces.' A sensible and direct warning to those who smoke and kid themselves it is harmless.

A SUITABLE DIET FOR SALESMEN TO INCREASE ENERGY AND ZEST

Salesmen need to give a 'lift' to their daily activities, especially when the flow of energy to the mind and body is low. Good nutrition makes a difference to growth rate, fitness, endurance, resistance to colds and other illness, recovery from disease. It has a great effect on appearance, morale and attitude.

The salesman who wants to be healthy and active in his profession should not take food for granted or avoid proper attention to the body's requirements. The body, sapping up great amounts of energy, needs the right foods to regulate the body processes and provide for the upkeep of the body structure.

A haphazard selection of foods does not always give the body the nutrients it requires. *Meal planning* is needed if food is to be good for health as well as a pleasure to eat. Plan for variety in the choice

---

* By J. De Witt Fox, M.D., F.A.C.S. Review & Herald Publishing Associa-tion. Washington, D.C.

of foods to prevent monotony. Eliminate costly foods which produce little health-giving value. Cakes, pies, carbonated beverages, chocolates, may taste nice, but they contribute little to your well-being and sometimes work against it.

Most people require three meals a day. It is difficult to fit all the recommended foods into less. Divide meals evenly without filling-up on between-meal snacks. Follow the *planned meals program* for better health.

SALESMAN'S PLANNED MEALS PROGRAM

BREAKFAST

Usually about 12 hours have passed since the last meal was eaten and the body needs refuelling. No breakfast or an inadequate one lowers efficiency and work output, increases fatigue and attracts the unwanted headache.

- Fruit or juice (orange, lemon, grapefruit, prune).
- Wholegrain cereal with milk and honey.
- Boiled egg.
- Wholemeal toast dry or lightly buttered.
- Beverage (no sugar) honey to sweeten.

LUNCH

Lunch is necessary to meet the body's needs for the afternoon activities. If sandwiches are substituted for the suggested lunch, do not eat white or brown bread (white bread dyed). Wholemeal sandwiches with date or salad fillings are best.

- Fish (grilled) with lemon juice.
- Salad or fresh fruit.
- One slice (wholemeal) bread dry or lightly buttered.
- Beverage (no sugar) honey to sweeten.

DINNER

This is the main meal of the day and the one which makes a healthy contribution to the body's nutritional needs. No matter how large the evening meal, it cannot compensate for a missed breakfast and inadequate lunch.

- Tomato Juice.
- Lean meat (grilled) or chicken (never fried).
- Green vegetables, carrots or cauliflower.
- Salad.
- Fresh fruit desert or cheese and plain crackers.
- Beverage (no sugar) honey to sweeten.

DYNAMIC IMPRESSION 3: SPEECH PATTERN

Your voice is an important success tool in selling. Voice quality indicates whether you are energetic or lazy, tired or rested, sincere or insincere in your attitude and the things you say.

Some salesmen have voice qualities that repel others. Sharpness, too-high pitch or fatigue of voice are the result of insufficient air and failure to get the voice out of the throat. Many people choke-off words, do not enunciate or articulate clearly. Some are classic mumblers, some shouters. Either way, it's an annoyance to the person listening.

The English language has four pitch levels. The more actively you move your voice up and down those levels (light and shade, rise and fall) the more attractive will be the sound of your voice.

You do not always hear the sound of your own voice as others hear it. Nasalization, slurred consonants, throatiness or raspiness go unchecked until you become aware of how poor your voice quality is. A fairly accurate assessment can be made of your voice by cupping the hands behind the ears (forming a shell). Push the ears forward slightly and speak. Use of a tape recorder is the best method of hearing the *real* you. Once you are aware of the weak areas of your voice, make every effort to improve them. An improved voice quality improves impressions made on those who are in a position to enhance your sales commissions.

CORRECTION OF SPEECH PROBLEMS

Begin a daily reading program: newspapers, magazines, books, reports relating to selling and marketing. Read aloud and in front of a mirror. Listen for sloppy speech habits, mispronunciation and too slow or fast reading pace. Watch the movement of your lips. Correct exaggerated mouthing of words. Set aside time each day for speech analysis and correction of speech problems.

Read slowly and enunciate words. Don't mumble, slur words or drop 'h's' and 'ing's'. Don't bury your chin in your chest. Hold reading material at eye level so the voice isn't constricted. Develop a well-modulated tone. Avoid a monotonous drone, too loud (or soft) volume, a harsh nasal sound. Develop a natural speech rhythm; a fluency of words producing easy-to-understand ideas. *The key:* enunciate and articulate in a normal volume. Maintain a well-modulated tone.

YOUR SPEAKING VOICE CONTRIBUTES TO YOUR INDIVIDUALITY

Everything that is of a distinctively individual character contributes to your individuality as a salesman. The one favorable means of projecting an effective individualism is that of speaking. What you say is important; *how* you say it even more so.

There are two times when it is especially important for you to make effective speaking impressions when selling. The first is when *greeting* your prospect, the second is during the *main text* or body of your presentation. Both should be developed and perfected.

A fluid presentation of ideas through words and phrases sparked by an inner excitement causing the voice to rise and fall in a melodic, vibrant and interesting way, projects individualism for you.

A pleasant speaking voice should be developed quickly by those lacking this necessary attribute. Begin a daily speech improvement program. Read (aloud) passages from books. Record them on tape. Replay the tape, listen for mistakes and correct them.

DEVELOPING A RESONANT AND WELL-SUPPORTED TONE

More than three-quarters of the sounds used in connected speech are voiced. They are sounds for which the vocal folds are brought together and made to vibrate. If this vibration is firm, it will be transmitted through the upper part of the body (chest area). Feel a constant vibration through to the end of each sentence spoken by holding your hand over your chest.

Pay attention to the quality of your voice as it reaches the lower pitch levels, particularly at the end of sentences. Don't let your voice trail away, become weak, toneless or scratchy.

Practise correct breathing. Don't take gulps of air through the mouth. Breathe evenly through the nostrils. Practise the five exercises for developing resonance and correct breath control for at least 10 minutes each day.

5 TECHNIQUES FOR DEVELOPING A RESONANT VOICE

1. Sit or stand in an easy, erect position. Inhale and exhale deeply and smoothly *10 times*. Don't pull back the shoulders and throw out the chest. This tenses the muscles of the throat making it difficult to produce a 'free' tone. The chest cavity should enlarge as you inhale. The abdominal muscles will contract as you exhale.
2. Inhale and on exhalation sound an open vowel as: *'ah'—'oh'*. Relax the throat muscles so the sounds come out without being flat or harsh. Repeat *10 times*. Quietly at first, then gradually increase volume as voice improves.
3. As you exhale, count slowly to five. Take a deep breath and repeat. Link the syllables, hold the long vowels and voiced consonants. Repeat *10 times*.
4. Repeat the phrase *'Ha-hah!'* many times, making the syllables by a sharp 'kick' of the diaphragm. Whisper at first, increasing the energy of the sound with each repetition until virtually shouting, then decrease back to a whisper. Make the sound so that you cannot hear an escape of breath on the initial 'h'.
5. Place the fingers on the lips and hum; place them on the top of the head and hum; place them on the nose and hum; place them at the back of the head and hum. Feel the vibration. Say the following words: ring, sing, moan, hum, wind, going, coming, throwing. Place your hand on your chest and repeat the exercise. Feel the vibration.

WORDS ARE TOOLS OF TRADE FOR THE SALESMAN

It is helpful to know that for the five hundred most commonly used words in the English language, the dictionary lists approximately 14,000 meanings. This rules out the false assumption that words can only be used in one way. Words have many meanings. Do you attach the *correct* meanings to words? Understand that words are your *tools* of trade and should be chosen carefully.

The salesman's 'thinking' must be so accurately trained that every time he opens his mouth to speak he will use words that indicate clearly and accurately what is actually intended. Misuse of words is common, hence poor communication, resulting in lost production, industrial disputes, poor customer relations and lost orders.

Unless you know exactly what you want to convey and express it in a comprehensible manner, you cannot expect the listener to interpret for you. How often do you say one thing and mean another? Make sense of your message. Make it accurate, intelligible and totally clear.

INCREASING YOUR WORD POWER

Every salesman should possess a good dictionary and a *Thesaurus of English Words and Phrases*. A thesaurus is a book of words grouped by ideas. With a dictionary you know the word and need to find its meaning so it is listed alphabetically. With a thesaurus you have the idea and you want the right words to express it so all the words and phrases are classified according to ideas.

Words are the salesman's valuable *tools of trade* and he must know the precise words to use to express the meaning he wishes to convey. A good thesaurus gives you a range of synonyms (words that have nearly identical or related meanings) so that you can say exactly what you mean. Thus, an expanded vocabulary helps the salesman to communicate his message easily, confidently and impressively.

THAT SPECIAL 'SOMETHING' PEOPLE LOOK FOR IN A SALESMAN

Every topic calls for its own type of word skill. Professional selling calls for use of a *special* word skill that can never be neglected by the sales professional.

Creating good first impressions requires the use of understandable words that have no ring of 'ordinariness' about them. Your communication of ideas—through the effective use of words—must have a ring of sincerity and authority. Customers require that your manner and words show them you are what they *hope* you are: honest, efficient, reliable and an authority on the product or service you are offering.

People you deal with in your day-to-day business affairs don't want you to talk above them and certainly not in any condescending manner. They do expect something 'above the ordinary' of you and they want to *hear* it. *Word skill* is that special 'something' that can put you and your message across in a dynamic way.

BUILD A DAILY WORD PROGRAM

Set a daily word-building program. Learn five new words each day. Write them down on 3 x 5 cards and study meanings. Drop them into your conversations and sales presentations.

When you read or hear words you do not understand, write them down and check the definitions in a dictionary. When you require other than ordinary words to convey a meaning, consult a thesaurus.

You have something of importance to sell others—your product—use important, *persuasive* words (but not too high-sounding or unfamiliar) to convey your message.

12 MOST PERSUASIVE WORDS IN SELLING

A psychology professor at Yale University has listed the 12 'most persuasive' words in salesmanship. They are:

1. YOU
2. MONEY
3. NEW
4. SAVE
5. RESULTS
6. EASY
7. HEALTH
8. SAFETY
9. LOVE
10. DISCOVER
11. PROVED
12. GUARANTEED

VOCABULARY EXPANDER

The following list of words is offered as a 'starter' to your word-building program. Transfer them onto 3 x 5 cards and research the meaning of each.

A:
Accelerate
Acceptable
Accessory
Accommodate
Allotted
Assignor
Assignee
Actionable
Absolutely
Affirmative
Adhere
Aesthetic

B:
Backlog
Beautifier
Brilliancy
Balloted
Bonuses
Bravura
By-product
Byword
Bravado
Boding
Bizarre

C:
Commission
Committee
Consummate
Calculus
Caliber
Captivate
Capsule
Cataclysmic
Chauvinist

D:
Deferred
Dilettante
Deficit
Distributor
Docketed
Depreciation
Deference

E:
Equitable
Especially
Enactive
Endorsee
Enunciable

F:
Flagrant
Flagging
Flamboyance
Flavorous
Flout
Forte
Formulary

G:
Gruelling
Gleaning
Glib
Glimmering
Garnishment

H:
Harassing
Habitually
Haply
Horrendous
Hypocrisy
Hypothesis
Hybrid
Hurly
Humoresque

I:
Irrelevant
Irreverent
Idiosyncrasy
Idiomatic
Ignoble

J:
Judicious
Jubilate
Joyance
Jostle
Jurisdiction
Juxtaposition

K:
Kindred
Knead
Knowable
Kudos

L:
Laden
Lambaste
Legalism
Liaison
Literalism

69

M:	P:	S:	U:
Machinator	Palatial	Sconce	Unagitated
Magnitude	Palaver	Scourge	Unabated
Mainstay	Parallelism	Seditious	Ultraism
Maintainer	Paraphrase	Sedulous	Ubiquitous
Malevolently	Perspicacious	Seer	Undiscerning
Maraud	Phonetics	Sequential	Usurp
Manipulator	Plateau	Sequacious	
Maneuvering	Plight	Severity	
Manageable	Pliable	Sham	V:
Materialize	Populous	Sibilance	Vacillating
Mediate	Potpourri	Signification	Vacuity
Mentality	Precaution	Simile	Vacuous
Mettlesome	Premonition	Splenetic	Variance
Mindless		Splendent	Vernacular
Monopolistic		Spiritualist	Voracity
Motivation	Q:	Stratagem	
	Quixotic	Stratify	W:
N:	Quittance	Sublimate	Wastrel
Nebular	Quintessence		Waxen
Nefarious	Quirk		Wheedle
Negate	Quotient		Writhe
Negatory		T:	Wry
Negotiable		Tableau	Wrangle
Neolithic	R:	Tactician	
Nominative	Rampart	Tarrying	X:
Nonplussed	Rancor	Tartness	Xero
Nurture	Ravening	Tangible	Xanthous
	Raucous	Tedious	
	Rationality	Telekinesis	Y:
O:	Rebut	Tenuous	Yearn
Oblivious	Recalcitrate	Torpidity	Yore
Occultism	Recourse	Tolerable	
Omen	Recompense	Torque	Z:
Omnipresent	Reiterant	Toryism	Zonule
Opinionist	Remonstrate	Transverse	Zymotic
Overzealous	Repressionist	Transitive	Zyme
Ozone	Repose	Transcend	

DYNAMIC IMPRESSION 4: ATTITUDE AND PERSONALITY

This last section of image development pertains very closely to the 'self' of you discussed at the beginning of this chapter. We will now deal with personality, that mysterious *aura* some people display distinguishing them from the vast majority of humans who seem to lack that special 'something'.

The purpose of getting to know your 'self' is to guide you in your journey through life. It is a sense of direction, a *knowing* what you can and cannot do. Knowing the self is the beginning of wisdom and the starting point of all success.

You require a first rate physical look to create a visual impact. Physical changes and developments (discussed earlier) are the easiest to bring about. The next change to make is one of attitude. *Think right!* Create the right image patterns in your mind and you will manifest the right outer conditions.

ATTITUDE ANALYSIS CHART

If your honest marking reveals a score of 10 or more 'no' and 'sometimes' answers, then you are in a rut, bored with your job and the quality of your life-style. A firm plan of action to get moving should be your immediate goal. Know what you want and go after it.

ESTABLISHED ATTITUDE	NO	SOMETIMES	YES
● Do you feel you would like to change jobs?	☐	☐	☐
● Do you feel you are underpaid?	☐	☐	☐
● Do you have trouble remembering names, faces, places, dates?	☐	☐	☐
● Do you have difficulty getting started in the morning?	☐	☐	☐
● Do you plan your day or let things happen as they may?	☐	☐	☐
● Do you feel insecure in the job you are doing?	☐	☐	☐
● Do you feel that people are talking about you behind your back?	☐	☐	☐
● Are you shy in the company of others?	☐	☐	☐
● Do you give thought to your future?	☐	☐	☐
● Have you considered further training to achieve your aims and objectives?	☐	☐	☐
● Have you stopped to consider the impressions you are creating?	☐	☐	☐
● Do you have a reading program?	☐	☐	☐
● Do you have specific ideas and convictions on local and international affairs?	☐	☐	☐
● Are you a reliable person?	☐	☐	☐
● Are you honest in your dealings with others?	☐	☐	☐
● Are you able to make decisions?	☐	☐	☐
● Are you easy to get along with?	☐	☐	☐
● Can you take criticism?	☐	☐	☐
● Do you think about the feelings of others?	☐	☐	☐
● Are you able to communicate your ideas to others?	☐	☐	☐

SCORE:

71

YOUR INNER BELIEFS ABOUT YOURSELF MUST BE UPDATED

Your behavioral patterns must come under close scrutiny. Why do you say and do the things you do? What makes you react in a particular manner? You'd better find the answers. Your personality hinges on your attitudes.

Self analysis is the key. Discover your plus and minus personality factors. Write down a list of your positive and minus traits—what you *think* you are and the traits you display to others. Also, mark the *attitude analysis chart* and you will have an accurate composite of the type of individual you are.

WHAT IS PERSONALITY?

Every human being has a so-called 'personality'. But what is it? To many people, personality is a mysterious 'something' quite difficult to define but easily recognizable in others. It has been described by some as: 'a series of personal traits.' But *what* traits?—read on.

Webster's *New World Dictionary* gives personality this description:

> *Habitual patterns and qualities of behavior*
> *of any individual as expressed by physical and*
> *mental activities and attitudes. The sum of*
> *such qualities as impressing or likely to impress.*

Perhaps personality is best described as expressing the qualities of the 'self'—pleasant or otherwise. It is the sum total of your estimation of yourself: thoughts, feelings, beliefs, skills, physical looks. You always express your feelings through your personality. Hence, an individual could be described as having confident, friendly, happy, enthusiastic, charming personality traits. Your personality then, is a clear reflection of your *inner* convictions and values.

THE TWO PERSONALITY TYPES

It is generally accepted that man has two types of personality: adequate and inadequate. One is valued, the other value*less*. Both personality types stem from 'attitude'. An individual's attitude or concept about himself creates a positive personality or a negative one.

ADEQUATE PERSONALITY TYPE: derived from a proper *value* being placed on the *real* self. You accept the fact that you are a totally unique human being with individual thoughts, feelings and beliefs as well as creative abilities. You see yourself as Infinite Intelligence created you: an expression of glorious Life encompassing beauty, wisdom, truth, love and creative genius. The Divine Energy is in your soul. Recognizing these truths, you place the proper value on the 'self' of you and without conceit or arrogance your *self* respect returns an acceptable adequate personality. It is a personality *alive* with the wonderful traits others admire and respect: enthusiastic, friendly, generous, loving, compassionate.

INADEQUATE PERSONALITY TYPE: reflects deep inner resentments and hostilities toward the self. The inner voice is saying: 'I'm no good. I'm worthless. I hate myself.' What you think (about yourself) you become. Imagine yourself to be inadequate and you'll become inadequate in everything you do. Self condemnation arises from a lack of *self* respect. A changed self concept (value placed on the self) brings a changed (affirmative) personality.

SELL YOUR TRUE PERSONALITY

Your true personality will shine when you gain a high estimate of yourself and approve of yourself as an individualized expression of Divine Mind. You are different from any other living person. You have unique capabilities. You are equipped to express this thing called Life in a brilliant and special way reserved *exclusively* for you.

Individuals who have control over their thoughts will have a pleasing 'open' personality. If your estimation of yourself is less than pleasing then you must change it and keep it changed. Self confidence is gained when you feel secure within yourself. It is reflected in your personality, your speech pattern, your health, your manner, (and of concern to every salesman) your ability to sell successfully.

You have a certain potential or capacity and you must know what that potential is. You must take full stock of personal assets and then use them to full advantage. If you extend yourself to the limit, the limits will recede, the boundaries will be pushed back while your potential rushes forward.

You have wonderful potential as a salesman to earn large amounts of money and to contribute to the well-being of your fellow man. You have a source of power that has only to be *recognized, approved* and *valued*—then *used*.

Psychologists inform us that in almost every sphere of life, success depends 80 per cent on personality and 20 per cent on acquired skills. This clearly indicates that the salesman must develop his personality to express himself fully and eliminate all inferior, inadequate and insecure feelings from his consciousness. *The key:*

● DEVELOP A SENSE OF *SELF* ESTEEM.

● HONOR THE QUALITIES-ATTRIBUTES AND SKILLS OF THE *SELF*.

● EXPLOIT THE CREATIVE ABILITIES OF THE *SELF*.

HOW NEGATIVE PERSONALITY DEVELOPS

Negative thoughts are the seeds from which poor personality traits grow: guilt feelings, envy, jealousy, conceit, intolerance are just a few which surface and project an uncomplimentary image. A poor personality is self inflicted—sometimes unconsciously—and is difficult to change once the mold has been cast. Attempting to bolster personality traits without changing the cause (attitude) is self-defeating.

73

Negative personality *can* be changed. It begins shining brightly when negative self concepts are eliminated from the mind and solid belief in the self is substituted. You talk, act and look according to the specific thoughts and images you hold in your mind. If your images are distorted and unrealistic, then your reaction to them will be inappropriate. The secret of personality change is to discover the calibre of thought and image held relating to the self and up-grade it. If you despise yourself, you cannot express a wonderfully-radiant personality. Your inner resentments deny you this.

ELIMINATE THE DETRACTORS

Now that you are aware of what creates a personality pattern, get to work eliminating detractors which spoil your image. Take stock of your personal assets and liabilities. Detractors to rid yourself of are:

STOCK PHRASES IN SPEECH

MUMBLING

CARELESS MANNERS

WEAK HANDSHAKE

HOSTILE ATTITUDE

SLANG EXPRESSIONS

DISORGANIZED ACTIONS

POOR VOICE QUALITY

TARDINESS—NO
    RESPECTER OF TIME

PROCRASTINATION

COLD MANNER

GLOOMY

THOUGHTLESS

SLOPPY DRESS AND
    GROOMING

REFUSING EYE CONTACT

CUTTING OTHERS OFF
    MID-SENTENCE

SELF REJECTION

ARGUMENTATIVE

UNCOUTH MANNER

NERVOUS SCRATCHING-
    BITING NAILS

EXAGGERATED GESTURES

GOSSIPY

ENVIOUS—JEALOUS

CRUEL

WHINING AND COMPLAIN-
    ING

UNPREDICTABLE

PERSONALITY COMPOSITE CHART

I AM		I WOULD LIKE TO BECOME	
Aggressive	☐	Pleasant	☐
Unreasonable	☐	Accepting	☐
Abrupt	☐	Good mannered	☐
Unappreciative	☐	Generous	☐
Lacking self confidence	☐	Confident	☐
Without faith in my ability	☐	Strong of mind	☐
Unhappy	☐	Joyous	☐
Unloved	☐	Loving	☐
Lonely	☐	Happy	☐
Hostile	☐	Friendly	☐
Superstitious	☐	Realistic	☐
Greedy	☐	Selflessness	☐
Dishonest	☐	Honest	☐
Fearful	☐	Powerful	☐
Insecure in job	☐	Secure in Job	☐
Unorganized	☐	Methodical	☐
Selfish	☐	Thoughtful	☐
Prejudiced	☐	Compassionate	☐
Lazy	☐	Energetic	☐
Frustrated	☐	Patient—Serene	☐
Unreliable	☐	Integrity	☐
Careless	☐	Dependable—Alert	☐
Inferiority feelings	☐	Mature	☐
Confused and anxious	☐	Constructive	☐
Cranky	☐	Serene—Calm	☐
Immature	☐	Flexible	☐
Envious	☐	Well adjusted	☐
Jealous	☐	Understanding	☐
Possessive	☐	Reasonable	☐
Boastful	☐	Humble	☐
Suspicious	☐	Trusting	☐
Cowardly	☐	Brave	☐
Bad mannered	☐	Courteous	☐
Criticizing	☐	Constructive	☐
Uninterested	☐	Enthusiastic	☐
Negative	☐	Affirmative	☐

SUMMARY OF IDEAS TO HELP YOU CREATE
DYNAMIC IMPRESSIONS

1. Get to know the *real* you. You are more than flesh and bone. You are consciousness: thought, perception, awareness. Ask yourself the question: 'Who am I?' Get to know your strengths and weaknesses.

2. Visual impact must be created during the first 90 seconds of meeting a prospect. Your first job is to sell yourself, your personality package: dress, grooming, posture, manner, etc. Where visual impact is lacking in a salesman, sales difficulties occur.

3. Monitor the image you are projecting to others. Remember: others are judging your performance and setting a low or high value on it. Eliminate nervous detractors and project an adequate personality.

4. Successful impressions are created by raising the standard of four aspects of you: DRESS AND GROOMING—GENERAL MANNER—SPEECH PATTERN—ATTITUDE AND PERSONALITY.

5. Your clothes tell a lot about your personality and character. Dress-up your visual image with well-cut clothes. Always dress in good taste.

6. Good grooming is essential for those dealing with the public. Hair, nails and body must be clean.

7. Your posture is a vital factor contributing to good health. Stand tall. Your walk indicates your state of mind. Don't lope along, droop the shoulders or sway from side to side when you walk.

8. Stem anxiety and worry by thinking affirmative thoughts. Expect the best and you will receive the best. You cannot win sales with a 'hang-dog' look.

9. Look after your health. Eat nourishing foods. Follow a suitable diet.

10. Watch your speech pattern. Increase your vocabulary. Words are your tools of trade. Develop a resonant, pleasant sounding voice. Project a strong personality. Display confidence in your true 'self'.

HOW TO APPLY
THE TECHNIQUES OF
PSYCHOLOGICAL SELLING

FORMULA

4

Affirmative Ideas in this Chapter

- A Short History of Selling
- The Psychology of Modern-Day Selling
- Analyzing The Two Divisions of Selling
- Gain A Realistic Attitude About Selling
- The Basic Needs of Humans
- The Consumer Market Requirements
- The Retail Trade Requirements
- The 6 Psychological Needs of All of Us
- The 3 Secrets of Psychological Selling
- Why People Buy
- Psychological Selling Is Not Taking—It's Giving
- The First Law of Psychological Selling
- Finding the Psychological Buying Motive
- The 5 Main Buying Motives
- Analyzing The Buying Motives
- 2 Buying Motive Examples
- If You're Getting Too Many Rejections Re-Check The Buying Motive
- Get To Know More About Your Customers
- Buying Motives Chart
- How To (Psychologically) Handle The Various Buyer Types
- The Male Response
- The Female Response
- Low Key (Psychological) Selling Vs High Key (Pressure) Selling
- Group Buying Motives
- How To Achieve Greater Selling Awareness
- Wake Up And Live
- How To Build Confidence In The Mind of The Buyer
- The Extent of External Forces
- Summary of Ideas To Help You Sell Psychologically

4

A SHORT HISTORY OF SELLING

The history of selling dates back to early, primitive man. He survived by living off the land. As he progressed, he began to move further afield to satisfy his curiosity and to seek better conditions and environment. The mountain people moved to the sea and here found others who lived by different means and conditions. The mountain people communicated their desire to exchange meat and skins for fish and nets. Thus began a system of barter. (The first long-distance trade began more than 10,000 years ago in what is now France. Written records of goods acquired through barter date back to 5000 B.C. in Sumeria.)

It didn't take enterprising men long to discover that the harder they worked, the more they caught and the more they had to trade, which ultimately brought greater advantages to their way of life.

Soon, these enterprising men began travelling to distant villages to exchange skins, feathers, beads, arrows, crude cutting tools and weapons. The exchange of possessions ultimately gave way to precious metals being used as a medium of exchange. With this new system came a *change* in selling motivation—greed. Dishonesty in selling came about.

Peddlers took to horseback, to boats to blaze new trade routes. Wherever settlements sprang up the trader was on hand to sell his tinware, cloth, flints, guns and medicines. With the arrival of the railroads, the numbers of travelling salesmen increased. Many of them with less than honest motives.

Drummers, droppers, exploiters, travelled far and wide to exchange and sell merchandise for exorbitant prices. As competition became keener and production methods more sophisticated, trick selling and high pressure tactics were employed. Many people were brainwashed with outlandish claims and tricked into buying goods they couldn't afford or pay for. To cope with this problem, clever businessmen offered a time payment purchase plan—with interest added.

History has recorded those companies that have followed the path of unethical trading practices. Hundreds of thousands of them are statistics buried in bankruptcy registrars.

The great merchant houses of the world have prospered because of customer acceptance based on fair value, ethical business practices, quality merchandise and service. The history of selling clearly indicates that to be successful, individuals as well as companies must adhere to honest selling methods. The customer must never be considered 'someone to take money from.' A fair and mutually beneficial exchange must take place bringing satisfaction to both buyer and seller.

The professional sales representative is a contributor, an adviser and counselor to his customers and clients. Their welfare is his concern. Perhaps the Rotarian motto sums up the attitude best adopted by today's psychological salesman: 'He profits most who serves best.'

While there are dishonest salesmen around the name of the profession will always have less respect than it deserves. Fortunately today, consumer protection bureaus keep a watchful eye on the trading practices of companies and those representing them. This was also the case in the first century. Roman writings of that time labelled dishonest traders 'vulgar persons' and the practice of reselling goods by trick means a 'degrading custom.'

Selling has played (and will go on playing) a vital role in the life of communities and nations. The art and science of selling will undergo further refinements as man grows mentally and spiritually.

Honest selling professionals have helped build our nation. They make possible advancements in design of merchandise that brings a high standard of living to the mass. History has also recorded the names of men, who, by their ability to communicate and motivate, were able to move a nation and turn dark hours into the sunlight of victory. This is the true art of *salesmanship* and there are many and varied examples to be copied by those who aspire to the winners' circle in the noble profession of selling.

THE PSYCHOLOGY OF MODERN-DAY SELLING

Enter the seventies and the introduction of a more challenging sales approach: *psychological selling*. Its basis is a thorough knowledge of human behavioral patterns: *why* people are as they are; *what* motivates them to certain action; *how* they can be motivated toward a specific end result. The study of human needs, habits and emotions is a deep study and one that should be undertaken by those desiring a career in selling.

The professional salesman is an individual who has come to terms with his own self; one who has learned to control his *own* emotional responses: fears, frustrations, anxieties, moods. In knowing the personal self, it is easier to understand the self of others. And this he must do— *accurately.*

> *You will find that the mere resolve*
> *not to be useless, and the honest*
> *desire to help other people, will,*
> *in the quickest and delicatest ways,*
> *improve yourself.*
>
> RUSKIN.

ANALYZING THE TWO DIVISIONS OF SELLING

Many changes have come about in the sales and marketing profession since the beginning of the nineteen-seventies. Selling to the 'wary' consumer has altered dramatically. The modern-day buyer has become much more sophisticated, better informed and technically knowledgeable. The product knowledge of the average consumer is often as good and sometimes better than the product knowledge of the average salesman. For this reason alone, there is a decided move on the part of managements to employ salesmen who are capable of researching, studying and assimilating large amounts of product information.

Recent developments in the advertising profession (geared to stimulate heavier buying demands by a discerning public) support the contention that salesmen today must be better trained and technically and psychologically equipped to handle the demands of an advanced-thinking public.

While the professional will have a broad knowledge of many subjects, the tendency is toward more 'specialist' selling knowledge. The entry of technology into the sales encounter has made it imperative that salesmen know how to cope with technically-oriented questions and objections. Degrees in engineering or business, while helpful, are not essential. But thorough product-knowledge training and indoctrination are an absolute must. And this is the distinguishing mark of the true professional: a constant striving to improve knowledge relating to his company, product and market, until he approaches perfection in his chosen field.

Professional salesmen and the selling profession can be divided into two specialist areas. They are:

(a) *The consumer market*—salesmen who sell to consumers.
   Speciality (outside) selling. Retail (inside) selling.

(b) *The retail trade*—salesmen who sell to resellers.

Each of these classifications has a separate set of required qualifications. As a general rule, nearly all sellers to users are specialists and therefore, their knowledge of the product or service offered is specialized. The salesman selling to the reseller has a more exacting job; he needs to know a great deal about the reseller as well as the consumer who eventually will use his product or service. Both types of sales professionals must be personally motivated by a strong sense of 'serving the needs' of their clients. And this is done with completely honest motives.

GAIN A REALISTIC ATTITUDE ABOUT SELLING

Psychological selling is an art as well as a science. It is not a profession for the weak minded, the physically lazy or those seeking 'easy' money or something for nothing.

A scientific and successful approach to selling is gained by those who understand that honor, self respect and a desire to help others are the basic requirements of the professional. Self confidence, courage, enthusiasm, determination, resourcefulness and integrity are allied factors which cannot be ignored. They must be *part* of the salesman's personality and character.

A realistic attitude is brought about when the sales representative recognizes the fact that he cannot sell every prospect he approaches. Selling is a *percentages game*. Therefore, the professional develops a realistic sales philosophy based on the law of averages: the more calls made to the right type of client, the greater the number of sales made. This attitude brings a degree of 'detachment' resulting in fewer disappointments, negative moods and self depreciation.

THE BASIC NEEDS OF HUMANS

The basic needs of humans are: food, clothing, housing, transportation and the exploitation of creative abilities. These human needs are sought in varying degrees by people everywhere; during every minute of every hour of every day salesmen are satisfying these needs.

However, one very important psychological (emotional) need which is often disregarded (and often the one most sought) is the need of *appreciation*. It is a fact of life that humans love to be loved, to be wanted, to be appreciated.

A compliment—sincerely expressed—has the power to change attitude, facial expression and physical bearing. Try it and see! Pass a compliment to your wife about her cooking, dress or personality. Watch her facial expression 'light up', notice her attitude change and sparkle, watch her posture straighten. Sincere praise is the best medicine I know for cheering up a person who is depressed. A word of caution: do not make this a game, passing insincere compliments to all-and-sundry. Give praise where praise is due. It must not be done with falseness or any ulterior motive.

> *What charms are there in the harmony of minds, and in a friendship founded on mutual esteem and gratitude.*

> DAVID HUME.

THE CONSUMER MARKET
—REQUIREMENTS—

1. *Thorough knowledge* of the product or service offered.
2. *Specific knowledge* of how it can be utilized.
3. *Understanding* of the requirements of the purchaser.
4. *Knowledge* of the territory assigned.
5. *Awareness* of market potential in assigned territory.
6. *Knowledge* of advantages and disadvantages of competitor products.
7. *Awareness* of the capability and reliability of client to pay for products or services offered.
8. *Knowledge* of time and motion expenditure: the capability to get things done in the shortest possible time.
9. *Knowledge* of policy, management structure and historical background of company worked for.
10. *Thorough knowledge* of the structure of a sales presentation incorporating the *AIDA* formula.

THE RETAIL TRADE
—REQUIREMENTS—

1. *Thorough knowledge* of the product and its uses including all technical data.
2. *Knowledge* of the market. (Awareness of social levels being sold to).
3. *Awareness* of all competitor activities: advertising, promotions, etc.
4. *Complete knowledge* of company: policy, historical, financial, image, goals.
5. *Background* on each client serviced: financial responsibility, average purchases, interview times, psychological makeup.
6. *Ability* to gather market research material on territory covered.
7. *Ability* to communicate to groups. Effective oratory ability.
8. *Ability* to relate product or service to the needs of the resellers' customers.
9. *Ability* to solve customer problems associated with the use of product.
10. *Thorough knowledge* of the professional selling procedure incorporating the *AIDA* formula.

The salesman who learns the art of 'appreciation' and applies it *sincerely* will win worthwhile business and personal friendships *and* sales. Learn to appreciate the personal qualities of customers and express your true feelings about them. Appreciate the time a buyer gives. *Thank* the buyer. Express appreciation for business received no matter how small the purchase. Express appreciation of valued friendships made. Your showing of this much desired need will return rewards far beyond your expectation.

THE 6 PSYCHOLOGICAL NEEDS OF ALL OF US

Six basic feelings and emotions are common to all people. A complete understanding of them will help you to better understand yourself and others.

Psychologists have defined them quite clearly and they are:

1. The need to feel secure.
2. The need to be appreciated.
3. The need to love, be loved and receive affection.
4. The need to conquer fear and worry and solve problems.
5. The need to create and exploit skills.
6. The need for new experiences.

These desires are the same in all of us: children, adults, male or female. It is necessary to understand the needs and drives before we can establish satisfactory human relationships. Psychologists point out that children who have been deprived of love are likely to become timid, shy and insecure adults *or* aggressive and hostile toward others.

Human beings cannot live harmoniously, beneficially or normally without affection and appreciation being shown to them. Approval of what we are and what we do from those we admire and respect brings out the best in us. Lack of it causes anxiety and discourages us from doing our best in work and personal dealings with others.

Security is a feeling all people strive to experience. We cannot work efficiently while under the threat of losing possessions, employment or loved ones. Fear of failure cripples the thinking processes and retards the creative genius within us.

New experiences give an emotional 'lift' to our lives and offer something to look forward to—something bigger and better. Restricting movement (travel) and interests (hobbies, sports, job, friends), keeps us from expanding our lives mentally, spiritually and physically.

These six 'feelings' we *all* desire and need in life. And the professional salesman will find he will be in a better position to help others if he makes a serious study of them.

THE 3 SECRETS OF PSYCHOLOGICAL SELLING

Although each of us has individual thought choice and individual expression of ideas and feelings, the vast majority of peoples around the world conform to 'patterns' of thinking and acting. Families, communities, nations, conform to certain beliefs whether they be social, political, religious or otherwise. We think individually *and* collectively on matters of personal importance.

Thus, the salesman becomes aware of the *first* secret of psychological selling: *human beings are highly amenable to the power of suggestion.* People can be swayed from one point of view to another, from one product or service to another and from one attitude or state of mind (negative or affirmative) to another.

Psychological selling secret *two* deals with the 'reasoning' factor: *human beings are easily swayed when the idea or thing presented offers a definite advantage to their way of life.* People are constantly searching for an easier and better way to live.

The *third* secret eliminates the need to 'sell' or pressure people into buying. It is this: *human beings will buy voluntarily if the idea or thing presented appeals to their ego, fulfills a specific need or enhances their self esteem.* Here they are again, study them carefully:

1. HUMAN BEINGS ARE HIGHLY AMENABLE TO SUG-GESTION.

2. HUMAN BEINGS ARE EASILY SWAYED IF AN ADVANTAGE IS EVIDENT.

3. HUMAN BEINGS DO NOT NEED TO BE 'PRESSURED' IF A PROPOSITION APPEALS TO THEIR EGO—FULFILLS A NEED—ENHANCES THEIR SELF ESTEEM.

WHY PEOPLE BUY

There isn't a customer alive who buys 'things' in order that the salesman might increase *his* income or personal needs. A customer buys because he wants to fulfill *his* desires and satisfy *his* needs. As simple a statement as this is, it is positively amazing how many salesmen begin a presentation thinking only of their own needs. This truth should be written on a card and read prior to beginning a sales presentation:

> *People do not buy products or services for the sake*
> *of buying them or to give seller satisfaction. People*
> *buy products or services for the sake of 'something*
> *to be gained' from them and to satisfy personal desires*
> *and needs.*

PSYCHOLOGICAL SELLING IS NOT TAKING—IT'S GIVING

The first rule to be learned in psychological selling is to think in terms of *YOU* (the customer) not *I* (the salesman). A common mistake made by many salesmen is to start the presentation with the selfish thought: 'what can I *get* from this customer?' Selling is a give-and-take arrangement between buyer and seller and not a one-sided proposition favoring the seller.

Eliminate selfish motives and think in terms of *mutual* benefits to be gained: a consideration of customer satisfaction *first* and then seller satisfaction. When both seller and buyer benefit, satisfaction is automatic. Dissatisfaction occurs when the buyer finds he has not benefited from the transaction.

Begin every presentation with the thought: 'How can I benefit you?' (The customer.) Think of it as:

THE *YOU* FACTOR

When the customer realizes that he has something to gain, he says 'yes' and the sale is concluded satisfactorily. The unselfish motive of the seller is rewarded (commission earned) automatically without necessity of using trick selling methods or pressuring the customer. It's a case of doing the *right* things to get the *right* results.

Every human looks for self advantages. Prior to the interview ask yourself: 'What benefits do I have for the customer?' FIND the customer benefits. INDIVIDUALIZE the advantages and SELL the YOU FACTOR rewards.

THE FIRST LAW OF PSYCHOLOGICAL SELLING

Find the YOU factor and supply it and you will have learned the first law of psychological selling. What benefits are there for the customer in the proposition you want him to accept? If this sale is concluded will the customer have a feeling of satisfaction or disappointment? Is your motive one of greed or customer satisfaction?

Your objective must be to genuinely help the other person by selling him goods or services that he can use and benefit by, not goods or services that are difficult to market or do not live up to promises made about them. This is where personal integrity enters selling—but does not end. Your selling motive must always be to SATISFY A NEED— FULFILL A DESIRE. Remember: whatever customers decide to do is due to *their* reasons—*their* needs, wants and desires—not yours. The psychological concept of selling holds that the selling process is not really selling at all but a *buying* process.

FINDING THE PSYCHOLOGICAL BUYING MOTIVE

The salesman is a professional adviser-counselor and therefore, should work with customers to assist them in the solving of business problems: matching the best possible product (service) to specific needs, thereby enhancing some aspect of their business or personal affairs.

Sometimes, the psychological 'need' of the buyer is an obvious one, often it isn't. Before the sale can proceed along satisfactory and scientific lines, the buyer's 'desire factor' must be established. How will the product (service) be used? What benefits will accrue to the buyer? Can the product satisfy stated wants? Starting with the premise that people buy to satisfy needs and fulfill desires, the seller must make a fast analysis of the BUYING MOTIVE(S).

Buying motives are found by a process of *adroit questioning*. The buyer reveals his needs and desires in answer to carefully-worded and subtly-presented questions. There are times, of course, when questioning is not required as the buying motive is an obvious one. For example, a customer wishing to purchase a staple food item, an item of toiletry, a particular stationery line, etc. Buying motives would not be *as* obvious in the desire to purchase: an automobile, a sewing machine, tools, certain hardware lines and building materials, etc.

THE 5 MAIN BUYING MOTIVES

There are five basic buying motives. People buy to satisfy at least one of them and sometimes a combination of them. The buying motives are:

1. GAIN
2. PRIDE
3. FEAR
4. IMITATION
5. PLEASURE

Discovering the buying motive and structuring a presentation around it, reduces the possibility of losing a sale. The possibility of closing is greatly enhanced because the seller is fulfilling his professional obligation: to service the needs of his customer and enhance some aspect of his business or personal life.

Analyze the customer's buying motive by getting answers to:

WHO is the buyer? (his status).

WHAT is it he requires?

WHEN does he wish to use the product or service?

WHERE will the product or service be utilized?

WHY should he buy the product or service? (advantages).

Quite often, this information can be established prior to meeting the customer. If this is not possible then the information can be gathered and quickly assessed *during* the presentation.

ANALYZING THE BUYING MOTIVES

The sales representative must understand WHY the customer is interested in his product or service or why he SHOULD be interested in it. Without this knowledge, selling becomes a 'hit-and-miss' situation with the salesman only *occasionally* satisfying the needs of his customers and thereby, only occasionally concluding sales successfully.

People are motivated to buy goods or services by internal (emotional) reasons and by external forces (influence of others). This is why the salesman must present the benefits of buying so that they meet the prospect's *precise* needs. He must build his appeal factors around the affirmative (gain, pride, imitation, pleasure) or negative (fear) buying motives.

The needs and desires of the buyer are always secreted within the five main buying motives. Analyze each of them in turn and you will find that (psychologically speaking) the *ulterior* motive(s) is always physical and or emotional gratification.

1. GAIN—to obtain a financial advantage and increase present worth.
2. PRIDE—to satisfy the ego. To fulfill creative urges.
3. FEAR—to stem competition or produce and market goods at lower cost.
4. IMITATION—to increase social standing, enhance the self image.
5. PLEASURE—to gain a more comfortable existence, experience happiness.

2 BUYING MOTIVE EXAMPLES

EXAMPLE 1: Customer 'A' enters a car dealership and proceeds to look over a bottom-of-the-line model. The salesman begins his presentation by pointing out the beautiful color range available, the advantages of adding luxury extras such as air conditioning, radio, leather upholstery to the car. The customer leaves without making a purchase and crosses the street to another dealer. Here, the salesman discovers (through adroit questioning) that the customer seeks a replacement automobile for his business. Realizing that the buying motive is GAIN (the car is to be used to make money) the salesman begins his presentation with a list of product *plus factors* geared to satisfy the buyer's desire: 'Mr. Buyer, this basic model has no frills or costly extras. Less maintenance means more time on the road instead of in the workshop. More miles per gallon of gasoline adds up to lower yearly operating costs. The sensible and practical seating arrangement means less tension and strain on the driver.' Satisfied that this particular model fulfills his requirements, the customer signs the deal.

EXAMPLE 2: Salesman 'A' enters the office of a buyer for a major department store. He is selling transistor radios and hoping for a large order. He plows his way through a presentation and at the end of it is surprised (and dismayed) when the buyer rejects his offer.

Salesman 'B' calls on the same buyer. He, too, is selling transistor radios. Knowing that he must find two buying motives (retailer and retailer's customers' motives) salesman 'B' proceeds to adroitly question his prospect. The buying motive of the retailer is obvious: *gain*. The second motive is found to be a combination of *pleasure* and *pride*. 'My transistor radio customers are mostly teenagers and they buy them to take to the beach. They love colorful looking units with as many gadgets on them as possible,' the retailer informs the salesman.

Armed with this information, the presentation of salesman 'B' proceeds along scientific and psychological lines. He presents the advantages supporting the buying motives of *gain, pleasure* and *pride*. Briefly, the presentation includes the following points:

GAIN: added profits for the retailer from greater volume of units sold of this unusually attractive and low-priced model.

PLEASURE: large speaker gives superior tone quality in this compact unit. Easy-to-operate dials with separate volume and tone controls give pleasurable hours of listening at low cost.

PRIDE: this radio has many features found only on more expensive models: ear plug, carrying case, electric and battery operated, luminous dial, speaker extension jack and 12 attractive colors to choose from.

Salesman 'B' satisfies the retailer's needs and convinces him that his transistor radios will fully satisfy the needs of *his* customers. The retailer recognizes the advantages of buying and the sale is successfully closed.

IF YOU'RE GETTING TOO MANY REJECTIONS RE-CHECK THE BUYING MOTIVE

Too many rejections mean that you aren't selling the customer the things he *really* wants. You are not fulfilling his idea of 'advantages to be gained.' Re-check the buying motive and be certain that you present product plus factors which answer *all* aspects of it. Do not clutter a presentation with points that are of little interest or advantage to the client. Give him every conceivable point which adds up to: 'this is too good to miss.' Check the buying motive by asking yourself the following questions:

(a) Is the customer seeking monetary satisfaction? (GAIN).

(b) Is he desiring to satisfy his ego? (PRIDE).

(c) Is he attempting to combat competition? (FEAR).

(d) Is he trying to increase his social standing, gain prestige? (IMITATION).

(e) Is he looking for a more comfortable, easier way of life? (PLEASURE).

(f) Is he motivated by interior desires or exterior influences?

GET TO KNOW MORE ABOUT YOUR CUSTOMERS

To become more effective in your dealings with customers, strive to *understand* them. Look for better ways to handle them when difficult situations arise. Analyze the way they think, feel and act. Develop an ability to 'read' their motives. Learning more about people is a matter of *observation* and a willingness to *listen*.

Study attitudes and actions—they go together like coffee and cream. Look for definite patterns of thought which motivate corresponding actions. Look for emotion negatives: envy, jealousy, greed, insecurity, prejudice, timidity, intolerance, etc. How *friendly* are your customers? Are they *sensitive* to the opinions of others? Do they become *upset* easily? What is the *tolerance* level of each?

Draft an image profile of each customer you call on. Write down a list of their strengths and weaknesses of character and personality. Find the best method of approach in each case. Your new-found knowledge will help you to deal with each customer psychologically and thus, *effectively*.

BUYING MOTIVE CHART

GAIN
- EXTRA PROFITS
- MONEY EARNED
- TIME SAVED
- INCREASED PRODUCTION
- LOWER OVERHEADS
- PRODUCT AND COMPANY RECOGNITION

PRIDE
- OWNERSHIP OF POSSESSIONS
- APPEARANCE
- SOCIAL STANDING
- JUDGEMENT
- CREATIVE ACHIEVEMENT
- LOVED ONES

FEAR
- LOSS OF STATUS
- LOSS OF SALES
- COMPETITOR GAINS
- LOSING OUT
- INABILITY TO PAY
- OVERPRODUCTION— OVERSTOCKED
- RIDICULE

IMITATION
- TO BE AS GOOD AS
- TO GO ONE BETTER
- TO SET PERSONAL STANDARDS
- TO GAIN PRESTIGE
- TO SATISFY EGO DEMANDS
- TO CONFORM

PLEASURE
- EASIER EXISTENCE
- HAPPINESS—CREATIVE FULFILMENT
- ENHANCE WELL-BEING
- REDUCE TENSION— FATIGUE
- BRING ADDED COMFORTS
- ENJOY NEW EXPERIENCES

HOW TO (PSYCHOLOGICALLY) HANDLE THE VARIOUS BUYER TYPES

There are hundreds of different buyer types: timid, aggressive, negative, impulsive, honest, dishonest, etc. Make a list of 'buyer types' you have met. Add to the list each time you meet a new type. Look for ways to handle each. Some of the more obvious buyer types are:

THE STALLER: he will think of every excuse in the book to avoid saying 'yes' and he can be the most frustrating individual to sell to. Always emphasize 'loss' caused by delay. Suggest that waiting will increase the basic cost as a price rise is imminent. Flatter his power of decision making by saying: 'A man with your decisive mind would not procrastinate in a matter of personal importance. Would you agree, Mr. Smith?'

THE METHODICAL: he needs time and re-statement to get your message in full. He is slow—very slow on the uptake. Go easy. Take the presentation step-by-step and get the prospect to agree with each point you make. Do not attempt to pressure this type of buyer or you will lose him. Be patient. Stay with him and he will come through with a firm 'yes' to your final close questions.

THE INSECURE: he really needs coaxing. He wants someone else to make up his mind for him. He will ask you question after question, hoping all the time that you will tell him he *must* buy. Don't leave the final decision up to Mr. Insecure or he will take the easy path out and tell you he'll 'think about it' and come back at some future time. Of course he never does come back and that's a prospect lost.

THE CONCEITED: he knows everything and could teach you a few things about selling—if you let him. Flattery will get you everywhere with this type. Keep patting his ego and concentrate on the immediate sale.

THE IMPULSIVE: get it over fast and don't waste time on unimportant points. He sees it, he likes it and he wants to buy it. *Pace* is the key here.

THE TALKATIVE: he's come in out of the rain and he'd talk the leg off an iron pot. Lead him back to your point system. Don't give him the (sales) reins or he'll ride off on your horse, forgetting that *you* wanted to sell him something.

THE SUSPICIOUS: he's a real 'motive' man. You'd better have the right answers or he'll make mince meat out of your arguments. He wants to know everything there is to know about you and your company. Have the answers ready and shoot them at him eye-ball-to-eye-ball. Don't flinch or lose eye contact or you are sure to lose him.

THE COMPLAINER: he's tried your product and it's 'absolutely useless.' He'll complain about every little thing. He needs psycho-analyzing. Find out *why* he feels as he does and what would really make him happy. When he tells you, sell him what he wants and he'll go away happy.

THE NODDER: he doesn't say very much, just shakes his head and grunts a lot. Pretty hard to communicate with this fellow. Throw a series of questions at him and wait for his answers. Look him straight in the eye and silently challenge him to open his mouth and speak.

The theory of buying behaviour and buyer types is built around ego gratification and self and projected image qualities. It's a matter of finding out what the customer wants. Knowing how he sees and values himself in terms of physical looks, personality traits and human values. It is the job of the master salesman to determine—through questioning, listening and observing—what the prospect's true motivations are and to build the sales presentation around them.

Well, there they are—at least some of them. I'm sure you will be able to add other buyer types to this list. The more kinds of people you meet and analyze, the more you learn how to handle people and the more success you have as a psychology-oriented salesman.

THE MALE RESPONSE

Because of differences in psychological make-up, the male buyer often has different buying motives and appeal reasons than his female counterpart. The male is more *objective* and tends to view things rationally and logically from an overall situation. He responds more to reason and is concerned with facts and logic. He is more of a gambler and will take a chance on something new more so than the female. For the most part he could be considered a *RATIONAL BUYER*.

THE FEMALE RESPONSE

Much more subjective than the male and tends to look at things in the light of how they will affect her personally. She buys more on *emotional appeal* than using logic. The female is more conservative and likes to feel she is buying a product that has general acceptance. Quite often is suspicious of new things and doesn't like to take too many chances, particularly with mechanical items. Instructions must be easy to understand and simple to apply. If it's too complicated she'll pass it up. Because of her psychological make-up she could be classified (usually) as an *IRRATIONAL BUYER*.

LOW KEY (PSYCHOLOGICAL) SELLING Vs HIGH KEY (PRESSURE) SELLING

Low-key selling is the favored form of salesmanship today. High-key or 'pressure' selling is a negative method whereby the salesman attempts by any means (fair or trick) to coerce the buyer into placing an order.

A low-key salesman is concerned with assisting his customers and gaining their confidence, not selling them products or services they do not need, cannot afford or might not use. The low-key approach leaves the prospect's door wide open to return at some future time and re-present the message. When the salesman knows that the prospect

GROUP BUYING MOTIVES

NOTE: all prospects have reasons for buying (or not buying) and they are based on rational or irrational motives (or both). Your job is to detect them.

GROUP	BASIC MOTIVE	REASON	INCENTIVE
Businessmen	Gain (rational)	Profit	Greater productivity and profit.
Professional men	Gain	Profit	Greater income.
	Pride (emotional)	Ego	Appeals to ego.
Trades people	Gain	Profit	Ways to increase earnings.
	Pride	Ego	Creative satisfaction in work.
Wholesalers	Gain	Profit	Ways to increase customers.
Retailers	Gain	Profit	Ways to increase customers, induce more purchases.
	Imitation (irrational)	Competition	Ways to be as good as or better than competitor.
	Fear (emotional)	Competition	Ways to combat customer loss.
Housewives	Gain	Spend less	Ways to save money and get better value for money.
	Pride	Ego appeal Creative satisfaction	Satisfy needs, wants and life-long dreams. Give ego satisfaction.
	Pleasure (emotional)	Enjoyment	Ways of doing things easier and happier. Enjoyment and peace of mind.
	Imitation	Ego	To keep up with friends, neighbors, relatives.
	Fear	Loss	Guarantee security.
Teenagers	Pleasure	Happiness	Ways to enjoy life.
	Imitation	Ego	Status raised among friends.
	Pride	Creative satisfaction	Ways to express creative urges.

has arrived at a 'just conclusion' and rejects the proposition, he 'thanks' the prospect and makes a tentative or firm date for a 'call-back'.

High pressure selling is short term selling. It is the quickest way to damage the image of a product and company and usually results in loss of customers. Some door-to-door salesmen use high pressure or trick means to close sales. While they may benefit financially, the reputation of the profession suffers.

Reject trick selling methods—dishonesty, cheating, lying, attempting to mentally blackmail people into accepting your proposition. Adhere to honest selling procedures and you'll build a strong reputation for yourself and your profession.

HOW TO ACHIEVE GREATER SELLING AWARENESS

Your selling ability is enhanced when you 'tune-in' to life. Brighten your eyes and sharpen your ears. Become mentally awake to things going on around you. The only way that the information of life can reach you is through your five sensory organs: *touch, taste, smell, sight, hearing.*

Greater use of your five senses sharpens your mind, brightens your personality and improves your communication with life. When you organize your sensory organs and use them as direct lines of communication *to* life you get more *from* life.

WAKE UP AND LIVE

Really *listen* when another person is talking to you. *See* and take note of the speech patterns, attitudes, mannerisms and personal habits of those you meet. Organize, assimilate and evaluate everything that can enhance your career as a salesman. Remember: the more you tune-in on people the more you learn about them. The more you tune-in on places and things, the more knowledgeable you become about places and things. The more you know about people, places and things, the easier it is to sell your ideas, products or services *and* yourself. The greater the awareness, the greater the power of perception or intuitive judgement. Look alive! Wake up and live!

HOW TO BUILD CONFIDENCE IN THE MIND OF THE BUYER

The success or failure of any business enterprise depends on the efficiency of the sales team. The salesman, whether he is behind the counter, selling from a van or operating as an accounts executive, must instill confidence in the minds of his customers. The more efficient, self confident, well dressed and groomed and personable the salesman is, the greater the customer confidence.

Appearance, behavior and ability, are plus factors every salesman must develop. A smiling face, a word of appreciation, a pleasant disposition, a genuine desire to be of service, a thorough knowledge of product and company procedures, an ability to make people happy, will prove to be priceless ingredients when the salesman is canvassing for new business.

THE EXTENT OF EXTERNAL FORCES

External forces that make up an individual's social environment include: nationality, area of residence, race, religion, education, occupation, income. The truth that a consumer is a product of his cultural and social environment is pointed up in his logic and value judgements projected in his purchases of products or services. He always reflects what he believes to be culturally and socially acceptable. An individual's attitudes and actions are influenced by many layers of society. These include the culture and subculture in which he lives: social class, friends and business associates, family and relatives. Social classes within cultures play an extremely important part in attitudes and behavior. Upper-class people may place value on status symbols such as expensive cars, luxury homes, boutique purchased clothes. Lower-class people may find satisfaction and take pride in neat, small homes and clothes they have made themselves.

SUMMARY OF IDEAS TO HELP YOU SELL
PSYCHOLOGICALLY

1. Selling is a noble profession. Honest selling professionals help to make a nation strong. Become an honest, professional salesman.

2. There are two divisions of selling: those who sell to the consumer market and those who sell to the retail trade. There are special requirements for each. Study them. Develop your ability in the area in which you work.

3. Psychological selling is an art as well as a science. Study people, know that you cannot sell everyone. A realistic attitude is necessary. Remember: selling is a percentages game. You win some, you lose some. The more calls you make, the more chances you have to convert prospects.

4. The one basic need that stands out above all others where humans are concerned is appreciation. Show others that you appreciate their abilities, personality, friendships and business they give you.

5. Always think in terms of the YOU FACTOR. Eliminate selfish motives. Your job is to service the needs of your customers. *Give* and you'll *receive*.

6. Look for the customer's buying motive. It could be GAIN, PRIDE, FEAR, IMITATION or PLEASURE. Perhaps only one, perhaps more than one. Find it and sell the *plus factors* to enhance it or the *incentives* to the motive.

7. Make a study of your customers and design image profiles on them. The more you know about customers the easier it will be to deal with them.

8. There are many types of buyers. Make a list of them and add to it each time you come across a new 'type'.

9. Low-key selling is the best method. Don't 'pressure' or mentally blackmail prospects into buying your product or service. Reject trick selling methods.

10. Tune-in to life and become more aware of what's happening around you. Make greater use of your five senses.

HOW TO JOIN
THE PROFESSIONALS
IN THE WINNERS' CIRCLE

❖

FORMULA

5

Affirmative Ideas in This Chapter

- What It Takes To Become A Winner
- Climbing The Ladder To Sales Success Through Dedication
- Character Is Priceless
- The Two Types of Character: Evident Character—True Character
- Personal And Business Integrity
- 12 Master Salesmanship Keys
- Master Salesmanship Keys Rating Chart
- Winning The Loyal Support of Others
- The Art of Self Discipline—A Winning Key
- Developing The Will To Win
- The Winner Never Quits—He Succeeds Through Faith Power
- Faith Power Changed The Course of Politician's Life
- How To Elevate Your Personal Power And Succeed In Selling
- How To Establish Self Confidence—The Winner's Trump Card
- How To Become A Winner By Making The Right Decisions
- 10 Steps To Right Decision Making
- The Winner Is An Accurate Listener And Absorber of Vital Information
- How To Work Effectively With Company Superiors
- A Word About Loyalty
- How To Secure A Balance In Your Home And Business Life
- How To Plan Immediate And Future Goals
- Set Rewards For Goals Accomplished
- Goals Chart
- Every Effect Has Its Cause—The Great Truth of Life
- 4 Areas of Development To Advance You Into The Winners' Circle
- 4 Personal Power Steps
- STEP 1: Knowledge of The 'Self'
- STEP 2: Knowledge of Human Behavioral Patterns
- STEP 3: Knowledge of Auto Suggestion
- STEP 4: Knowledge of Oratory Skill
- Reaping The Riches of Life For Positive Effort
- Be An Improver And Become A Winner
- Sales Image Profile Chart
- The Professional Salesman's Creed
- Summary of Ideas To Put You In The Winners' Circle

5

WHAT IT TAKES TO BECOME A WINNER

A successful career in selling requires that you have an ability to lead—yourself *and* others. You must be able to *self motivate,* to push yourself to victory when your world is tumbling around you. The true mark of a winner is 'guts'. More refined terms for the winner's special needs are:

- A COMPLETOR OF TASKS BEGUN
- A POWERFUL IMAGINER
- AN HONEST AND FAIR TRANSACTOR
- A SECURE AND CONFIDENT PERSUADER
- A DEDICATED AND HARD WORKER
- A DECISIVE AND INTELLIGENT THINKER

Enthusiasm and the desire to become part of a company team are other 'ingredients' for success in a profession which, although hectic, varied and stimulating, is always rewarding in a creative way.

In the selling profession there is room at the top for the person with drive and imagination. Youth is no barrier to promotion if you have the ability to do the job well. The winners' circle is open. But like all master salesmen who belong to it, you must be prepared to work hard, dedicate unflagging interest and be able to produce top sales.

A top sales earner may work an average of 50 hours a week in the office as well as out in the field prospecting, following-up leads, researching the market and selling. The rewards include a great variety of challenges, intellectual stimulation and excellent remuneration. In the final analysis, a salesman's right to stay in the winners' circle is governed by his performance. *Results* are the only yardstick.

CLIMBING THE LADDER TO SALES SUCCESS THROUGH DEDICATION

There are specific personal qualities that equip a man to become a successful selling professional. Many of them have already been mentioned, but the one that stands out is the salesman's attitude toward his own profession. All salesmen must contribute to the standing of their profession by adopting an attitude of *proud professionalism;* a genuine desire to be a credit to the industry to which they belong.

There is a big difference between a member of the selling profession and a true professional. Being a member of the profession does not in itself guarantee that an individual will remain a professional. It is the attitude toward the profession he has elected to join that determines whether a salesman can be classified as a professional or a pedlar and order taker.

The true professional is motivated by a spirit of service, a desire to raise the standard of living for his fellow man. The unprofessional salesman is motivated by selfish desires to 'get rich quick.'

The overall record of the 'pro' is a record of contribution, of giving time, talent and genuine service to his customers and to the industry to which he belongs. He is a person dedicated to higher ideals because he understands that personal integrity and honesty are the keys to continuing success in selling.

CHARACTER IS PRICELESS

Most of us have a better side which, consciously or unconsciously, we present to others. Our participation in life consists of thoughts, words, attitudes, convictions and actions. The two aspects of an individual are sometimes in sharp contrast. The person who seems to be mild mannered can, upon being provoked, exhibit violent temper. The individual who speaks of honesty and integrity is not always the person who *acts* in an honest manner.

Strong character is a priceless ingredient for the salesman. He cannot be bought or swayed to partake in dishonest dealings. An individual with strong personal integrity commands respect. Honest thoughts and deeds enhance your self power. People know that they can count on you; that your word is your bond.

Building a valuable reputation in the profession is a goal which should be placed high on your achievements list. Design your character to include honest thoughts, feelings and actions. Do not compromise high ideals for any reason. Do not sell your integrity or you sell your soul.

I cannot imagine how any salesman who is not able to be honest with himself and honest in his dealings with others, can ever hope to gain the confidence of those he must count on to help him succeed. Many of us like to think that we are honest, but I wonder how many of us would really measure up if our thoughts and actions were scrutinized? The character-conscious salesman must monitor his own motives and make the necessary adjustments if motives and actions are less than honest.

The truly effective salesman who is going to make it to the top and stay there, will give his full attention to the development of a strong, forthright and honest character.

The value of a man is secreted within
his true character. Never 'sell' your honesty and
integrity like common merchandise or you have 'sold'
your soul, for they are God's most precious gifts
to you. Remain honest in your thought and action and
resist compromising your high ideals. Strong character
is your strongest sales aid.

THE TWO TYPES OF CHARACTER

There are two basic types of character. They are:
1. EVIDENT CHARACTER
2. TRUE CHARACTER

Evident character is the one you outwardly show to others. It may or may not be your real character. If your evident character is one for show purposes only then it must be analyzed and changed. You fool yourself to think that others cannot see through your sham. *Be* the person you *say* you are. There is no room in the winners' circle for the sham salesman.

True character is what you really are at *all* times. You display your inner thoughts, feelings and beliefs. A true character is often a negative one: thoughts and actions. The ideal character to develop is a true affirmative character: honest thoughts, feelings, beliefs and actions. Show that you are a person of your word, that truth is the basis of your personal philosophy. Your outer wrappings must match your inner feelings and beliefs. A true, affirmative character breeds self confidence, a bright personality, a respected name and a happier existence.

PERSONAL AND BUSINESS INTEGRITY

Integrity builds strong character. An individual who has high ideals and sticks to them is a man worth knowing and doing business with. Personal integrity in a salesman strikes others immediately and makes them *want* to do business with him.

The desire for feeling worthy and being 'accepted' by friends, family and business associates is the driving force behind most of our actions. The dependable person, the one who sticks by his word, who refuses to compromise ideals, who cannot be tempted, is well on the road to self confidence, power, control and success in his personal and business dealings.

12 MASTER SALESMANSHIP KEYS

KEY 1:

— AIMS & OBJECTIVES —

Every salesman must have a list of aims and objectives. To do so is to clarify your present situation and to lay the foundation stones for future success in selling. Make a list of your aims . . . the things you want to achieve in the selling profession.

One of your aims might be to achieve a high level of self confidence. Another, the ability to speak before a group. Perhaps your aim is to work for a company where opportunities of advancement are many. Whatever your aims, they will not take shape until you put them in writing and then *do* something to achieve them.

KEY 2:

— INITIATIVE —

Initiative is essential for the attainment of success in selling. It means to do the right thing without being prompted. It means to have a definite purpose in mind and to turn ideas into organized effort bringing about a successful end result. It means to move into action without waiting for the other fellow to get you started. Initiative is the major quality required at the leadership counter. Persons with initiative make good leaders.

KEY 3:

— IMAGINATION —

A salesman must develop an imagination that enables him to understand the needs, objectives and emotional moods of his customers. He must see the other person's point of view, anticipate his actions and reactions. This takes imagination.

The salesman can create anything he can 'image'. All new ideas stem from the imagination of creative thinkers. Leaders of business, industry, finance, musicians, artists, writers, actors, use their creative faculty of imagination to become great in their respective fields. Man's success or failure lies in the degree of development of his imagination.

KEY 4:
— KNOWLEDGE —

There are two types of knowledge: general and specialized. Knowledge will not attract riches unless it is organized and put to use through practical plans. Successful salesmen never stop acquiring general and specialized knowledge. New methods of selling, new products, new marketing ideas, fall into the category of specialized knowledge. Community, national and international affairs, music, art, literature, fall into the category of general knowledge.

Knowledge in the field of selling is gained through: individual experience; training programs; newspapers and business journals; books; product research. The greater the accumulated knowledge the greater the opportunity of advancement.

KEY 5:
— INTEREST —

Interest—genuine interest—is a desire to gain knowledge about a particular subject, person or place. It is *caring* for something or someone. It is a desire to serve, to help. Are you interested in the needs of your customers? Are you concerned about their attitudes when things go wrong? Do you *really* care about people? Gain an interest in life. Observe, listen, participate in and experience this wonderful thing called life by being INTERESTED in life.

KEY 6:
— ENTHUSIASM —

Enthusiasm is motivated energy. It is a state of mind that inspires and 'incites' an individual to 'action'. Enthusiasm is contagious. People love to be around others who are enthusiastic. Enthusiasm for your work, for other people, for life, develops a dynamic personality. It brings health, happiness and financial rewards. Get on fire! Recharge your thoughts with the magic of enthusiasm.

KEY 7:
— PATIENCE —

Patience is a virtue. Wanting something immediately, refusing to listen to the other person's point of view, making demands, attempting too much too soon, are forms of impatience that make enemies in business.

Be prepared to listen to the other man's requests. Be tolerant of his opinions. Don't be too quick to pre-judge others. No human is perfect. Our aim is to grow into a state of perfection. Therefore, tolerate the faults of others. Don't condemn them. Don't be too hasty in condemning yourself for your own mistakes. Be patient! Success will come to you in due course if you apply the principles of life.

KEY 8:
— APPRECIATION —

Learn to appreciate the talents and good points of others. People love to be appreciated for their real worth. Place a value on others and show them that you appreciate their friendships and their acts of kindness. Appreciate the customer who gives you business. Appreciate your employer, your wife, your family.

KEY 9:
— SELF CONFIDENCE —

Self confidence is confidence in the real SELF of you. Place a value on your magnificent mind and what it can accomplish. Eliminate fear from your consciousness. Fear is the basic cause of all failure: the fear of poverty; the fear of criticism; the fear of ill health; the fear of job loss. You are a unique individual with nothing to fear but your own negative thoughts. Build a confident attitude producing the success you desire.

KEY 10:
— PERSISTENCE —

Persistence is staying power. Those who give-up at the first sign of failure never amount to anything. Edison experienced 10,000 defeats before perfecting the electric light. Keep going. Don't allow others to sway you from your aims in life. There are millions of failures in the world—those who tried once and gave up. Don't add your name to the failure list. There is no such thing as permanent defeat. Within each failure lies the 'key' to future success. The wise salesman profits by all his mistakes and failures and, through observation, by the mistakes and failures of others.

KEY 11:
— HONESTY —

There is no substitute for honesty. No one will entrust you with merchandise, money or credit unless you are an honest person. No one will put you in command of staff unless they are satisfied that you are honest. Honesty is not something you say or something you claim to be. It is a definite state of mind that produces honest actions. Be honest, even to the smallest detail in all your personal and business affairs.

KEY 12:
— BELIEF —

The first law of mind is the law of belief. As a man believes so he becomes. Gain solid belief in the power of affirmative thought. You will establish a successful selling career if you backstop your efforts with strong belief in your ability to win. Believing in your ability to succeed is your first step toward success.

MASTER SALESMANSHIP KEYS
RATING CHART

KEY	ATTRIBUTE	POOR	FAIR	GOOD
1	AIMS AND OBJECTIVES			
2	INITIATIVE			
3	IMAGINATION			
4	KNOWLEDGE			
5	INTEREST			
6	ENTHUSIASM			
7	PATIENCE			
8	APPRECIATION			
9	SELF CONFIDENCE			
10	PERSISTENCE			
11	HONESTY			
12	BELIEF			

WINNING THE LOYAL SUPPORT OF OTHERS

Customers and fellow employees will give you their loyal support if you show them that you have a sincere interest in their welfare. To be successful in human relationships it is necessary to have a deep understanding of and appreciation for the interests, feelings and ambitions of others. It is human nature for you to want to help someone who has helped you, to like the person who sees superiority in you. It is also human nature for you to take the opposite attitude and *dislike* those who show antagonism toward you.

You must draw friendliness from others, not wait for it to come. Make the first move in your *friendly* and *open* greeting. Get people on your side. You need people to succeed as a salesman. The more loyal support people give you because they genuinely like you, the more successful you will become. Follow the 5 steps:

1. Warm to people immediately you meet them.
2. Always greet others with a smile.
3. Listen to the needs, wants and desires of others with interest.
4. Show concern for the other person's welfare.
5. Be prepared to help others without expectation of personal gain.

THE ART OF SELF DISCIPLINE—A WINNING KEY

The star salesman 'acts' in an affirmative manner at all times because he has learnt the art of self discipline: thoughts, emotions. Self discipline training corrects, molds, strengthens and perfects your self and projected image. Your self power cannot be developed if you lack thought discipline.

When you control your emotions you are immune to disparagement, you are unfearful of challenge, you are below no one, you cannot be shaken and you are in control of every situation. Your self-power attitude comes alive and generates an attitude of poise, strength and confidence.

Much of our thinking is uncontrolled. We give far too much time to daydreaming, wishing, hoping. Mind discipline is thought control: focusing the mind on a given desire until ways for its realization have been discovered and put into action. Self discipline teaches the salesman to channel the energy generated by affirmative thoughts into positive doing. It teaches the salesman to carry through with tasks. It smooths life's highway and speeds his journey accurately toward the targets he has set.

DEVELOPING THE WILL TO WIN

> '*Never look down to test the ground*
> *before taking your next step;*
> *only he who keeps his eye on the far*
> *horizon will find the right road.*'
>
> DAG HAMMARSKJOLD.

This quote from the late Dag Hammarskjold, Swedish statesman and secretary general of the United Nations from 1953 to 1961, should be typed on a 3 x 5 card and carried in the pocket of every sales representative—particularly those desiring to enter the winners' circle.

The will to win—personal motivation—is not to be overlooked in the quest for success in selling. Incentive motivation requires a *desire factor* to support aims and objectives. To succeed in any endeavor, there must be a specific *desire* to succeed—a *reason*. When you present a strong reason to win, it becomes your strength of purpose, your thing to fight for. No army could engage in war without its soldiers being motivated by a strong conviction in what they are to fight and possibly lose their lives for.

Give yourself a strong reason, a motivating factor for wanting success in your chosen profession. Your will to win is strengthened when you know *why* you want success and what it will mean to you once you have achieved it. Lack of a strong *desire factor* is the main reason people fail. They have nothing worthwhile to fight for.

Be certain that your motivating factors are sound and realistic before undertaking difficult tasks. You will reduce the risk of failure and save valuable time and energy. The questions to ask yourself are:

1. *What* is it I want? (Goal).
2. *Why* do I wish to accomplish it? (Desire factor or motivation).
3. *How* will I go about it? (Plan of action).
4. *When* do I expect to complete it? (Actual time and date).
5. *Who* can assist me to succeed? (Professional adviser).

THE WINNER NEVER QUITS—HE SUCCEEDS THROUGH FAITH POWER

Don't allow lack of faith in your own ability to stop you in your tracks. Fill your mind with *faith power* and you'll last the distance. You can't succeed in life unless you believe you have the ability to succeed. You go where your thoughts are. If you imagine that you are going to fail, you might toil 15 hours a day and yet you will not succeed. If your basic premise is negative, your conclusion must be negative. The cause is within you and is generated by your beliefs.

Faith is the power within you which will lift you up and set you on the path to the fulfillment of your desires. Back your aims and objectives with solid faith and life will not deprive you of the realization of your fondest dreams.

You desire to live and to express yourself creatively in the wonderful world of selling. Divine Life is seeking expression through you in the form of your desires. Therefore, there is nothing holding you back except your faith-*less* attitude. There is a force within you capable of great works—*faith power*. Cease dissipating your energy and stifling the *life force* within with negative thoughts, feelings and beliefs. Your faith must be placed in the workings of your conscious and subconscious mind and in the truths of Divine Intelligence which never change.

FAITH POWER CHANGED THE COURSE OF POLITICIAN'S LIFE

They called him the Great American Loser. I well remember working as a speaker for him when he contested the California gubernatorial elections. He lost. And the defeat was a bitter one for the man who had been Vice President of the United States under Dwight D. Eisenhower.

Many people felt that Richard M. Nixon's political career was finished. And it well might have been had it not been for the amazing faith power of this strong, decisive and ambitious leader.

In 1968 he moved into the nation's number one executive position with the smallest popular mandate since Woodrow Wilson's in 1912. Many people thought he'd last one term in office as President. Again, the doubters were wrong. In 1972 Richard Nixon was swept into power for a second term with one of the largest Presidential landslides in American history.

Richard Milhouse Nixon may not go down in American history as the 'most loved' President, but he must surely be recognized as the man with the strongest faith in his ability to succeed as a politician. A *faith* every sales individual would do well to emulate. Faith expands your life beyond ordinary limits. You can accomplish much with it—little without it.

> *All the scholastic scaffolding falls, as a ruined edifice, before one single word—faith.*

NAPOLEON.

HOW TO ELEVATE YOUR PERSONAL POWER AND SUCCEED IN SELLING

The ability to reason logically instead of emotionally (man is a highly emotional creature) is the fastest route to acquiring self power and success in selling. It is the principle of accepting *reason* as the authority in determining one's opinions or courses of action to follow. It is the use of common sense and sound judgement when making decisions.

Thinking in terms of specifics, of reasoning things through to a logical conclusion, eliminates unrealistic 'hoping' and 'wishing' for success to overtake you. Rational thinking reduces costly mistakes, wrong decisions and moves being made. It helps you to achieve maximum cooperation from others and projects an individuality that marks you as a person others want to know.

Your rationalization of problems and analysis of important decisions to be made, reduces frustration, anxiety, tension and fear of failure. Instead of trying to side-step or avoid the challenges of life, you find yourself wading through them. To become a rational thinker is to learn how to succeed in selling *and* in life.

HOW TO ESTABLISH SELF CONFIDENCE—THE WINNER'S TRUMP CARD

Your personality and character reveal the type of 'thinker' you are. Negative thinkers are individuals plagued by fear. They have little self respect for their abilities, concepts and actions. The development of self confidence begins with the elimination of FEAR. You cannot succeed in selling if you carry inner fears; you cannot succeed in living if you are plagued by fear.

Fear is another term for ignorance and superstition. Get the truth about yourself. Know that you are your own worst enemy by holding to fearful thoughts, feelings and beliefs. You will not rise above the things you fear until you change your concepts about them. Change your thinking (negative) and you will eliminate that dreaded demon fear.

Place a proper value on the self of you. Know that no situation is beyond your grasp or self defeating until you believe it to be defeating. Know that success is yours when you cease holding yourself back because of a timid, shy and apologetic manner. Frustration and anxiety are the seeds of creativity attempting to break through your consciousness into the light of achievement. The only thing holding back creative success is your attitude about its possibilities—your fear of failing. Lack of self confidence is your enemy and you cannot win success (your friend) until you get your attitudes on an affirmative level. Confidence is knowing the true self and valuing the self.

Self confidence may be mistaken for egotism and conceit if it is not accompanied by humility. Don't be frightened to place a high value on your skills, but remember: your abilities are the *gift* of Infinite Intelligence and you have a duty to use them for the good of yourself as well as for the good of your fellow man.

HOW TO BECOME A WINNER BY MAKING THE RIGHT DECISIONS

Nothing of value can be achieved in life without making the *right* decisions. Procrastination is more energy consuming than decision making. Mental stalling robs you of opportunity. It was General MacArthur who said: 'In this life there is no security, only opportunity.' The salesman who is frightened to make decisions cheats himself of the opportunity to become a *great* salesman.

Make up your mind to become a decisive, strong, forthright personality. Take on the challenges of life as they present themselves. Don't run away from problems, they'll follow you wherever you go. They become your shadow and refuse to dissolve until you raise the courage to deal with them. Failure to deal with problems and make vital decisions keeps a potentially good salesman from the winners' circle.

Put problems in writing. Reduce them to simple statements which can be analyzed. Clear your mind of fear. Never attempt to solve problems while you are in a poor state of health or emotionally upset. Avoid making decisions based on opinions or hearsay. Don't jump to conclusions before you have the facts. Get into the habit of deciding on small things. Gradually decide on more important issues and as you persist in this way, you will find an automatic response triggered each time a problem arises or a decision has to be made quickly. Follow the 10 steps to right decision making.

10 STEPS TO RIGHT DECISION MAKING

1. Write down problems which require a decision.
2. Analyze the problem after calling for the facts. (Not hearsay).
3. Don't make impulsive decisions. Check all facts.
4. Eliminate worthless opinions. Don't be pressured into deciding.
5. Argue the pros and cons after presenting an alternative course of action.
6. Review all information and come to a conclusion.
7. Convert the decision into action.
8. Believe in your final decision.
9. Hold to your final decision.
10. Set a time limit on all decisions to be made. Do not procrastinate.

THE WINNER IS AN ACCURATE LISTENER AND ABSORBER OF VITAL INFORMATION

To listen accurately is to really *hear* and *absorb* important messages and information necessary to your success in selling. The first requirement is strict concentration and discipline of the emotions.

Far too many salesmen are guilty of 'poor listening' of not *accurately* getting the message. Wrong names, addresses, delivery times, misunderstandings relating to pricing, payment and quantity are the end result of 'half' listening to customers' requests.

Clear your mind of insignificant and unrelated thoughts when talking to customers. Focus your attention where it belongs—on your customer. Discipline your mind to listen, to *really* hear and absorb everything being said.

We tend to filter out the things we don't like to hear. We select for retelling only those things we feel are important. If we fail to understand or think the point unimportant, it gets lost in the retelling. We cannot eliminate all distortion in our communication but we can eliminate most of it by *concentrating* on what the other person has to say and *taking it in*.

During an *average* waking day we spend the best part of it *listening*. Consider these statistics:

9 per cent of our day we spend *writing*.
16 per cent of our day we spend *reading*.
30 per cent of our day we spend *speaking*.
45 per cent of our day we spend LISTENING.

Nearly half of our day we spend listening; but how much do we really hear and understand? Poor listening lessens our ability to evaluate the message as it should be evaluated (accurately) and because of this to react efficiently and effectively.

The rules to apply when meeting and talking to others are:

1. GET THE NAME. *LISTEN* FOR IT.

2. *REPEAT* THE NAME FREQUENTLY THROUGHOUT THE CONVERSATION.

3. CONCENTRATE ON WHAT IS BEING SAID. *FOCUS* YOUR ATTENTION.

4. GET *INTERESTED* IN WHAT IS BEING SAID. BE MENTALLY ALERT.

5. BUILD A MENTAL PICTURE OF THE PERSON SPEAKING. *RELATE* UNUSUAL FEATURES TO HIS NAME.

6. DON'T TRUST VITAL FACTS, FIGURES, DATES TO MEMORY. WRITE THEM DOWN.

HOW TO WORK EFFECTIVELY WITH COMPANY SUPERIORS

Managers are paid for an important ability—to make accurate decisions. Therefore, the salesman can establish a firm company foothold if he abides by the decisions made by company superiors. Company policy is set after much deliberation. The salesman who goes against policy is headed for trouble—and another job.

The rebellious salesman, one who irritates customers, disregards management decisions, causes friction within the sales team, is in line for the *firing* line, not advancement.

The quality of performance of any follower depends on his degree of acceptance of his leader's decisions. The rule: *follow the leader.* Someday you may become a leader and ask others to follow your policies, decisions and methods of operation.

Gain the confidence of company superiors by attending to your duties in an enthusiastic way, a manner that suggests to them that you are a self-starter, a reliable and conscientious worker. Exude charm and get on friendly terms with those you work with. Avoid gossip or being too friendly with female members of the staff. Watch your manners. Remember, your image is on display and management is judging your projected image qualities.

Get to know *all* executives in your company. Know them by name and position. Understand their function within the organizational structure. Make a point of greeting them with a cheerful 'hello' and a bright smile. Don't hesitate to seek advice from your sales manager when difficulties arise or when advice is needed. You will be in line for promotion if you adhere to these six suggestions:

1. Be well informed.	4. Be skillful in your work.
2. Dress immaculately.	5. Be cooperative at all times.
3. Be socially refined.	6. Be diplomatic and charming.

A WORD ABOUT LOYALTY

Loyalty to his company is the mark of the 'pro'. By skillful use of public relations (affirmative attitudes and actions) the professional salesman is able to convince his company superiors that he is (and must be) just as loyal to company interests as he is to the interests of his customers. Every sale must be of mutual benefit to buyer and seller. Every sales manager worth his salt knows this and realizes that following this philosophy builds goodwill between company, sales representative and customer.

Goodwill is built out of respect—the result of loyalty on the part of the salesman. Company superiors recognize *customer loyalty* as being part and parcel of *company loyalty*. Salesman loyalty is honest thought producing honest action on behalf of the employer. It means sticking by company policy and helping to further the aims and objectives of the company *and* the customer.

> *To God, thy country, and thy friend*
> *be true, then thou'lt ne'er be false*
> *to any one.*
>
> VAUGHAN.

HOW TO SECURE BALANCE IN YOUR HOME AND BUSINESS LIFE

The quality of each family depends on human relationships. Where there are differences of opinion, concessions may be necessary. Misunderstandings, grudges, hurt feelings, arguments, can be avoided by adopting a 'give and take' attitude—by compromise instead of domination of the marriage partner.

The wise businessman does not allow the negative aspects of his business life to trespass his home affairs. Temper tantrums, criticism of employer, fellow workers or customers, must not be inflicted on the family. This rule should be observed in reverse: keep family differences from the ears of employer, friends, fellow workers and customers. An harmonious blend of family and business life can be brought about by the practice of commonsense, thinking and acting.

An emotionally disturbed salesman cannot function efficiently, creatively or successfully. Whatever the state of family affairs, free the mind of them once you have closed your front door and started your business day. A negative consciousness sours your personality, causes stomach disorders and headaches and reduces your effectiveness as a communicator and motivator.

Refuse to be drawn into heated arguments with business associates or family members. Mentally slugging it out leaves you emotionally and physically tired and depleted of vital energy. When you become involved in a shouting match you discard control and lose your self power. You succeed only in antagonizing others *not* winning them over. Their antagonism eliminates any self power you may have had over them. Talk out problems. Remain in control of the situation. Instead of shouting, ranting and raving, exude charm, pleasantness and

112

amiability. Face every problem-situation in this manner, maintaining control of the conversation and action in which you participate. You'll experience better human relationships, be emotionally free to exploit your creative skills, be less prone to ill health and you'll live a lot longer and enjoy life more.

HOW TO PLAN IMMEDIATE AND FUTURE GOALS

A balanced life—where harmony and well-being prevail—occurs when creative desires are fulfilled. Anxiety, tension, worry and frustration become a thing of the past when you release your creative mechanism and head toward planned targets. The important thing to do is to start planning and involving your attention on chosen projects. Select your targets and *begin*.

Use the cybernetic technique of doing the *right things* at the beginning (setting plans) so that end results take care of themselves. Remember, cybernetics means helmsman; *you* are the guiding force directing your mind to the accomplishment of your goals. The computer programmer feeds the computer with a 'plan' or program enabling the complex mechanism to accomplish its goal. You must design a program of attitudes and habits to support your aims and objectives and then install them in the memory of your mental computer (subconscious mind). If your programming is 'on the ball' you will get a success-response. If it is not, then you will get a failure-response.

List your goals and a plan of action to accomplish them. Begin by thinking of things within easy reach, things you feel you can accomplish without too much effort or time involvement. Write them down on a goals sheet. Place a time limit for their completion. Separate your goals into three time zones:

● 1 YEAR GOALS ● 5 YEAR GOALS ● 10 YEAR GOALS

The smaller and easier goals will fall within your one year time zone, more difficult goals within the five year zone and the most difficult within the ten year period. Write your goals in detail then reduce them to a couple of sentences. Write them in simple terms without confusion or vagueness. Your desires must be specific. You must know *exactly* what you want. Reduce your goals into subgoals to bring quick successes.

After listing your goals within time zones, develop a plan of action to accomplish them. List the names of people you can enlist to help you achieve them. Review your progress. Make changes if you feel your goals are unrealistic or cannot be completed within the time you have allowed.

SET REWARDS FOR GOALS ACCOMPLISHED

When your goals plan is completed and your plan of action developed, analyze each goal and find the *desire motive—why* you want to accomplish it. Look for the reward at the end of the goal— the benefit. Keep your 'reward' in front of you to spur you on to success.

GOALS CHART

Name: ....

	1 YEAR	Time Limit	5 YEAR	Time Limit	10 YEAR	Time Limit
MAJOR AIMS						
SUB GOALS						
ACTION PLAN						
PROGRESS REPORT						

Goals and subgoals can be programmed for fast successes in every area of your life. But you must not stop with their planning. You must go on to achievement. Fix your attention on your target areas, involve your skills in hitting your targets and experience the rewards of creative accomplishments.

EVERY EFFECT HAS ITS CAUSE—THE GREAT TRUTH OF LIFE

Nothing happens in life by so-called 'luck' or chance. Things 'happen' because they are designed to happen. The 'effects' of your life (successes and failures) have their beginnings in your consciousness— your thoughts and feelings. Plant the seeds of success in your deeper mind and support them with faith.

Plot your own Goals Chart and begin your plan of action *today!* Produce *right* thinking, *right* plans and you will experience *right* results.

4 AREAS OF DEVELOPMENT TO ADVANCE YOU INTO THE WINNERS' CIRCLE

The psychological drive to succeed should be the feature of every salesman's philosophy: a desire to expand knowledge in every possible area of human relations; a seeking of personal motivation to justify the long and difficult climb to success in selling and in attaining life's riches.

If you are going to develop yourself into a person of noticeable personal power then you will require something to build on and something to move toward. Your basic personality and skills are the starting point and upon these things you begin your development program. Your aims and objectives are your target areas to build toward.

When you develop yourself to the degree that your personal power is recognized by others, you will experience better customer relations and business dealings with others. You will find that others begin to court you. Your personal magnetic aura will draw others to you, make them want to know and do business with you. This is the power you must strive to develop and use. It is a respect that must be earned, but once gained it makes others want to perform *for* you instead of against you.

When you develop the four personal power steps listed, you will notice an immediate change in your relationships with others. Your striking personality will cause others to seek a bond with you. You will be the person others seek out to gain advice and to buy from. You will be the authority, the respected adviser and counselor.

---

4 PERSONAL POWER STEPS
1. KNOWLEDGE OF THE 'SELF'.
2. KNOWLEDGE OF HUMAN BEHAVIORAL PATTERNS.
3. KNOWLEDGE OF AUTO SUGGESTION (THE POWER OF PERSUASION).
4. KNOWLEDGE OF ORATORY SKILL (COMMUNICATION).

STEP 1: KNOWLEDGE OF THE 'SELF'

Discover your own weaknesses and strengths of character and personality. Why do you say the things you say, do the things you do and respond the way you do to the remarks and actions of others? What motivates you to action? Self analysis is the way to find out all you should know about yourself. The better you understand your own thinking and acting patterns the better you will be able to deal with others in selling. Become consciously aware of your thoughts, feelings and actions.

STEP 2: KNOWLEDGE OF HUMAN BEHAVIORAL PATTERNS

Make a study of people. Strive to understand human emotions and what makes people think and act as they do. Study facial expressions, posture, walk, mannerisms, dress and grooming habits, attitudes, emotional responses. Look for hidden meanings. People do not always say what they are really thinking, do not always express their true feelings. Become a psychoanalyst, a clairvoyant. When you can adequately judge character you will have fewer disappointments and lose less valuable time when dealing with others.

Look for the patterns of behavior in people. Note their prejudices, moods, responses and direct actions. Find the WHY factor in behavior and you will be equipped to psychologically deal with others in an accurate and successful way.

STEP 3: KNOWLEDGE OF AUTO SUGGESTION

What thoughts and ideas easily sink into your own subconscious? What ideas impress you, take hold and incite you to action? What can you implant in the minds of others to bring desired responses? Auto suggestion is positive repetition—a continual implanting of affirmative suggestions until a desired reaction is brought about. As selling is a positive function (encompassing positive product, positive attitude, positive approach), the master motivator knows that he must not allow negative ideas to enter his own or the customer's mind during the presentation.

The technique of *repetitive positive statement* and repeated suggestion of *positive ideas* will produce the actions desired. The power of suggestion is a potent tool to bring success in personal relationships and in all business dealings. It is the motivating force behind all successful achievement.

STEP 4: KNOWLEDGE OF ORATORY SKILL

It is essential that the sales professional develop the ability to express his ideas logically, authoritatively and fluently. Oratory skill is the mark of a leader. The spoken word is a powerful way to convey ideas from one mind to another. Every good salesman must depend upon it for a large measure of his success. *What* he says and how he says it must have a profound effect on the prospective customer; the force and clarity of the spoken message must incite the customer to take positive

116

action—to say 'I'll buy.' (Oratory skill is covered in greater detail in chapter 14.)

REAPING THE RICHES OF LIFE FOR POSITIVE EFFORT

Every man seeks to increase his income and enjoy more of the 'good things' in life's rich garden. To succeed is your birthright. I've yet to meet a man who said he would rather be poor than rich, uncreative than creative, unhappy than happy and a failure instead of a success. The day I meet *that* individual I'll call for the man in the white jacket and show him a screwball.

Fortunately, there is a scientific way to gain the benefits and riches of life. Many of them have already been pointed out in earlier chapters, others will follow. Noticeable changes will occur when you *apply* the techniques in your daily activities. Dedicate your life to expressing your *true* potential. Express *more* of what is in you. Don't allow fear of past defeats to drag you down and jam your mental computer. It's future success that should be consuming every minute of every hour of your day. Coordinate your mind with all that is good, pure, true, noble and right and you will reap the magnificent joys of life. And these will be your inspiration for greater good.

BE AN IMPROVER AND BECOME A WINNER

The sales professional by instinct is an improver. He knows he must develop every aspect of his true self. He is not complacent, but enthusiastic in his desire to become a top salesman. Mediocrity is not for him; greatness within his profession is. He is prepared to spend time and money on furthering his aims. He attends lectures on selling and marketing, builds a library of books on selling and human relations, invests in sales training programs to learn new techniques and polish his presentations and personality.

The individual aspiring to the winners' circle embarks on a personal development program geared to take him step-by-step up the ladder of success. He does it because he knows he must. He works hard, adapts to change and dedicates his life to the accomplishment of worthwhile aims. He is a person who can lay claim to the following valuable traits:

- Dynamic *communicator.*
- Powerful *motivator.*
- Efficient *planner.*
- Effective *organizer.*
- Excellent *orator.*
- Consistent *performer.*
- Self *starter.*
- Brilliant *negotiator.*
- Responsible *counselor.*
- Patient *listener.*
- Sincere *helper.*
- Tireless *researcher.*
- Ideas *creator.*

SALES IMAGE
PROFILE CHART

THE SALES WINNER	THE SALES LOSER
Low Key	High pressure
Product oriented	Uninformed
Individualist	Non-entity
Amiable	Rude
Considerate	Inconsiderate
Cooperative	Argumentative
Reliable	Unreliable
Decisive	Indecisive
Ideas Creator	Lazy thinker
Tactful	Tactless
Secure	Insecure
Loyal	Lack of integrity
Charming	Sour disposition
Tolerant	Intolerant
Respectful	Disrespectful
Industrious	Lazy
Well dressed and groomed	Poor appearance
Helpful	Selfish
Courteous	Brash
Humble	Self-centered
Friendly	Distant
Consistent performer	Inconsistent performer
Ambitious	Lacking ambition
Organized	Disorganized
Energetic	Listless
Punctual	No sense of time
Healthy	Unhealthy
Compassionate	Cruel
Sensitive	Insensitive
Dynamic personality	Timid-shy
Truthful	Liar
Leader	Follower
Observant	Disinterested
Affirmative thinker	Negative thinker

= sales professional	= non professional

THE PROFESSIONAL SALESMAN'S CREED

I AM COURTEOUS AT ALL TIMES.

I PRESENT MYSELF AS A FRIENDLY ADVISER TO THOSE NEEDING MY ASSISTANCE.

I ACT WITH HONESTY IN ALL DEALINGS WITH OTHERS.

I AM A PERSON OF MY WORD. MY PERSONAL INTEGRITY CANNOT BE BOUGHT.

I GIVE OF MY TIME FREELY WITHOUT LOOKING FOR MONETARY REWARD.

I RESPECT THE OPINIONS OF OTHERS.

I SEE GOOD IN OTHERS AND VALUE THEIR FRIEND-SHIPS.

I AM LOYAL TO MY FRIENDS AND BUSINESS ASSOCIATES.

I AM DECISIVE. I MAKE THE CORRECT MOVES QUICKLY WHEN REQUIRED TO DO SO.

I AM TACTFUL AND DO NOT OFFEND OTHERS.

I DISPLAY A SENSE OF HUMOR TO CHEER OTHERS.

I AM A SINCERE PERSON.

I APPRECIATE THE ABILITIES OF OTHERS AND TELL THEM SO.

I AM RELIABLE—ALWAYS PUNCTUAL.

I AM NOT PREJUDICED AGAINST ANY PERSON FOR ANY REASON.

I AM ALWAYS WELL DRESSED AND GROOMED.

I AM DEDICATED TO MY PROFESSION AND CONDUCT MYSELF WITH DIGNITY.

I AM FULLY INFORMED ON CURRENT AFFAIRS AND KEEP UP-TO-DATE WITH WORLD EVENTS.

I ALWAYS ADOPT AN ATTITUDE OF WILLINGNESS AND I AM COOPERATIVE.

I MAINTAIN HARMONIOUS RELATIONSHIPS WITH EVERYONE.

I NEVER GOSSIP OR TELL UNTRUTHS.

I DIRECT ALL MY ENERGIES TOWARD CONSTRUCTIVE, CREATIVE ACHIEVEMENT.

I ACT CONFIDENTLY AND CORRECTLY IN ALL SITUATIONS.

I HAVE SOUND PERSONAL VALUES AND A REALISTIC AND AFFIRMATIVE SPIRITUAL PHILOSOPHY.

I AM WORTHY OF THE TITLE OF 'SALES PROFES-SIONAL' AND I VALUE THIS TITLE.

SUMMARY OF IDEAS TO PUT YOU IN
THE WINNERS' CIRCLE

1. A 'winning' salesman is a self-motivator. Results are the only yardstick to measure ability. It takes hard work and 'guts' to succeed.

2. Adopt an attitude of *proud professionalism*. Being a member of the selling profession does not mean that you are a true professional. Dedicate yourself to raising the standard of the sales profession.

3. Strong character is a priceless ingredient. Allow only honest thoughts and deeds to take place in your life. Check your sales motives.

4. Develop the will to win and reject any idea of defeat. Give yourself a strong desire factor (motive) to succeed. Fight for it.

5. Faith power is a miracle worker when the going gets tough. Place faith in the workings of your (affirmative) conscious and subconscious mind.

6. Think in terms of specifics. Reason things through. Rationalize when problems seem unsolvable. Eliminate daydreaming, wishing and hoping for things to come right. Take your problems apart. Analyze them.

7. Fear is another term for ignorance and superstition. Gain self confidence by knowing that you are part of the Divine Plan. Your abilities are a gift of the Great Giver.

8. The biggest percentage of your day is spent listening. But how much do you *really* hear and absorb? You cannot be effective as a sales representative unless you listen to what the customer requires. Get the message. And get it right.

9. You'll get along better with family, friends, business associates, if you follow the loyalty path. Goodwill is built out of respect. It is not possible to respect another if he lacks personal loyalty and integrity.

10. Improve yourself: develop skills, expand knowledge. Plan goals and know where you are headed in life. Be an improver and become a winner.

BOOK TWO

Selling—successful selling—takes powerful personal incentives to keep you going when others are quitting around you. The stronger the incentives, the longer you will last and the more successful you will become. Do not let others pull you down to their (NEGATIVE) level. Keep your thoughts high, your actions honest and you will win—if not today, then tomorrow. But you WILL win.

HOW TO BECOME A
POWERFUL COMMUNICATOR
AND MOTIVATOR

Affirmative Ideas in this Chapter

- The Technique of 'Getting Through' To People
- An Exercise To Help You Become An Effective Communicator
- The Art of Successful Communication
- Methods of Communication
- If You Want To Become A Good Communicator Get People To Like You
- How To Open Communication Channels
- When Communicating, Make Your Words Meaningful
- Don't Violate The Rules of Good Grammar
- Effective Communication Ideas
- Select Favorable Surroundings To Communicate Your Message
- The Art of Conversation
- Talking Is Only 50 Per Cent of Communication
- Establish A Communication Link With Customers And Management
- Your Communication Effectiveness Sets The Pattern of Your Selling Success
- Communication And Motivation Go Hand In Hand
- The Art of Successful Motivation
- What Motivates People?
- You're In The Business of Winning Not Losing Sales
- Basic Human Motives
- Certain Items Need Little Motivational Selling—Others A Great Deal of It
- The First Rule of Persuasion
- The 3 Appeals To Motive
- Self Motivation
- Give Yourself Personal Motives To Succeed
- Incentive Changed Poor Sales Performance And Made Sandy Top Man In His Sales Team
- Paderewski's Personal Motivation To Win Brought Fame And Fortune
- Motivating Subordinates
- Incentive Motivators
- Summary of Ideas To Help You Become A Powerful Communicator And Motivator

124

6

THE TECHNIQUE OF 'GETTING THROUGH' TO PEOPLE

Now with an understanding of yourself and *how* and *why* others think and act, you are in a favorable position to develop your power of communication—the technique of 'getting through' to people.

Communicating effectively isn't all that easy. It calls for clear thinking, affirmative application and constant practise. To succeed in selling, just knowing product plus factors isn't enough. You've got to be able to clearly express yourself. Nothing can be more frustrating than knowing *what* you want to say, but being unable to say it in a concise and effective way.

We spend 84 per cent of our day communicating: listening, writing, speaking. Obviously, if our ability to speak and write our thoughts is ineffective, then many doors to challenging and worthwhile positions will be closed.

The sales representative must be able to 'speak his mind' in a clear and concise manner to business associates, customers, individuals and groups. Verbal communication means that you state your thoughts and feelings so that the hearer knows *exactly* what you mean. Poor verbal communication occurs when you state one thing and intend another. Thus, the customer misinterprets your intention.

Just being a good craftsman is not enough—not nearly enough—if you desire to become a *top professional salesman*. You will be meeting people and influencing their lives. Therefore, you will have to enunciate your ideas and philosophy in a dynamic way. Develop the art of communication. Learn to express your ideas clearly, in easy to understand words.

AN EXERCISE TO HELP YOU BECOME AN EFFECTIVE COMMUNICATOR

Select editorials from magazines or newspapers and read them aloud. Practise correct reading, without stumbling over words or sentences. Join thought groupings together. Look for the correct meaning and emphasize words which point up the meaning.

When you are proficient at reading a particular piece, write down your impression and opinion of it. Now express it in your own words. Say the *same* thing but in different words, expressing other ideas which add up to the same conclusion. Be accurate in the retelling. Don't stray from the main points or 'color' the piece with your own convictions if they do not follow the author's original intent.

This same exercise can be applied to books, reports, films, etc. Try your interpreting skill on friends. Ask them to criticize your ability to communicate ideas, messages, stories.

Remember: communication of ideas must be *clear, concise* and stating exactly what you mean—not what you *think* you mean. If the person listening to your ideas cannot grasp the 'meat' of what you are saying then poor communication is the result.

THE ART OF SUCCESSFUL COMMUNICATION

If you're going to get satisfaction out of selling you've got to develop the art of communication. The art of communication is the art of expressing your ideas in such a way as to impress others with your knowledge, conviction and manner of presentation. It is a two-way exchange of understanding. Just talking to people or worse, talking *at* them, is not communication. But talking *with* them, intently listening to their views, then expressing your own, clearly, easily and dynamically, is true communication.

The individual who puts his case and then allows the other person to put his and *listens* to it, makes friends and enhances customer relations. Effective communication requires effective listening. When you get the message 'right' you are in a position to pass it along to others correctly. The art of successful communication includes the ability to:
- (a) DEVELOP VALID IDEAS AND OPINIONS.
- (b) EXPRESS VALID IDEAS AND OPINIONS.
- (c) LISTEN FOR VALID IDEAS AND OPINIONS.
- (d) RETELL ACCURATELY THE IDEAS, OPINIONS AND MESSAGES OF OTHERS.

METHODS OF COMMUNICATION
- (1) BY SPEECH: person to person, lectures, recordings, broadcasts.
- (2) BY GESTURE: signals via facial expression or body expression.
- (3) BY WRITING: letter-report-book-news article-telegram.

IF YOU WANT TO BECOME A GOOD COMMUNICATOR GET PEOPLE TO LIKE YOU

If you're going to become a good communicator then you've got to get people to like you or else they won't listen to you in the way you want them to listen. Naturally, you won't get every person you meet to like you, but you can win the majority to your corner by making an effort to like them. A healthy mental approach to other people returns their respect for you.

Be yourself! Human relationships are based on *reactions* of people to each other. Others will be attracted to you if you display your true qualities, not false ones. Any attempt to win friendships by forcing a false personality, by trying too hard to impress, makes others suspicious of your motives. Your powers of communication are blocked if those you are talking to 'tune-out' or refuse to believe and accept your point of view.

HOW TO OPEN COMMUNICATION CHANNELS

Though you may not always be aware of it, others sense your true attitudes. False praise or untruthful words boomerang. Your spoken words must match your deep inner thoughts. The channel of communication between mind and mind must be free from negative thinking. You cannot afford to have customers suspicious of the things you say.

Clear the way for an open flow of ideas when communicating to others. Release negative thoughts and feelings and fill your mind with illuminating, friendly, honest and enthusiastic thoughts. Your affirmative consciousness will be 'sensed' and reacted to in a like manner, allowing the free-flow of ideas from one to the other.

WHEN COMMUNICATING MAKE YOUR WORDS MEANINGFUL

The great actor John Barrymore learned to use words as 'tools' from Margaret Carrinston, his voice coach. She instructed Barrymore to take a piece of fruit in his hand and tell her what he was holding. 'A red apple,' he told her, in a flat, expressionless tone.

The voice coach made him recite that line for three weeks until he made that apple sound the most delicious red apple in the entire world. 'That woman taught me to make love to words,' Barrymore said.

The way you express words can make a product sound interesting, inviting and a *must* to own. The way you express them can also detract from the product's image. It's in the *way* you express yourself. Use the *right* words to convey appealing ideas to the buyer. And use them 'lovingly'.

The ability to communicate through the spoken word is a measure of a salesman's efficiency. The salesman whose spoken words cannot be understood or are 'unappealing', is in for a difficult time. He can and *should* improve his performance by practise.

DON'T VIOLATE THE RULES OF GOOD GRAMMAR

A sincere, enthusiastic and well organized sales presentation can be ruined by incorrect grammar. Violating the rules of good grammar adds a jarring note to your presentation and if it occurs frequently makes the prospect wince. If this is one of your faults change it and quickly!

Because we do not always hear ourselves as others hear us, we should check our speech patterns often. Eliminate too many superlatives, check vocabulary and make sure you understand the words you use. Build your presentation around clear, easy to understand words. *Be aware of incorrect grammar.*

There are three methods of correcting faulty speech patterns:

1. Buy a book on good English and study it.
2. Enrol in a course on basic English and join a public speaking group.
3. Practise reading into a tape recorder and correct speech faults.

In many ways, proficiency in English expression is one of the most important of all skills to the salesman. Without it, he cannot communicate and motivate effectively. The salesman must be able to think analytically and present his thoughts without losing the main points or diminishing their effectiveness by speaking incorrectly. The force and clarity of what the salesman says must have a profound effect on the prospect. It can only have a negative effect if the presentation is incorrectly phrased, poorly spoken and the English battered.

Prior to making a sales presentation ask yourself the following questions:

(a) What am I trying to say?
(b) What do I want the prospect to *think* and *do* when I've finished speaking?
(c) Will the message be easily understood in the manner I intend presenting it?
(d) Is my grammar correct? Choice of words suitable?

EFFECTIVE COMMUNICATION IDEAS

The most precious possession we humans have at our command is the ability to communicate. We do not always use it as effectively as we should. Poor communication occurs when the speaker implies something and the listener takes it to mean something else. Salesmen are often guilty of this practice. Lost time, aggravation, customer dissatisfaction, financial loss are results of a break-down in communication between sales representative and buyer.

A report read to a group of executives can end up with many different meanings when it is taken by the executives and related to others: details are omitted; a different point of view is given; facts and figures are distorted. Poor communication can be reversed by *proper listening* and correctly getting the message before retelling it. This method ensures that the communicator *fully understands* the message and repeats it accurately.

Points to remember when *receiving* messages:

1. WRITE THE MESSAGE DOWN.
2. ASK QUESTIONS IF UNCERTAIN AS TO FACTS AND FIGURES.
3. UNDERSTAND WORDS, MEANINGS, CONSEQUENCES OF MESSAGE.
4. REPEAT THE THEME OR 'MEAT' OF THE MESSAGE BACK TO THE SPEAKER TO MAKE SURE YOU HAVE IT CORRECT.

When *communicating* ideas follow these points:

1. NEVER REPEAT A MESSAGE OF IMPORTANCE UNLESS YOU *KNOW* IT IS ABSOLUTELY TRUE AND CORRECT. IF THIS IS NOT POSSIBLE, BEGIN WITH: 'I BELIEVE THIS TO BE TRUE . . .'
2. KEEP YOUR TALK ORDERLY. DON'T RAMBLE.
3. DON'T USE WORDS YOU DO NOT UNDERSTAND.
4. MAKE SURE YOU CONVEY WHAT YOU MEAN, NOT WHAT YOU *THINK* YOU MEAN.
5. IF YOU PRESENT OPINIONS (OR THE IDEAS OF OTHERS) SUPPORT YOUR STATEMENTS WITH INDISPUTABLE FACTS.
6. EMPHASIZE AND *RE-STATE* IMPORTANT FACTS. CALL FOR QUESTIONS TO ENSURE THAT YOUR MESSAGE IS UNDERSTOOD.

SELECT FAVORABLE SURROUNDINGS TO COMMUNICATE YOUR MESSAGE

When communicating with others in person, select the best possible surroundings. In most rooms in which we communicate there is approximately 40 decibels of intensity. To effectively present a message we must talk-through this distracting noise level. In office buildings or stores, salesmen must contend with phones ringing, office or store workers chatting, outside street noise, continual interruptions by staff members and customers. If you are selling, getting the other person to listen and concentrate on your presentation is often quite difficult. It is not possible to eliminate all noise when communicating, particularly if you are visiting a prospect's place of business. If you find that noise is a problem, request the meeting be held in a relatively noise-free room.

THE ART OF CONVERSATION

From our private world of thoughts, feelings and beliefs, we express our opinions—likes and dislikes—to others. We pass along ideas, attempt to impress others and motivate them to our way of thinking. The greater our knowledge, exerience and vocabulary, the easier it is to communicate with others—to talk to them easily and naturally. By developing the art of conversation, self confidence, enthusiasm, understanding, tolerance and personality are enhanced.

Our failure to understand one another is the cause of all human problems. We do not listen accurately; we do not effectively use the language we have been taught. Troubles stem from wrong and dishonest use of words—a lack of spoken integrity.

When conversing at social or business functions, keep your message, idea, statement of fact or question simple. Reduce the speed of your normal speech pattern (people talk too quickly). Enunciate and articulate so that your partner or audience hear every word. Emphasize important words and phrases. Hold eye contact with those you are talking to. Don't fidget. Stand still. Keep to the point. Don't ramble. Get others talking about their favorite subjects. Remain poised when asking or answering questions. Don't get flustered or stumble over words. 'Tune-in' on people. 'Feel-out' their likes and dislikes.

The most important point to remember in carrying a conversation is to have 'points of view' on a variety of subjects. Read newspapers, magazines, books. View films, television programs. Listen to radio broadcasts. Attend public lectures. Make a list of subject headings on 3 x 5 cards and write short statements concerning your feelings on each subject: politics, philosophy, advertising, selling, marketing, business, entertainment, travel, censorship, religion, education, the arts, etc. Know your subjects. Research them. Play heavily on facts in preference to hearsay or opinions. Present your points in a rational, calm and friendly manner. Avoid arguing at all costs. Arguments will not win friends and influence people in the way you want them to be influenced.

TALKING IS ONLY 50 PER CENT OF COMMUNICATION

The art of conversation goes hand in hand with the art of listening. Everybody warms to a good listener. A good listener shows that he is *interested* in us and our ideas. He is paying us a compliment. Listening is the other half of communication. Life is action and reaction. When two people are having a conversation together the listener *responds* to the talker. Some salesmen think they must talk *all* the time during a presentation. Don't be guilty of talking too much and listening too little. Listen and you might learn something about the needs, desires and feelings of the other fellow.

Listen for ideas you can use. Listen for the other person's point of view. Withhold evaluation until you fully comprehend the message. Our greatest fault: we don't hear people out. We jump to conclusions and *think* we heard the message right. Concentration is the most potent listening weapon. This is the basis of psychotherapy: a person talks, another listens. You do not learn while you are talking. You have an opportunity of learning a lot if you listen.

ESTABLISH A COMMUNICATION LINK WITH CUSTOMERS AND MANAGEMENT

A lack of regular communication with customers and with company management lowers a salesman's morale, prevents feedback of valuable market information, loses major accounts through poor complaint handling and inconsistent service contact.

The salesman must keep 'in tune' with both customer and his home office to know exactly what is going on. There must be no communication gaps which allow for mistakes, misunderstandings or lost business. The more informed a salesman is on new products, new marketing methods, new advertising campaigns, new pricing structures, the better equipped he is to make full use of this information in the field. In turn, the more informed he is about customer complaints, competition, buying trends, the more vital information he is able to pass back to company management.

Your motive for better communication will be your desire to relate to people. Bridge the communication links between seller, buyer and management. Make it a part of your normal day, to search-out problem areas with customers, to file reports on difficulties encountered and to seek ways to solve them.

YOUR COMMUNICATION EFFECTIVENESS SETS THE PATTERN OF YOUR SELLING SUCCESS

We have discovered that in selling it is important to 'sell' your personality. The *powerful* personality you must develop can bring 'acceptance' during the first few moments of meeting a client. Beyond that, your ability to communicate the advantages of your product becomes the deciding factor as to a 'yes' or 'no' response.

Your job is to make prospects *want* to do business with you. To have this necessary effect on prospects, you must communicate your ideas in a pleasing, forthright, personable and convincing way. The greater your communication skill, the more prospects will listen to your sales message and act on it in the *affirmative*.

Your speech and actions based on attitudes, knowledge, skills and habits cause you to be accepted or rejected, liked or disliked. No matter how much a prospect desires a product he'll buy it elsewhere if he doesn't like you or thinks that you are incompetent and unable to service his needs efficiently. Unless you make your mark with personality and with a powerful communication style you'll miss more sales than you make. Your *effect* on people determines your sales volume and your dollar earnings.

There are five vitally important factors which contribute to your skill as a communicator. They are:

1. THE WAY YOU **LOOK.**
2. THE WAY YOU **THINK.**
3. THE WAY YOU **TALK.**
4. THE WAY YOU **REACT.**
5. THE WAY YOU **LISTEN.**

COMMUNICATION AND MOTIVATION GO HAND IN HAND

You cannot motivate a prospect to the action you desire unless you have communicated your message in such a way as to make him *want* to act in the affirmative. Communication and motivation are *one*; they cannot be separated when it comes to selling.

Communication is the ability to express valid ideas and opinions. Unless this is accomplished by the salesman the prospect must react in his own favor and say 'no'. Effective communication results in effective motivation. The two cannot be treated as separate sciences for one relies on the other.

The gentle art of being persuasive (the effect) has its success deeply rooted in the message (the cause). The law of cause and effect is an important factor in communication and motivation. Make sure your message is *right* and your motivational power will be enhanced and work in the affirmative.

A buyer is influenced by both rational and emotional wants. You should attempt to look at things from *his* point of view and help him to solve his problems and fulfill his wants with the products or services you represent. Persuade him to accept your proposition through appeals to reason or emotion or through a combination of both. When the prospect is convinced that your products or services offer the best possible solution to his problems, he buys. A case of effective communication and motivation.

THE ART OF SUCCESSFUL MOTIVATION

Motivation is getting things done through our own powers (self-motivation) and inciting others to act in the way we want them to act (persuasion). The art of successful motivation is to:

    (a) SWAY WITH VALID IDEAS AND OPINIONS.

    (b) CONVINCE WITH VALID IDEAS AND OPINIONS.

    (c) CHANGE WITH VALID IDEAS AND OPINIONS.

Motivating others is not a matter of being heavy handed, laying-down-the-law or mentally forcing others to your point of view. Mental coercion brings resentment and stubborn resistance on the part of those it is tried on. A subtle approach, tactfully suggesting, gently leading others without making it obvious is the psychological approach to motivation.

Threats, over-aggressiveness, sternly presented or embarrassing words must be eliminated entirely from the salesman's thinking and approach. People can be led—they resist being forced to accept a point of view or directive. Lead—don't push, lean on, force or challenge others to 'do as you say.'

Study the behavior of customers. Know how far you can go with each when attempting to 'change' their attitudes and actions. Note their 'pressure' points: the precise moment resentment and hostility arise.

Any kind of pressure on the part of the salesman is usually regarded by the prospect as 'unreasonable force' and an immediate *resistance block* is established. The prospect is 'on-guard' and his suspicion of the salesman's intentions makes it difficult (if not impossible) to 'sell' him.

WHAT MOTIVATES PEOPLE?

In a short, simple sentence people are motivated by a 'what's in it for me' attitude. If you want prospects to accept your product or service then you must give them a good reason for buying it. We know that people do not buy things just for the sake of buying them. They make decisions and carry through on actions because they have a vested interest in the outcome of them. The challenge to every salesman is to learn the *interest* or *motive patterns* of prospective customers. Know *what* motivates them to say 'yes' or 'no'.

This is not as difficult as it may seem. Motives are a driving force within *all* humans. People have 'wants' and they wish to satisfy them. Find the motive *behind* the want, then present *incentives* to satisfy the motive. For example: a prospect desires to purchase a block of land. His motive is to build a house on it for his family. His incentive to buy the land and build the house is the love of his family and a desire to please them; to give them happiness and security. In return, he receives emotional satisfaction by fulfilling his needs, wants and creative urges.

From this example, we readily see that both motives and incentives are the keys to persuasion. Two steps to follow are:

1. FIND THE MOTIVE(S) BEHIND THE DESIRE TO PURCHASE.
2. SUPPLY AN INCENTIVE(S) TO THE MOTIVE(S) TO FULFILL THE DESIRE.

Present incentives that inspire and offer a definite gain or a guarantee of gain. If you want to convince the prospect that what you offer is worthy of his consideration and purchase, then offer him suitable *incentives* to buy—compensations for his financial expenditure.

Don't be guilty of losing sales because you fail to understand the emotional side of selling; it's as important as gaining product knowledge. The more you know about the emotional 'make-up' of your customers, the easier and quicker it will be to motivate them to buy your products or services. Return to the chapter on buying motives and study it again. Remember, the first law of psychological selling is to *satisfy needs*, to *fulfill desires*. And this is done by thinking of the customer's requirements—not what 'I' want but what the customer *needs*.

YOU'RE IN THE BUSINESS OF WINNING NOT LOSING SALES

Millions of dollars are lost to business every year because sales representatives are ineffective as communicators and motivators. Salesmen must develop the ability to 'read' human-emotion patterns and know how to deal with them.

All human beings, regardless of job held, are in the business of selling. Every time an individual presents an idea to another, he is 'selling' a point of view and attempting to motivate that person to

BASIC HUMAN MOTIVES

Behavioral scientists have discovered four major desires common to
all people: *physiological* needs, *social* needs, *psychological* needs,
creative needs. Buying decisions stem from these and they are made on
rational and or emotional grounds. Some of these basic human wants
are:

I Want To Be Important
I Want To Be Respected
I Want To Be Successful
I Want To Exploit Creative Abilities
I Want To Earn A Great Deal Of Money
I Want To Travel
I Want To Improve My Health
I Want To Change My Job
I Want To Develop My Appearance
I Want To Solve My Problems
I Want To Have Variety In My Life
I Want To Improve My Knowledge
I Want To Have Luxury Possessions
I Want To Love And Be Loved
I Want To Assist The Welfare Of Others
I Want A Better Work Environment
I Want To Start My Own Business
I Want To Develop My Personality
I Want To Develop My Business Contacts
I Want Peace Of Mind And Freedom From Fear And Worry
I Want Security And Financial Investments
I Want To Be Happy
I Want Others To Like Me
I Want To Make New Friendships
I Want To Be Kind
I Want To Be Generous
I Want To Be Humble
I Want To Be Courteous
I Want To Be A Good Conversationalist
I Want To Develop Organizational Ability
I Want Encouragement
I Want To Be Appreciated
I Want A New House
I Want A New Car
I Want New Clothes
I Want To Lose (Or Gain) Weight
I Want To Change My Life-Style And Experience New Things

accept it. Selling 'points of view' to others, is no different to the sales-man selling product or service 'points of view' to prospective buyers. Whether a person is motivated to 'buy' depends, to a large extent, on the effectiveness of the communication of incentives to the buying motive.

CERTAIN ITEMS NEED LITTLE MOTIVATIONAL SELLING—OTHERS A GREAT DEAL OF IT

While it is true that the essentials of life—food, clothing, housing—require little more than 'service' selling, the comforts and conveniences of luxury goods and services require motivational selling. The basic 'appeal' and 'benefit' factors must be put in such a way as to 'stir' the customer emotionally. As an example: a suit costing 80 dollars might well-satisfy the average buyer and therefore require only 'service' selling. A 350 dollar suit offered to 'Mr. Average Buyer' would require motivational selling. A sense of pride (of ownership) and prestige appealing to the buyer's ego would be the incentives to purchase.

An automobile equipped with the bare essentials would be satis-factory transportation for the 'average' individual. The same auto-mobile equipped with every conceivable accessory and costing hundreds of dollars more, would require a salesman to alter his approach. He would have to motivate the prospect by supplying incentives, emotional appeals, to satisfy and justify the added expenditure.

THE FIRST RULE OF PERSUASION

Motivation is the WHY of human behavior. The first rule: find the *WHY FACTOR*. The why factor is the cause, reason, purpose for buying. The buying reason must be discovered before effective measures can be taken to persuade, influence or direct the prospect's course of action. People have countless wants and needs. Your job is to discover them.

Motivation is twofold, derived from an individual's (internal) needs or desires—*motives*—or activated by incentives from outside the individual. Become a practical psychologist and investigate the cus-tomer's motives. Offer him incentives to fulfill his needs and you will have applied the first law of motivation: finding the WHY FACTOR and supplying it.

THE 3 APPEALS TO MOTIVE

Motive is a power which operates on the will of man, causing him to act. When a salesman presents his proposition he bases his 'appeal' factor on whatever will incite the prospect to buy. Failure to present a motive for buying is a sure way to lose a sale. No salesman calling himself a professional has the right to attempt to sell anything unless his presentation can offer suitable reasons *why* the prospect should buy. *All sales presentations must present satisfactory buying reasons*. These reasons come in the form of *appeals* to the prospect's buying motive(s).

There are three basic *appeals* to motive and these are:

1. INSTINCT   **2.** REASON   **3.** EMOTION
    APPEAL   APPEAL   APPEAL

INSTINCT APPEAL: causes most people to purchase the necessities of life: food, clothing, housing, methods of transport.

REASON APPEAL: savings, property investments, business equipment, mechanical and electrical appliances appeal through logical reasoning.

EMOTIONAL APPEAL: a great many goods and services are sold on emotional appeal: insurance, education, books, films, music, art, luxury items. Religion is 'sold' on emotional appeal. Love and marriage are based on emotional appeal.

SELF MOTIVATION

Applying the techniques of self motivation are the same as those for motivating others: find out what things you want in life, supply an incentive to get them and persistence, confidence and hard work will guarantee the accomplishment of them.

Surprisingly, many people find themselves frequently bored, irritated, listless, lonely and lacking in ambition. They worry, are frightened to make decisions, hate getting up in the morning and dread the thought of another day at their place of employment. They live within the confines of a failure consciousness pattern and their discontent with life keeps them from experiencing the joys of creative living.

People caught up in this negative 'roundabout' seldom reach the heights of creative and financial success. And the reason for it is because they are not *self* motivated. They lack a *reason* for changing their 'way of life'.

Only your acute awareness of your own attitudes, beliefs, needs and desires can lead to self improvement and eventually success in life. You've got to be analytical and utilize creative psychology to delve into yourself to find your motives for living, for enhancing your life and securing your future.

Lay your motives for success out in front of you and find strong incentives to satisfy them. This is the form your training for success in selling must take. If it doesn't, your progress will be as slow as the tortoise, instead of as fast as the hare.

GIVE YOURSELF PERSONAL MOTIVES TO SUCCEED

An individual's personal motivation can be assessed by examining the amount and *kind* of interest he has in the various aspects of his job and personal activities. The well-motivated person has more intense interest in things than the less-motivated one.

The salesman who loves his work because it is 'fun to do' is a better worker than the salesman who works because 'necessity' demands it. The former does what is expected of him and *more* because he *wants* to; the latter does what is expected of him only because he knows he must to keep his job.

Look at your own personal motivation and determine whether you are an eager performer or one who has to be motivated by others to get the job done. Give yourself strong reasons for spending more (productive) time and effort on your job as a professional salesman. Incentive motivation spurs you on to greater heights, greater achievements and rewards you with financial security, job security and creative satisfaction.

INCENTIVE CHANGED POOR SALES PERFORMANCE AND MADE SANDY TOP MAN IN HIS SALES TEAM

During a lecture tour in 1972 I addressed a group of salesmen in Toronto. In the course of a discussion later at a dinner, a young man told me that he had great difficulty getting started each day.

He told me he looked for 'any excuse' to get out of calling on prospects. 'I have no incentive to sell,' he said. 'Get one!' I told him. 'Look for personal incentives that incite you to action. If you can't get excited about your work then you should make a job change.'

This remark seemed to move him. 'No! I couldn't leave my job. I like it too much,' he said. What a contradiction, I thought. I felt that in this case it wasn't a matter of lazy attitude producing lazy actions, it was a case of no incentives. I told him to make a list of the things he'd like to have and accomplish. Once this was done, he was to take them, one at a time, and use each as an incentive to get himself moving. I instructed him to think of each prospect as having the vital key to the accomplishment of each desire and with every call made, the possibility existed that this customer would hand him another key to success.

The technique worked. Young Sandy is top man in his company's sales team. He acquired reasons to sell and with incentives firmly in his mind his right attitude produced right actions.

PADEREWSKI'S PERSONAL MOTIVATION TO WIN BROUGHT FAME AND FORTUNE

Before Ignace Paderewski became famous as a musician, he had been advised by famous authorities on music in his day, that he had no possible future as a pianist. The professors at the Warsaw Conservatory, where he went to study, pointed out that his fingers were not well-formed and it would be better if he concentrated on composing music.

'I want to be a great pianist', he told them. And pianist of world renown he became. Paderewski practised arduously for hours every day. He was tortured with pain from swollen fingers. Often, during concerts, blood seeped from his injured fingers.

Paderewski persisted with his dream because his incentive motivation—creative fulfillment, recognition—was stronger than the motivation to quit.

Develop a strong desire, a personal motive, to support your dreams and aspirations. You will find that the stronger the motive, the easier and quicker the road to accomplishment. Without it, life becomes hazardous, unsteady and fraught with fear, frustration and anxiety. If you want to win, develop the will to win and support it with *real* and realistic reasons.

MOTIVATING SUBORDINATES

There is a leader behind every successful venture. Leaders are recognized for the ability to decide and act in an affirmative manner. They are respected for their ability to motivate others to action.

A leader must motivate his followers to become loyal assistants. The leader who applies the YOU FACTOR technique—offers incentives to fulfill motives—has no trouble getting others to cooperate and do the things that must be done.

Learn to express yourself to those you want to have follow you. Let them know your aims and objectives. Find out theirs. Impress upon them the 'returns' (what's in it for them) if all objectives are met. Give praise to those who do their jobs well. Appreciate the work they do and tell them so. Compliment subordinates on: dress, grooming, attitude, loyalty, intelligence, honesty, willingness to work hard, etc.

Create a friendly atmosphere between subordinates in which it is easy to exchange ideas and feelings. Because no two people are alike, we can make ourselves 'easily understood' and 'easy to listen to' only by adjusting ourselves to each individual that we talk to; by 'sensing' emotional responses and not treading on the other person's self esteem.

Unless you communicate your message clearly to the other person you cannot hope to motivate him. Listen to his arguments, resentments, grievances. Perhaps there is truth in what he is saying. Motivating subordinates depends on your personal charm and the ability to enter into the interests, points of view and objectives of others.

INCENTIVE MOTIVATORS

- PRIDE OF ACCOMPLISHMENT—SELF SATISFACTION.
- PUBLIC RECOGNITION.
- RESPECT OF LOVED ONES AND BUSINESS ASSOCIATES.
- FULFILLMENT OF CREATIVE URGES.
- HAPPINESS—JOY—HARMONY—BALANCE IN LIFE.
- FINANCIAL SECURITY FOR SELF AND FAMILY.
- PHYSICAL ASSETS: HOUSE—BOAT—CLOTHES—TRAVEL, ETC.
- IMPROVED MENTAL AND PHYSICAL APPEARANCE—ZEST FOR LIVING.
- JOB ADVANCEMENT.
- POSITION OF STRENGTH TO HELP OTHERS IN LIFE.
- A FULL AND PRODUCTIVE LIFE.
- GREATER SELF POWER—MASTERY AND CONTROL OVER CIRCUMSTANCES.

SUMMARY OF IDEAS TO HELP YOU BECOME A POWERFUL COMMUNICATOR AND MOTIVATOR

1. Good communication calls for clear thinking and accurate listening. Expression of your ideas must be in easy-to-understand words. Know exactly what you want to say. Effective communication is the ability to express valid ideas and opinions.

2. If you want to be a good communicator you must get people to like you. Display a friendly attitude towards everyone. Be yourself. Do not force your personality on others or they will become suspicious of your motives. Others can 'sense' your true attitudes.

3. Don't violate the rules of good grammar. Correct your speech faults.

4. Communication is a two-way thing. You must *listen* before you can react intelligently. Select favorable surroundings. Prepare your message prior to delivering it.

5. Communication and motivation go hand-in-hand. You cannot hope to motivate others if you do not communicate your message in a concise easy-to-understand and dynamic way. Develop the ability to *sway* with valid ideas and opinions and *convince* and *change* with valid ideas and opinions.

6. People are motivated by a 'what's in it for me?' attitude. Find the buying motive and supply incentives to fulfill the motive.

7. Certain items such as food, clothing, housing, do not need motivational selling. But luxury items usually do. The first rule of motivation is to find the WHY factor—the reason for buying. Motive is a power which operates on the will of man, causing him to act. Get your customers to act in the way you want them to act by supplying logical reasons.

8. Self-motivation helps you to succeed. Give yourself incentives to accomplish the things you want. Know *what* you want and the reason you want it.

9. Paderewski the famous musician persisted with his dreams because the incentive to win was stronger than the incentive to quit.

10. There is a leader behind every successful venture. Leaders are recognized for their ability to think and act affirmatively. Also, for their ability to motivate others to action. Apply the YOU FACTOR to get others to do the things that must be done. Help fulfill the desires of others.

HOW TO BE YOUR OWN
PRODUCT AND MARKET
RESEARCH ANALYST

Affirmative Ideas in this Chapter

- The Value of Product Knowledge
- How To Find Product PLUS FACTORS
- Gaining A Superior Product Knowledge
- Product Analysis Questions
- Prepare Your Own Product Plus And Negative Factors List
- Lack of Information Brought Company To Its Knees
- Plus And Negative Factors
- Use Imagination And Hunt For Selling Plus Factors
- 3 Examples of Creative Imagining
- Get To Know Your Customers' Appeal Motives—Match Them To Plus Factors
- Questionnaire
- Obtaining Plus Factors On A Service Industry
- Value Analysis—Determining The Worth of Products And Services
- Know The Company Manufacturing And Marketing The Product You Sell
- Discover And Project Company Policy
- The Value of Market Research
- The Common Law of Business Balance
- The 4 Analysis Areas
- Successful Ways of Gathering Market Research Data
- Market Research Questionnaires
- How To Get The Market Edge And Exploit Your Product
- Keep A Check On Product Life Cycle
- Sales Trend Report Cards
- Every Salesman Should Be A Market Research Gatherer And Analyst
- Sample Sales Trend Card
- Writing Sales And Marketing Reports
- Sample Activity Report
- Activity (Sales) Reports
- Defining Some of The Problem Areas
- Preparatory Planning And Forecasting
- Summary of Ideas To Help You Gather Valuable Product And Market Research Facts

7

THE VALUE OF PRODUCT KNOWLEDGE

Every product (or service) offered to the public has 'in-built' benefits which, once discovered, are valuable sales tools to increase business to existing customers and generate new customers and clients. These in-built benefits are called product *plus factors.*

Every product has some form of *advantage,* every service some *benefit* to satisfy a need and fulfill a desire. The duty of the professional salesman is to discover and 'sell' product advantages and benefits.

Without knowing what his product can do—its *performance value*— a salesman must 'shoot-in-the-dark' when trying to combat customer objections. Customers with special needs cannot be dealt with efficiently or satisfactorily by the salesman lacking product information. They feel they are dealing with an order-taker instead of a specialist. Lack of sufficient product knowledge defeats the true purpose of the sales representative which is to be a professional adviser and counselor. Good product orientation can boost sales performance and selling morale and increase customer satisfaction. The value of product knowledge cannot and should not be questioned. It must become an accepted and *important* part of every salesman's specialist training.

HOW TO FIND PRODUCT PLUS FACTORS

Product plus factors are *advantages of use.* They are the in-built incentives which motivate customers to purchase products. The best sources of enquiry when seeking plus factors are:

1. **THE ADVERTISING DEPARTMENT.**
2. **COMPANY BROCHURES.**
3. **THE PLANT FOREMAN.**
4. **THE SERVICE DEPARTMENT MANAGER.**
5. **RESELLERS OF THE PRODUCT.**
6. **USERS OF THE PRODUCT.**
7. **A THOROUGH PERSONAL ANALYSIS OF THE PRODUCT.**

For obvious reasons, the *advertising department* is the best source of enquiry. If this is not possible, check advertising material and brochures. Many hours of thought have gone into producing a *brochure* extolling the virtues of the product. Technical data and the various benefits of use will be listed. A visit to the *plant* and talks with the plant foreman and those who actually make the product is time well spent. The *service department* is the place to discover the weaknesses of a product. *Resellers* and *users* will have definite views and these are important sources when putting together a product plus factors list.

If possible, always use the product yourself. What do you like and dislike about it? Pull it apart and become aware of the components that make it work. Look for quality construction and life expectancy.

GAINING A SUPERIOR PRODUCT KNOWLEDGE

The sales professional is a skilled researcher and analyst. He evaluates customers' needs and is imaginative enough to persuade his customers that his product can meet their needs; he matches plus factors to needs and instead of talking 'sales' he talks 'benefits', 'services' and 'fulfillments' of desires, wants and requirements. This intelligent, creative and scientific approach to selling wins—in addition to extra sales and commissions—valuable friendships.

A *superior* knowledge of the product's plus factors is the best possible defense for handling customer objections. Instead of trying to avoid 'hard-line' objections, the psychologically-trained salesman welcomes them because he knows he can handle them honestly and satisfactorily. In addition to having plus factors, products have *negative factors* or weaknesses associated with them. These must be known also, and suitable answers given should customers refer to them. The industry sales specialists are superior product analysts generating a high level of enthusiasm among customers through their vast knowledge of product facts.

PRODUCT ANALYSIS QUESTIONS

Your product (or service) is a commodity others will purchase if you can supply solid reasons why they should buy. Buying reasons are to be found *within* the product itself. Find suitable answers to the following list of ten questions:

1. What is there about the product (or service) that makes it 'special' and worthy of purchase?
2. What specific function(s) does it fulfill?
3. What is its reliability factor?
4. What after-sales service is offered?
5. Can spare parts be purchased to repair it?
6. What performance guarantee is there?
7. What is the expected life of the product?
8. What negative factors are there?
9. How does it compare to its nearest competitor?
10. Is the price fair and just—'value' for money?

Armed with the answers to these important questions, your selling confidence is given a boost and you are in a better position to handle any sales situation that may arise.

PREPARE YOUR OWN PRODUCT PLUS AND NEGATIVE FACTORS LIST

Prepare a list of your product(s) (or service) plus and negative factors and a separate list of competitor products and their plus and minus factors. Compare them and build a strong case for your own product. It is important to know what your competitor products can and cannot do. Don't be an 'Ostrich' salesman. Burying your head in the sand and ignoring your competitors won't make them go away or lessen their sales impact.

It is a good idea to prepare a questionnaire covering points on which you know prospects will question you. Lost sales should not occur because you do not have sufficient product knowledge. Your safeguard in this respect is thorough research and analysis of your product or service. You cannot know *too much* about your product. You can know *too little* and this is often (too often) the case with tyro salesmen. The only safe formula to success in selling is to raise the level of your product knowledge and keep reinforcing it with new facts as the product is developed and refined.

LACK OF INFORMATION BROUGHT COMPANY TO ITS KNEES

I was called in to remedy a sales situation that had the sales manager baffled. 'Sales have dropped off drastically over the past two years and if this trend keeps up we'll be out of business in another year,' he told me. After calling a series of meetings with the twelve-man sales team, I was astounded to find that eight out of the twelve had no knowledge of their company policy and couldn't answer a simple questionnaire I gave them to fill-out on the product's obvious advantages.

PLUS FACTORS	NEGATIVE FACTORS
Advantage of use—what it can do.	Disadvantage of use—what it can't do.
Quality of workmanship in assembly.	Poorly assembled.
Quality materials used in product.	Inferior components used.
Long life of article.	Built-in obsolescence.
Reliable performance.	Unreliable performance.
Excellent service facilities.	Poor service facilities.
Performance guarantee.	Worthless guarantee.
Spare parts available.	Shortage of parts.
Does the job it was built for.	Does not function well.
Surpasses competitor products.	Does not come up to competitor products.
Value for money.	Overly priced—poor value.
Many colors available.	Small range of colors.
Various sizes available.	Inadequate range of sizes.
Continual development of product.	Short run. Product to be phased out.
Easy to order. Ample stocks.	Hard to obtain replacement stock.
Lives up to advertising claims.	Does not live up to advertising claims.
Specifications correct.	Specifications incorrect.
Attractively packaged.	Unattractive packaging.
Excellent advertising and promotion.	No reseller support: advertising-promotion.
Need established through market research.	No market research to establish need.
High profit margin incentive.	Low profit margin.
Superior product image.	Poor product image.
Easy to sell.	Difficult to sell.
Many special features.	No special features.

I related this information to the sales manager and suggested that an immediate training program be established to ensure that each man becomes fully conversant with his company and its product and able to satisfactorily handle possible objections.

The program was instigated and each man went through a vigorous indoctrination of company policy and product selling points. A sales manual was prepared and supplied to each salesman. Sales situations, including handling of objections, were simulated at workshop sessions and a product knowledge test was given. The subsequent result was a tremendous increase in sales and profits and a far happier sales team. The company has reversed its liquidity situation and is now operating economically and profitably.

Blame for this situation (for the most part) rests with management. While a degree of blame rests with each salesman, management has a responsibility to ensure that its representatives have *all* available company and product information and use this information to advantage.

USE IMAGINATION AND HUNT FOR SELLING PLUS FACTORS

Selling points are found within the 'structure' of your product. They are also found in your imagination. Combine your imagination with the use of your five senses to discover unusual selling points. What can you *see, touch, taste, smell* or *hear* in connection with your product that could be used to advantage?

Creative imagining will bring appealing ideas to mind. Present these to prospects to get them involved *in* and excited *about* your proposition.

3 EXAMPLES OF CREATIVE IMAGINING

1. A candy salesman had difficulty selling a particular line of chocolates. His company added more tasty ingredients. The salesman didn't just *talk* about them he opened a box and invited his customers to *try* them. Then he invited them to try the chocolates with the old ingredients. The comparison test brought big orders —and extra commissions for the imaginative salesman.

2. An imaginative travel agency salesman asked his company to install a floor to ceiling mirror across the full width of a wall in his office. Across the full width of the opposite wall he had a mural painted of a Honolulu beach scene. He placed his desk in a strategic position so that clients facing him could see their reflections in the mirror with the beach scene behind them. *They were put in the picture.* They could actually see themselves on the beach at Waikiki. This salesman's package tours to Hawaii are always a 'sell-out'. A case of creative imagining and a sure technique for increasing commission earnings.

3. A watch salesman increased sales on a new shock-proof watch by applying the creative imagining technique. Instead of telling his prospects that the face-glass is shatterproof, and the case

shockproof, the salesman uses a small rubber hammer to prove his point. As he delivers his presentation he pounds the sample watch with the hammer. A startling and attention-getting sales presentation is the result. And one that earns big commissions.

GET TO KNOW YOUR CUSTOMERS' APPEAL MOTIVES—MATCH THEM TO PLUS FACTORS

When you have gathered a comprehensive list of product plus factors, match them to the specific needs of your customers. Some plus factors will have more appeal than others. Some will be important, others not so important. To assist you to match customers' motives to plus factors, complete the questionnaire. (List all customers in your territory and complete a questionnaire sheet on each.)

QUESTIONNAIRE

CUSTOMER NAME: ....

QUESTION	ANSWER
1. What buying motive(s) most influence this customer?	
2. What series of plus factors would appeal to his buying motive(s)?	
3. Is the customer familiar with every aspect of my product or service?	
4. What plus factors can be 'pushed' to help him sell more of my product?	
5. How can I best present the product to allow him to 'experience' the benefits?	
6. What is the customer's most pressing problem in connection with sales?	
7. Is my customer favoring a competitor product and if so, why? What can I do about it?	
8. What complaints is he receiving about my product? Is he satisfied with the way my company handles service complaints?	
9. Does the customer have sufficient brochures and technical data to help him resell my product?	
10. Am I properly assessing buying motives and matching the right plus factors?	

OBTAINING PLUS FACTORS ON A SERVICE INDUSTRY

Securing valuable knowledge to sell intangibles is much the same as gaining it for a product. There may be slight differences in emphasis, but the basic principles of gathering the information remain the same.

The questions to be answered are: what specific function or important role can my service fulfill? Is its cost in line with the service it offers? How does it rate with competitor services?

Intangibles take many forms such as travel, insurance, entertainment, advertising, correspondence courses, certain forms of investment, industrial cleaning, industrial and private protection, etc.

A client seeking insurance is not buying a piece of paper with a policy printed on it. He is buying protection. Benefits that adequately cover this are put before the prospect. The benefit factors are gathered from the service offered and matched to the buyer's motive or reason for buying.

Selling a service is a matter of knowing what the prospect intends doing with the service, whether he is in a position to pay for it and whether the service offered can satisfy the demands that will be made on it.

VALUE ANALYSIS—DETERMINING THE WORTH OF PRODUCTS AND SERVICES

Value analysis is a modern management tool aimed at finding cheaper and more efficient ways of doing things and determining the actual value of the product or service being offered. It's a method of *fact finding*: securing every piece of information about the product, so it can be clearly defined as to *what* it does and then sold in precise easy-to-understand terms.

It is also a method of finding out whether there is any real value in putting time, effort and money into a product in the first place or whether it is worthwhile in continuing with a particular product.

Value analysis is the study of the relationship between the design, function and cost of material of the product or service with the purpose of cutting down cost without restricting performance values.

The sales representative is free to make his own value analysis of the products he represents and come to a conclusion about them. This is one step beyond product research and it should be done to increase selling effectiveness. It helps to substantiate in the mind of the salesman confidence in his company's merchandise or services offered to the reseller or to the public.

A timely word about *value* is within the text of the John Ruskin philosophy. It's worth writing on a card and reading when 'price' is raised as a customer objection. (See page 151.)

KNOW THE COMPANY MANUFACTURING AND MARKETING THE PRODUCT YOU SELL

In addition to knowing all there is to know about your product or service, gain a thorough understanding of the company that *makes* the product you sell. The objective here, is to help you understand the purpose of the company and its trading philosophy.

Buyers want to do business with individuals, not impersonal conglomerates, whose sole interest seems to be making money instead of extending friendly, helpful service and top quality goods and services in *return* for money.

Knowledge of your company can be used as excellent supporting points for presentations and used to promote a healthy public image and customer relationships. Information to be found should include:

    (a) When was the business started and why? (Company history).

    (b) Who remains of the original founders and staff?

    (c) What products or services are still being sold that helped start the business? What do you know about current products?

    (d) What interesting facts are there associated with the company's growth?

    (e) What is the company policy?

    (f) What development plan does the company have?

    (g) How does the company treat its employees and customers?

    (h) What do you know about company executives?

DISCOVER AND PROJECT COMPANY POLICY

Objectives, in terms of finance, production, distribution, development and research, service, warranty, customer and staff relations, advertising and image projection, promotion, the 'why' and the 'what for' of the company's existence all emerge in the company policy—its reason for being. Yet, it's surprising to find so many salesmen and sales managers ignorant of the philosophy behind the policies of their respective companies.

Most policies are tied-in with the sales direction (or they should be) and when a clear path is set, deciding *what* to sell, *how* to sell it, at what price and in what quantities, the overall policy can be utilized to greater advantage by the sales team.

Progressive salesmen and sales managers should make every effort to get a clear picture of the policy of their company and to use it to set a firm sales direction. Questions to ask are:

    (a) What is the purpose of my company?

    (b) What do we hope to achieve by being in business?

    (c) What aims and objectives have been set by management?

    (d) Are these plans being met successfully?

    (e) What long-range development plans are there?

    (f) What is the basic trading philosophy?

    (g) What is the company attitude toward its staff?

    (h) What company image has been established?

THE VALUE OF MARKET RESEARCH

Today's business environment is a great deal more sophisticated than it was ten years ago and its rate of change will be even more rapid over the next ten years.

Research figures indicate that only 3 per cent or so of new ideas generated by a company become commercially successful. New product failure is often as high as 85 per cent and every 25 years approximately 90 per cent of all business concerns started within that time span, fail. Ninety-five per cent of all business failures are due to 'bad management' or what amounts to poor planning, poor decision making and inadequate market information.

While the above figures may seem alarmingly high, they are given to indicate the pressing need for management (and salesmen) to better understand the workings of market research and place more importance on its value to business success.

Market research can bring the answers to many complex questions. Such factors as:

1. The general trend of business.
2. The changing public tastes and preferences.
3. The requirements and needs of customers in specialist areas.
4. The response of customers to new product ideas.
5. The size and potential of a new market area.
6. The effect of competitor products.
7. The growth pattern and age, income and buying patterns of consumers in selected areas.
8. The acceptance of company and product image.
9. Advertising copy testing.
10. Distribution and price research.

Market research is geared to eliminate many of the risks involved in deciding on new product distribution, pricing, promotion, advertising and sales forecasting. It offers a feedback system to reduce management mistakes. It is a systematic gathering and analysis of pertinent data to assist in the solving of problems in the marketing of products and services. It is the road map, the guiding point for management to proceed along *safer* and *surer* roads to marketing success.

THE COMMON LAW OF BUSINESS BALANCE...

It's unwise to pay too much, but it's unwise to pay too little. When you pay too much you lose a little money, that is all. When you pay too little, you sometimes lose everything, because the thing you bought was incapable of doing the thing you bought it to do. The common law of business balance prohibits paying a little and getting a lot. It can't be done. If you deal with the lowest bidder, it's well to add something for the risk you run. And if you do that, you will have enough to pay for something better . . .

JOHN RUSKIN.

151

THE 4 ANALYSIS AREAS

Marketing is the final link between the producer and the consumer. It is the 'instigator' of information required to broaden the scope of the producer's business. The four areas for analysis are:

1. RESEARCH OF THE PRODUCT:
    matching plus factors to consumer needs: size, shape, color, ingredients, uses, etc.

2. PROMOTION—ADVERTISING:
    media selection, copy testing, image development, value of special promotions, etc.

3. PRICING:
    costs, values, potential sales, competitor pricing, etc.

4. DISTRIBUTION:
    selecting outlets, best and cheapest means of delivery, packaging for shipping, etc.

SUCCESSFUL WAYS OF GATHERING MARKET RESEARCH DATA

Market research has a big future in the business of selling. The more information gathered, the easier it is to function and sell those products and services the consumer needs, wants and will buy. There are many techniques for gathering data. The best approach is the questionnaire. A list of simple, concise, easy to understand questions will receive fairly honest answers. The deep emotional response questions will not fare as well. As a general rule, they are ignored, answered dishonestly or skimmed over. The trap to avoid is not to put the answers you seek in the mind of the respondent. Questions should be cleverly presented to draw 'attitude' responses.

MARKET RESEARCH QUESTIONNAIRES

Questionnaires must be specific and call for *one* answer to each question. Do not present more than one question in each phrase. Avoid ambiguous wording, leading questions, too personal questions or using trade or technical terms which might be unfamiliar to the respondent. Place interesting and easy to answer questions at the beginning to gain interest. While this section of the book makes no claims to expert design and interpretation of market research questionnaires, the suggestions are 'guides' for the use of salesmen and sales managers. A large company structure (usually) has a market research department or independent market research company in its employ. The most successful approach, in this case, is to 'leave it to the experts'

152

to design survey material. However, the following questions will serve as a guideline:

(a) Have you heard about our product?
(b) Would you consider trying our product?
(c) What are you seeking in this type of product (service)?
(d) Do you consider the product is fairly priced?
(e) Are you attracted to the product by its packaging?
(f) What suggestions do you have to improve our product?
(g) If you have used our product would you rate it poor-fair-good-excellent?
(h) What brand do you now use?

HOW TO GET THE MARKET EDGE AND EXPLOIT YOUR PRODUCT

New products (or existing ones) must be exploited after they reach the reseller. Store positioning of your product is, therefore, vitally important to its *rate* of sale. Poor product positioning can be overcome by constant checking and rearranging.

New products require the best possible positioning (along with display material) to reinforce media advertising. Insignificant placing (particularly in hidden corners or 'blind' spots) reduces the effectiveness of the overall campaign to promote a new line.

Every salesman has a responsibility to 'service' his company's products after they have been sold to the trade. Rearrange stock and replace damaged goods. Seek the permission of the store manager to place your products in more advantageous positions. Support the display with advertising literature and promotional materials.

KEEP A CHECK ON PRODUCT LIFE CYCLE

The life cycle of the majority of products is quite short and getting shorter with each ensuing year. There is no fixed law on this, nor any set time for particular products to fade and die. The rate of product degeneration is governed by the rate of technical change and market acceptance. A new product's life span is much shorter in today's highly competitive market than it would have been 20 years ago.

Customers are attracted to new products and invited to 'change' brands every day of the week by companies with ingenious marketing and advertising techniques. No company can expect to gain a stranglehold on the market and retain it permanently. New products have a typical pattern of development consisting of four stages:

STAGE 1: Market introduction of new product.

STAGE 2: Growth rate as sales are gained through consumer acceptance.

STAGE 3: Sales peak or maturity level.

STAGE 4: Decline and fall as competitor products flood the market. Sales figures drop, product is edged out and replaced.

SALES TREND REPORT CARDS

Keep a card system listing details of sales trends in your territory. Write down details of each customer's weekly or monthly purchases. Watch for slackening interest in particular lines. Find out why sales are decreasing: lack of consumer interest, poor product display, new product competition, service difficulties, customer dissatisfaction, life cycle on the fall, etc.

Be your own product and market analyst. The more information you have at your command, the more positive steps you can take to keep your company products or services 'alive' and earning the profits and commissions necessary to your personal success and the success of your company.

EVERY SALESMAN SHOULD BE A MARKET RESEARCH GATHERER AND ANALYST

Valuable feedback information on your territory can help to increase your sales and commission earnings. It is suggested that a weekly

---

SAMPLE
SALES TREND CARD

NAME: ....

ADDRESS: ....

PHONE: .... EXT: ....

CONTACT: .... POS. HELD: ....

PRODUCTS: ....

COMMENTS: ....

AVERAGE MONTHLY SALES

YR.	JAN.	FEB.	MAR.	APR.	MAY	JNE.	JLY.	AUG.	SEP.	OCT.	NOV.	DEC.	TREND

market report be filed with the sales manager detailing the following information:

1. Company and contact visited.
2. Demonstration given—receptivity and result of call.
3. Customer complaints and special requests.
4. Customer ideas for better promotion, advertising and marketing of product.
5. Competitor activity within the territory.
6. Prominence of products displayed.
7. Comments of consumers relating to product or service.
8. Trend of sales and sales forecast for following month.
9. Definite market changes.
10. New market opportunities.

Products which aren't exploited to their fullest, stand little chance of remaining top sellers in the ever-changing market place. Services that do not actively exploit markets are bound to fail. The salesman who is alert to market conditions and changes, who brings information of these conditions and changes to the attention of management, places his company in the best possible position to grasp market opportunities when they arise. The rewards to the salesman are obvious.

Markets, like products, are continually changing. Keeping track of these changes through the sales team is an excellent way for the small to middle-size company (unable to afford an independent market research team) to gain the information it needs.

WRITING SALES AND MARKETING REPORTS

Sales and marketing reports are the control instruments in modern management. A salesman's field report, giving all details of importance concerning his territory, is a valuable means of communication between the salesman, customers and the sales manager. It brings to the awareness of management, product acceptance, territory conditions, trends and changes.

Good report writing is similar to good letter writing. Both indicate in concise terms what the writer is actually thinking. The sales or marketing report should be written in a business-like, free-flowing style yielding data that can be used by the company in market analysis and by the sales manager to lend proper support to his team.

Every report should have a beginning, a middle and an end. That is, it must tell a story and draw a conclusion. Haphazardly written reports are valueless. Information must be accurate, not based on hearsay, someone's opinion or guesswork. The three rules to follow for good report writing are:

1. Be concise and clear in your meaning.
2. Be accurate with your facts.
3. Tell a story and draw a conclusion.

SAMPLE ACTIVITY REPORT

DAILY ACTIVITY REPORT

NAME:

DATE: **STATE:**   **AREA No:**

SPEEDO: FINISH
START
DAYS MILEAGE

AREAS VISITED:

ACCOMPANIED BY:

POTENTIAL OF FIRM

A $3,000+
B $2,000—$3,000
C $1,000—$2,000
D $ 500—$1,000
E $ 250—$ 500
F   Below $250

Date of Call	Duration of Call	Type of Call	Reason and Appt.	Products Presented		Result of Call Achievements Decisions Made	Order Value	Future Action Date of Next Call	Potential	Name of Company	Contact's Name
				Main	Others						

Total Duration

Total No. of Calls

TELEPHONE NEGOTIATION CALLS (not appointment making calls)

ACTIVITY (SALES) REPORTS

In addition to a weekly market report, a daily or weekly activity report should be filed with the sales manager to assist him in the evaluation of your territory. Most companies supply printed daily or weekly activity report forms. It's been suggested that these are used as a 'spy system' to check on the activities of salesmen. The outcome of a report is certainly evidence which can be checked by a sales manager, but the express purpose of the report is to know *exactly* what is happening within a given area. It is feedback information a sales manager must have if he is to lead a dynamic and successful team.

Take the time to file a suitable report. Instead of labelling it the 'swindle sheet' or the 'spy system', think of it as an information link to assist your sales manager to help you develop your territory.

Type your report. Keep a copy for your own file. Present the original to the sales manager prior to a scheduled sales meeting. When stating facts, state the source. Describe methods you followed in any experiments or surveys conducted. State what action you think should be taken and when. Attach your market report to your activity report.

DEFINING SOME OF THE PROBLEM AREAS

Selling is a highly competitive profession. But herein lies the challenge and creative satisfaction of selling. Indeed, there are many problem areas and situations to master. You will be faced with stiff competition from other salesmen and their offerings. You will have sales targets to reach, customer objections to handle and the job of finding a never-ending stream of new customers. You will need to be on your toes 365 days a year researching, planning, organizing and studying your company methods and policy, your customer wants, and market trends. The end result will be determined by your efficient organization of time and work.

You will be required to make immediate and accurate decisions on many problems which will confront you. You will be restricted by these problems unless you take immediate action to dissolve or overcome them. The first step to 'freedom' in selling is to define possible sales-problem areas and know what courses of action will be necessary should they arise. Some typical problems associated with selling are:

● Organization of time (too much work, too little time to accomplish it).

● Company and product orientation lacking because no internal training scheme provided.

● Reseller or consumer resentment toward company or product. (Poor public image).

● Lack of sales direction from sales manager.

● Inefficient handling and shipping of product to reseller or consumer.

- Poor servicing facilities.
- Highly competitive market.
- Insufficient advertising, promotions, point-of-sale material, direct-mail campaigns.

If you wish to succeed as a master salesman plan your sales program in advance. Allow for unexpected things to happen. Even the best of plans can be upset. Accurate planning and forecasting will give you a better-than-average chance of succeeding where others fail.

PREPARATORY PLANNING AND FORECASTING

Planning is predetermining a specific course of action to follow. Your personal planning should involve the identification of sales problems and logical ways to solve them. Your immediate plan is to increase sales and profits and thus, commissions. Sales targets should be set, customer lists brought up to date, prospecting lists assembled and time expenditure for 'return' analyzed.

You will be required to *forecast* (as accurately as possible) market trends in relation to consumer acceptance and possible sales volumes of your company's products. This will require assembling all available facts about new prospects, market competition, possible outlets and market growth.

Once you have this 'inventory' of your territory, decisions can be made and specific actions taken to develop your territory to its full potential.

SUMMARY OF IDEAS TO HELP YOU GATHER VALUABLE PRODUCT AND MARKET RESEARCH FACTS

1. Every product or service has 'in-built' benefits. Discover them and use them as valuable sales tools to increase commissions.

2. Product or service plus factors are advantages of use. These are found by thoroughly *researching* the product or service. Advertising brochures and people who use the product or service are the best sources of inquiry.

3. Draft a product analysis sheet and discover buying reasons: value, reliability, service, guarantee, function, etc. List both plus and minus factors.

4. Use your imagination and make greater use of your five senses to become aware of marketing possibilities. Find unique methods of presenting your product.

5. Get to know your customers and their motives for buying. Match motives to product appeal factors.

6. Know the background of your company. Study its trading methods. Know its policy. What image has been established and why? What aims and objectives are there? Get a clear 'operations' picture of your company.

7. Market research is a valuable aid to management to reduce the risks involved in presenting products and services. Marketing is the final link between the producer and the consumer. Valuable research material helps to present a better product at a cheaper price.

8. Products must be kept in prominent view after they have been sold to the reseller. Check your products and their positions in the reseller's store. With the permission of management, enhance displays and give your products the best possible chance of creating visual impact.

9. Every product has a life cycle: introduction, growth rate, maturity and fall and decline. Keep your eye on the life cycle of each product you sell. Look for sales decline and find the reason behind it.

10. Report filing helps the salesman and the sales manager to better understand territory trends. Keep accurate records.

159

HOW TO PROSPECT AND OPEN UP NEW CHANNELS OF BUSINESS

FORMULA

8

Affirmative Ideas in this Chapter

- Increasing Sales Productivity
- Time Is The Salesman's Most Precious Commodity
- Average Salesman's Work Day
- Turn Unproductive Time Into Prospecting Time
- How To Identify Unproductive Time
- 8 Time Wasters To Avoid
- How To Be A Clock Watcher And Increase Commissions
- Self Organization To Double Your Effectiveness
- 10 Effective Daily Work Habits
- Effective Planning
- Salesman's Facts File
- Sample Prospect Rating Card
- Keep Your File Active And Up-To-Date
- The Requirements of The Master Prospector
- How To Identify And Qualify Prospects
- 5 Proven Methods of Prospecting
- Prospect Method 1: Company Leads
- Prospect Method 2: Direct Contact Leads
- Prospect Method 3: Advertising Leads
- Prospect Method 4: Directory Leads
- Prospect Method 5: Referred Leads
- How To Get Appointments With Prospects
- 4 Points To Follow When Calling For An Interview
- Ideas Worth Effecting
- Good Telephone Technique
- Sample Appreciation Cards
- 3 Prospecting Elements To Consider
- Summary of Ideas To Help You Become A Master Prospector

8

INCREASING SALES PRODUCTIVITY

Every company is anxious to increase sales. Every salesman must have the *same* aim. It's surprising how many salesmen use the alibi that they are 'too busy taking orders' to think about prospecting for new business. The specialist salesman—the master communicator and motivator—cannot afford such an attitude. Prospecting is an integral part of the selling function, the life-blood, the *essence* of successful selling.

The salesman who uses the excuse 'lack of time' to avoid seeking new business does himself and his company a disfavor. Sooner or later, existing customers will reduce orders or drop-out entirely. The thinning ranks of established accounts become so acute in terms of sales volume, the sales manager has no alternative but to insist that new accounts be signed-up or the salesman resign his position.

Sales, of course, can be increased by hiring extra salesmen to prospect for new business, leaving the existing sales force to concentrate on servicing established accounts. Where money is no object, this is often a suitable, convenient and financially sound arrangement. But what about the small company with limited financial resources and manpower? The challenge is to increase sales productivity by carefully planning each day's activities: more calls, less wasted time and energy. The salesman must apportion his actual selling time where it will do him and his company the most good.

163

Time expenditure must be analyzed and each hour of every day used to produce the maximum sales benefit. More time should be spent with 'profitable' accounts, less with small buyers, time wasters and those who are 'occasional' purchasers. This method will increase sales dollars, ensure time for a continuous injection of new business and boost the salesman's morale and weekly pay check.

TIME IS THE SALESMAN'S MOST PRECIOUS COMMODITY

TIME is a most important success factor. Time means *energy output* for creative and monetary return. Every minute of every day should be spent creatively, productively and rewardingly.

This is not always the case, as the time expenditure figures for the average salesman's work day indicate. Too little time is spent *selling* and far too much time devoted to areas that could be left to non-work hours: prior to 9 a.m.—after 5 p.m.

AVERAGE SALESMAN'S WORK DAY

·18 PER CENT PLANNING THE SALE *(Arranging brochures, samples, price lists, setting appointments).*

·23 PER CENT GETTING READY TO SELL *(Waiting to see clients, chatting to buyers, transport time).*

·*36 PER CENT ACTUAL SELLING TIME* *(Taking orders, closing the sale).*

·23 PER CENT REVIEWING THE DAY *(Turning in orders, sales reports).*

TURN UNPRODUCTIVE TIME INTO PROSPECTING TIME

Investigate your work day. Complete a time and motion study on your daily activities. Add-up unproductive times and devote them to prospecting. Besides generating new business, increasing sales and your commission earnings, you are building a secure sales future— today's prospect is tomorrow's customer. No salesman can 'perform' unless he has a steady stream of customers to call on.

The successful salesman is the enthusiastic prospect chaser. The larger the selection of prospects, the more qualified buyers will be developed and the higher the closing average. Successful prospecting is the result of consistent effort, proper value given to time and a sincere desire to build *future* business *now*.

HOW TO IDENTIFY UNPRODUCTIVE TIME

Non-productive time is brought about (consciously or unconsciously) by disorganization, mental and physical laziness and ignorance of professional selling techniques. Eight reasons for 'time wasting' are given. Study them and eliminate them from your work day if they apply.

8 TIME WASTERS TO AVOID

1. SELLING TO THE WRONG MAN.
2. POOR ITINERARY PLANNING. (Long distance travel/low sales return).
3. LONG CHATS WITH CUSTOMERS AND PROSPECTS.
4. TOO MANY BREAKS—LONG LUNCH PERIODS.
5. ATTEMPTING TO SEE CUSTOMERS WITHOUT PRIOR APPOINTMENTS.
6. FORGETTING TO BRING SAMPLES—BROCHURES—PRICE LISTS.
7. INSUFFICIENT PRODUCT/SERVICE INFORMATION REQUIRING A CALL BACK.
8. LATE FOR APPOINTMENTS.

HOW TO BE A CLOCK WATCHER AND INCREASE COMMISSIONS

In adding up the score, we find that only 36 per cent of the average salesman's day is spent in *actual selling*. Those sales representatives being paid salary and commission for their efforts must surely suffer as a result of lost selling time. As an example: a salesman earning (on an average) 50 dollars a week in commissions for approximately 36 per cent of his time spent in actual selling, could increase his earnings by *doubling his actual selling time*. By how much his earnings would increase is purely theoretical. But assuming his capacity to earn 50 dollars in just over a third of his working week, one might assume that he could greatly increase his commission earnings by increasing selling hours and thus multiplying the number of calls made.

Charles Roth in his book, *Selling 365 Days A Year,* points out that 'champion salesmen' sell *all* the time. The professional is a clock watcher. He knows the importance of time because it means commissions won or lost. Time must be *managed,* not allowed to slip by and wasted. Sales can be increased and commission earnings doubled (or trebled) through efficient time management resulting in increased productivity.

Arrange more calls each day than you are now doing. Cut down on extensive travelling time by grouping calls in outlying areas and servicing them on a specific day. If an account isn't profitable, spend little time on it. Identify accounts who can be sold quickly and those that take up more time than is profitable. Eliminate long chats, too many coffee breaks, extra long lunch breaks. On recurring sales, it is often possible to write orders by phoning the customer or having him mail in his order.

Estimate the sales volume of each customer. Design a time chart and designate a specific time to spend on any one account. When calling on customers adhere to your time schedule . . . be a *clock watcher.*

> 'The man who is always killing time is
> killing his own chances in life. The
> man destined for success *makes time
> live* by making every minute useful.'
>
> ARTHUR BRISBANE.

SELF ORGANIZATION TO DOUBLE YOUR EFFECTIVENESS

Disorganization creates frustration, tension and fatigue as well as poor sales performance. Salesmen must establish effective daily work habits. Trusting things to memory, hoping, wishing or anticipating that things will happen without proper thought and action brings failure conditions into the business activities of the mentally and physically lazy and disorganized sales representative.

Follow the '10 Effective Daily Work Habits' and you will establish order, balance and harmony into your work routine. The constant urges to do better, to accomplish more, to get organized and stay organized, are the priceless assets of the truly self-motivated salesman. It makes him a *profitable* user of time and energy.

---

10 EFFECTIVE DAILY WORK HABITS

1. PLAN EACH DAY'S ACTIVITIES. MAKE A LIST OF *ALL* THINGS TO DO.
2. SET A DAILY SALES TARGET.
3. DO NOT LEAVE YOUR OFFICE WITHOUT BRO-CHURES—SAMPLES—PRICE LISTS.
4. KNOW YOUR CUSTOMERS' INTERVIEW TIMES. PHONE FOR APPOINTMENTS.
5. PLAY THROUGH THE INTERVIEW IN YOUR MIND FIRST—THEN PRESENT IT.
6. SET ASIDE TIME TO PROSPECT—TO SELL *NEW* CUSTOMERS.
7. CHECK YOUR PROJECTED IMAGE. LOOK LIKE A SUCCESSFUL SALESMAN.
8. 'TUNE-UP' YOUR ATTITUDE. REMOVE *EMOTIONAL* SCARS—MOODS.
9. BE PUNCTUAL FOR APPOINTMENTS. WATCH YOUR CLOCK. ARRIVE EARLY.
10. SET A RETURN INTERVIEW TIME WITH YOUR CUSTOMER. KEEP THE 'SALES DOOR' OPEN AND YOU'LL HAVE A FULL APPOINTMENT SCHEDULE EACH DAY.

EFFECTIVE PLANNING

Establish a personal 'facts file', a system designed to keep your finger on the pulse of your business activities. The better organized you are the greater success you will have in selling. *The key*: organize —plan—execute.

Purchase a 3 ring loose-leaf notebook, two sets of 3 x 5 cards (different colors), chronological dividers, a card file box and an appointment book. Collect relevant information to your profession and file it in your loose-leaf binder. Make a list of existing customers and prospects and keep a card on each one. Log times, places, events, etc. in your appointment book. Your facts file should include the information listed below.

SALESMAN'S FACTS FILE

SALES TREND CARDS: customer purchase records, etc. (See chapter 7.)

PROSPECT RATING CARDS: relevant details on prospects: marital status, number of children and ages, place of employment, approximate income, car driven, clubs, organizations, lodge memberships, church affiliation, community activities supported, hobbies, sports played, own or renting home, prospect rating—A (excellent) B (fair) C (poor) etc.

MARKET REPORT: feedback on market trends, competitor activity, etc.

ACTIVITY REPORT: activities relating to company business. (See chapter 7.)

PRODUCT FACTS FILE: brochures, price lists, all data to assist in the selling of products or services.

NEW DEVELOPMENT FILE: new ideas in your field reported in magazines, newspapers and trade journals.

APPOINTMENT BOOK: list all appointments and 'things' to do each day.

SAMPLE

PROSPECT RATING CARD

NAME: .... AGE: ....

ADDRESS: ....

HOME PHONE: .... BUS. PHONE: .... EXT: .....

BEST TIME TO CALL: .... EMPLOYED BY: ....

POSITION HELD: ....

APPROX. SALARY: .... CAR DRIVEN: .... YEAR: ....

MARITAL STATUS: .... CHILDREN: .... AGES: ....

OWN HOME: .... RENT: ....

CHURCH: .... ORGANIZATIONS: .... CLUBS: ....

COMMUNITY ACTIVITIES: ....

HOBBIES: .... SPORTS PLAYED: ....

COMMENTS: .... CALL BACK DATES: ....

RATING: (A EXCELLENT) ☐ (B FAIR) ☐ (C POOR) ☐

(NOTE: additional headings and information can be carried to the reverse side of the card.)

KEEP YOUR FILE ACTIVE AND UP TO DATE

Bring your file up-to-date each month. Check call-back dates and write them in your appointment book as they fall due. After the call has been made, make a notation on the back of the prospect's card as to the result. Your records are worth their weight in gold if you keep them up-to-date and properly indexed. A master prospector takes note of every detail learned on each call and files the information for future use.

Don't try to keep call-backs stored in your memory. Write them down with a short comment on the result of the previous call. With dozens (perhaps hundreds) of names in a prospect file, it's impossible to remember every relevant piece of information.

Make persistent, systematic calls on all individuals listed. Don't let your prospect file gather dust. No matter how you go about it, the possibilities for finding leads are unlimited. Somewhere, sometime, if you look often and hard enough, you'll find people eager to purchase your goods or services. Your job, as a master prospector, is to keep *looking*.

THE REQUIREMENTS OF THE MASTER PROSPECTOR

Successful prospecting is an *action* proposition: positive thinking, positive believing and positive acting. To become a *master prospector* requires a great deal of staying power—persistence. You must gain a strong desire to create and build a steady stream of new customers to your present list. Your sincere desire to *act,* to bring this about, will assure your place in the ranks of the top income earners.

Be ever-alert to *changes* within your community. Look for new faces, new sources of business, new ideas. The more you see that is new, the more you have to *act* on.

Your ability to be successful as a sales prospector, will depend on the following:

(a) *AN ALERT MIND:* use the five senses to *hear* more, *see* more, *touch* more, *taste* more and *smell* more. Open your mind to changes going on about you. Take advantage of them.

(b) *INITIATIVE:* be a self-starter. Don't rely on others to do your work for you. Prospecting requires a great deal of cold canvassing. Use your initiative and lead yourself to success in your profession.

(c) *PERSEVERANCE:* you'd better be able to 'stick-with-it' and keep on keeping on. Be a fighter, a winner. Don't give up trying. Your persistence must bring success.

(d) *ORGANIZATION:* get yourself organized. Know exactly *what* you are going after, *when* you will go after it, *why* you are doing it and *how* you will accomplish it. *Plan your work and work your plan.*

(e) *INTUITION:* 'sense' new situations. Get your power of ESP working for you. Newspaper stories, magazine articles often 'tip-off' future happenings. Put your creative imagining to work and act on hunches.

HOW TO IDENTIFY AND QUALIFY PROSPECTS

Your prospect file (if it's to be a valuable sales aid) must have a workable rating system to qualify potential customers. If a prospect has been checked-out and rated 'poor' then it's best to eliminate his card from the file. Otherwise, it becomes cluttered with hundreds of worthless names producing an extremely confusing system.

A prospect rated 'fair' should be next in line for action taking. Identify his need and if you can fulfill it, move him into the 'excellent' category. If you cannot satisfy his desire factor then disqualify him from your file. More time will be required to work on the 'top-rated' prospect. If he, too, is 'beyond reach' then eliminate his name. If the 'excellent' rated prospect becomes a customer then transfer his card to your 'existing' customer file.

How is it possible to identify and qualify prospective customers? Quite easy, question them. A series of well-chosen questions will bring the answers you seek. Sometimes, advance information from friends, company and customer referrals or advertising leads indicate that a prospect is eager to purchase your product or service. In this case, the enquirer is rated as an 'excellent' prospect.

Don't waste *too* much time on 'poor' or 'fair' category prospects. They can wear-down your energy, reduce actual selling time and strike at your self confidence. The key to productive prospecting is to see enough of the *right* people. These will come from your 'excellent' category and hopefully, end up in your permanent customer file. These prospects *want* to buy, can *afford* to buy and (usually) *do* buy if your proposition is sound and well presented.

There are five aspects to be considered when rating prospects. They are:

1. The prospect's financial capacity to pay for your products or services.

2. His basic *need* for the item or service offered.

3. His motive(s) for buying.

4. The incentives that could 'close' him.

5. Does he have the authority to buy?

Category one and five require close examination. There are those who would *like* to buy your product but if they do not have money to pay for it, have a poor credit rating or do not have the authority to make a decision to buy, then you are *wasting* valuable sales time.

5 PROVEN METHODS OF PROSPECTING

To close sales you must have genuine buyers. And the only *sure* way to find them is to prospect for them. *Positive prospecting* is finding a steady-stream of logical buyers—people who have the inclination and the financial capacity to buy whatever it is you're selling.

You must forge the first link in an endless chain of prospective customers. The first link can be started by canvassing existing customers and seeking their referrals. The second link, through your efforts of *observation* and cold canvass. The third link, from advertising leads, and so on. The five prospecting methods listed are basic ones and easy to apply. However, it is suggested that you develop further methods to find new customers. A certain percentage of 'existing' clients are lost each year (for various reasons) and you need to replace them as quickly as possible without a drop in your sales volume.

There is a big difference between a 'list' of people to see and a list of qualified prospects. Qualified prospects are the ones with true buying potential. A mere list of people to see, those who haven't been rated properly (or not at all), cost you and your company valuable time and money.

The prospecting techniques given in this chapter are comprehensive and practical. However, they will be of little use unless converted from theory into *action*. Regardless of how you feel toward prospecting, don't put it off. It must be done. Your future as a successful salesman hinges on your customer list.

Study the five proven methods of prospecting and use them and you will be assured of a secure sales future. The methods are:

1. *COMPANY LEADS*: supplied by your company and through employees in other divisions and departments of your company.

2. *DIRECT CONTACT LEADS*: your own source of research and discovery.

3. *ADVERTISING LEADS*: advertising, promotions and direct mail campaigns conducted by yourself or your company.

4. *DIRECTORY LEADS*: professional, business, trades, phone directories, newspapers, magazines, trade journals.

5. *REFERRED LEADS*: existing customers, friends, business associates, new acquaintance referrals.

PROSPECT METHOD 1: COMPANY LEADS

Most companies supply leads that come via phone, letter or personal visits by customers to the company's factory, warehouse or office. Sometimes, sales managers will label them 'house accounts' and they will be serviced by the salesman in whose territory they fall or they will be handled personally by the sales manager.

Company leads may or may not be qualified leads—*sure* sales. Quite often, they turn out to be 'shoppers' or 'lookers', people who haven't the slightest intention of making a purchase. Where a telephone number is supplied, the salesman can personally qualify company leads when setting appointments. Don't be too anxious to quit these leads. Successful prospecting requires insight, confidence, perseverance and initiative. Whether the lead supplied to you sounds interesting or not, *check it out*. Motivate yourself to follow-through.

170

Sources for leads exist in many different departments of your own company. It is advisable to meet the various department heads and to elicit information on prospects they may know. Each department (usually) has its own list of customers which the sales department may not directly be involved with. As an example, a large company selling a variety of products may have separate divisions, each with its own salesmen and mailing lists. Check to see if there are worthwhile sources of business among these lists. Your company service division is another worthwhile 'leads' possibility. Take advantage of the various 'company sources' of leads and turn your prospect file into a rich reservoir of names for future sales and added commissions.

Departments or divisions of your company to be checked-out include:

- ADVERTISING DEPARTMENT.
- ACCOUNTS DEPARTMENT.
- MARKET RESEARCH DEPARTMENT.
- TRAINING DEPARTMENT.
- SERVICE DEPARTMENT.
- CUSTOMER RELATIONS DEPARTMENT.
- SHIPPING DEPARTMENT.
- SEPARATE SALES DIVISIONS.

PROSPECT METHOD 2: DIRECT CONTACT LEADS

The direct contact leads approach is perhaps the most successful in the long run. Direct leads are those the salesman discovers and follows-up himself. It is a practical method of producing a healthy list of class 'A' prospects and eventually new customers.

Direct contact leads are found by using your power of *observation*. An 'observation' tour of your territory will bring awareness of: new stores, new houses, new television aerials, 'for sale' and 'vacancy' signs, etc.

By observing changes in your territory, your alertness will bring new customer possibilities. Keep your eyes and ears open and use every opportunity to meet new people and become involved in new situations.

Thorough knowledge of the prospect must be gained to determine if he can benefit from the product or service you wish to sell him. This information can easily be gained by writing him, telephoning him or meeting him face-to-face via 'door-knocking'. If the prospect turns out to be 'unsuitable', ask him to recommend a friend or business associate who might profitably use your product or service. This 'spring-off' approach often turns up new customers. Other direct contact sources are:

CURRENT CUSTOMERS: these are an excellent source, particularly if they are satisfied with the service you have given. Don't neglect them. You can be sure other salesmen won't. Current customers are perhaps the best single 'leads' source. However, few will volunteer names, you will have to ask for them.

OTHER SALESMEN LEADS: salesmen of noncompeting companies are good 'leads' sources. Cultivate salesmen of noncompetitive products or services and reciprocate by giving them leads and information when requested.

COMPETITOR LEADS: trace the movement of opposition companies. Know what they are doing within your territory, the special promotions they put on, the direct-mail campaigns mounted and the new products released. Watch for stores promoting new lines. They are sources to follow-up to place and promote your own products.

SOCIAL CONTACTS: become a joiner of clubs and associations. Meet as many people as possible on a social level. But don't be aggressive or 'use' club memberships to pressure people into doing business with you. Use clubs and organizations as a means to swell your friendships. If you consider a club member to be a good prospect, then contact him during business hours, not at your club. Separate your business life from your personal life and you won't be called a 'bore' who tries to exploit friends.

COLD CANVASS: plain old door-knocking it's called and it's not the most popular method of finding new customers. Regardless of how you feel about this technique, it still remains the backbone of hard-line prospecting. The idea is to think of *everyone* as a prospect and to systematically cover every business or home in a given area. The time and energy this method eats up is considerable and care has to be taken to ensure that the financial return matches the time and energy output.

CIRCLE OF INFLUENCE: this means to approach virtually everyone you do business with where you are the center of influence: butcher, baker, milkman, barber, other salesmen, banker, electrician, grocer, lawyer, retailers, etc. If they cannot be rated 'A' then ask them to suggest names of people within their circle of influence. This method creates a source from which good prospects will constantly flow. A suggestion: always have a supply of business cards handy to give out to people you meet. If possible, get theirs and transfer the information to prospect cards.

PROSPECT METHOD 3: ADVERTISING LEADS

It will pay you to know what advertising is being planned by your company. Obtain reprints of advertisements (possibly with your name printed on them) and mail them to prospects. Enclose customer reply cards. If these are returned, they will represent grade 'A' prospects. A meeting with the advertising department is helpful and could mean 'first priority' in handling advertising leads. Thought should be given to placing your own advertisements in local papers. The return, more often than not, outweighs the cost.

SPECIAL PROMOTIONS: conventions, exhibits and trade fairs in which your company participates, are useful places to find prospects.

Attend them if you can, even if you aren't a delegated representative of your company. Exchange business cards with everyone you come in contact with and try to qualify them on the spot. If this is not possible, write, phone or call on them as soon as it is convenient to do so.

DIRECT MAIL: it is often worth the expense to mount your own direct mail campaigns. A well-presented brochure with interesting information helps to keep your name in front of the prospect and aids you when calling him for an appointment—the prospect knows you through your mailing piece. Ask your company to contribute to the cost of your personal mailing. It's worth talking to the sales manager about. (Insurance companies frequently contribute to the cost of direct-mailing for their salesmen.) Customer reply cards or coupons should be part of your mailing piece. And it is important to follow-through a few days after your letters have been posted. Reply cards should be dealt with first, then systematically call those who have not responded to your mailing. Plan repeat mailings every month or so. The key to assuring direct mail success is to limit the number of letters sent on any one occasion. To mail hundreds of letters at one time would require a team of salesmen to work several weeks to follow-up with phone and personal calls. Send out a dozen or so letters at a time. When you have followed-up and qualified these, send out another dozen. Special-occasion cards (birthday and Christmas, etc.) are good public relations gestures for the customer-conscious representative. It costs money to do it, but it's money well spent.

PROSPECT METHOD 4: DIRECTORY LEADS

TELEPHONE DIRECTORY: classify all potential buyers who have need of your product or service and then make a search of the business section of your local telephone directory. Establish a list of companies or individuals in order of apparent potential. If, for example, you are selling insurance, you might take a specific section of the directory and organize a list of doctors to call on. If you are selling typewriters and office equipment, turn to the section in the directory listing 'public stenographers' and cold-canvass them.

NEWSPAPERS AND MAGAZINES: these are excellent sources of information for the serious prospector. Peruse your daily newspapers and clip articles of interest on business mergers, new business openings, business expansion and development, staff promotions, engagements, wedding announcements, births, winners of contests, etc. Send the articles to the persons concerned. Attach your business card and a short note of 'congratulations' to the article. Your thoughtfulness will promote good will and increase your circle of friends and prospects. Magazines and trade journals should be researched in the same manner.

PROFESSIONAL—BUSINESS AND TRADES DIRECTORIES: every city publishes business, trades and professional directories. Specialized groups of trades and professions are listed and useful information is supplied making it easier for the salesman to classify and rate prospects. Placing advertisements in trade journals (for those in a service industry) is useful. Insurance, real estate, investment (where acceptable), cleaning, vending services, car hire, etc., are logical services to advertise. Lists of potential customers such as personnel officers, purchasing officers, department heads, sales managers are often to be found in articles or advertisements in trade journals. Business and financial news items are well worth reading. Government departments, Chambers of Commerce, libraries, clipping services can be utilized to advantage, particularly bulletins and magazines published by Chambers of Commerce and the various departments of Government. Collect them. Read them. Make use of them.

PROSPECT METHOD 5: REFERRED LEADS

The referral system can be put to work every minute of every hour of every selling day. Every person you meet throughout your work week has his own circle of friends and business associates—they are all *potential* customers. If they don't offer suggestions as to where or with whom you might generate business, then ask them. (Politely and subtly, of course.) The best kind of referral is a formal introduction (by a friend or customer) to another through a letter, phone call or personal appearance. Set up a lunch date if you feel it warrants it and this will allow ample time to get to know the prospect. Additional contacts to investigate and to get referrals are:

● Salesmen and people you knew in a former job.
● School friends.
● People you have met in clubs, lodges, civic organizations.
● Trades people you have hired.
● Professional people you have hired. (Doctor, banker, lawyer).
● People you have met while on your vacation.
● A fellow church member.
● *All* people you do business with.

HOW TO GET APPOINTMENTS WITH PROSPECTS

Getting in to see the prospect is the first step in the *action* of selling. It can be accomplished in any one of four ways:

1. REQUESTING AN APPOINTMENT BY PHONE.
2. REQUESTING AN APPOINTMENT BY LETTER.
3. A MEETING TIME SET BY A FRIEND.
4. DIRECT CANVASS.

APPOINTMENTS BY PHONE: with this method it's easy for the prospect (or his secretary) to say 'no' and leave it at that. Good phone prospecting is an art. *What* you say and *how* you say it can bring quick success or prompt failure. The telephone is a cold, impersonal instrument which must be used in such a way as to 'peak the curiosity' or 'excite' the prospect to the degree that he responds favorably to your request for an appointment. The trick here, is to give him just enough information to make him want to hear more. Always have a specific time for the appointment you desire: 'Would four tomorrow afternoon be suitable, Mr. Brown?' Once you have your appointment set, don't engage the prospect in idle chit chat. Stay on the line long enough to tell him *who you are, what company you represent, what benefit you have in mind for him and a suggested time for both of you to meet.* Thank your prospect for his interest and hang up.

APPOINTMENT BY LETTER: the same rules apply when writing for an appointment. Keep your letter short and to the point. Give only enough information to arouse the reader's interest, to present a *you* factor, a reason *why* it is important to see him. Specify a time for the meeting and suggest that this be confirmed by his secretary (or by a phone call from yourself). A request for an appointment can be made on your behalf by your company. A letter from the sales manager (or someone in a senior position) is liable to bring a quick response.

MEETINGS SET BY FRIENDS AND ACQUAINTANCES: don't be shy about asking friends, acquaintances or relatives to introduce you to people they feel could benefit from the use of your product or service. If possible, have your friends write formal letters of introduction or set appointment times by phoning the prospect in your presence. It's a good idea to say a quick 'hello' to the prospect at this time.

DIRECT CANVASS: by means of letter, phone call or a personal visit to the prospect in the hope of getting an immediate appointment or a future one. The salesman explains to the prospect's secretary that he is in the area and would like to have a quick chat to her boss as he has an 'interesting proposition' to present to him. The opening sentence is important. Direct calls without prior appointments are risky. Secretaries (or prospects) usually look upon them unfavorably. Therefore, know what you are going to say and say it with warmth and charm of manner.

---

4 POINTS TO FOLLOW
WHEN CALLING FOR AN INTERVIEW

1. Obtain the name and title of the right person to talk to.

2. Suggest a specific time and date for the interview.

3. Know where you want the interview to take place: customer's office, a job site, your factory, a restaurant.

4. Make arrangements for others to be in attendance if this is necessary.

IDEAS WORTH EFFECTING

SEE THE RIGHT PERSON: valuable time is saved by seeing the *right* person, the person able to make a decision. It takes less effort to sell the right person than the wrong one. The person not able to make a key decision will sometimes make excuses, put you off or suggest you see someone else. This time wasting can be prevented by finding out prior to the interview the name of the key decision maker. He can then be called, qualified and an appointment made to see him.

RESPECT OF PROSPECT'S TIME: If you are unavoidably detained and know that you will be late for an appointment, call the secretary of the person you are to see and explain the situation. Reliability, courtesy and a healthy respect for other people's time will warrant their respect of your professional attitude and performance. Don't overstay your welcome once you are face-to-face with a prospect. His time is valuable and so is yours. When you have presented your message and the result known, thank the prospect for his time and take your leave.

APPRECIATION FOR COURTESIES SHOWN: a handwritten note or card thanking the prospect for his time and consideration of your proposition is a thoughtful way to show your appreciation. A small gift for the prospect's secretary or a 'thank you' card to her is a good public relations touch worthy of consideration. Make it a practice to show appreciation to *all* friends or business associates who help you. A personalized card serves as a quick, valuable, attention-getting method of promoting good will and extra business. It is preferable to hand write a personal note to a secretary or friend. However, to a business associate, it is customary to type your message on a plain white card or note paper.

GOOD TELEPHONE TECHNIQUE

There are many advantages to be gained by correct use of the telephone to identify and qualify prospects. It allows you to screen prospects in advance, to know that you are seeing the right man and gives you an idea as to the prospect's attitude toward your product. It also allows you to ascertain whether others should be present at the meeting and which samples, brochures and promotional materials to take along. Get the name of the key man from the switchboard operator, *not* his secretary. After the operator has given you the buyer's name she will put you through to his secretary. A confident, direct and friendly approach to the secretary will (usually) get you through to her boss. However, she may want to know the nature of the call in an attempt to protect the 'time' of her boss. When you talk to a secretary begin with: 'Hello, I'm John Brown from XYZ Company. I'm calling to make an appointment with Mr. Jones for Thursday at three. I wanted to check the suitability of this time with him.' If Mr. Jones is in and the salesman has a pleasant telephone voice and technique, he will be put through without difficulty. Don't demand to talk to the secretary's boss or be abrupt with her. Courtesy, politeness and confident, friendly opening statements work wonders. Remember, it's charm of manner that wins young ladies' hearts.

Dear Miss Williams:

Thank you for your generous efforts on my behalf. I certainly appreciate your efficient handling of the situation.

Warm wishes,

Bill Brown

Bill Brown.
XYZ Company.

Mr. John Jones
Purchasing Officer
Johnson Brothers Services Inc.
231 Stanley Street
Bakerstown, Ontario 2321

Dear Mr. Jones:

A short note to 'thank you' for the generous time you spent yesterday and the courteous consideration you gave to my proposition.

Trusting I can be of service to you and your company in the future.

Very truly yours,

Bill Brown

Bill Brown.
XYZ Company.

3 PROSPECTING ELEMENTS TO CONSIDER

Three prospecting elements in common are: *planning, timing* and *follow-up*. A well conceived plan of action is the first element. Never prospect aimlessly. Plan who you will see and when and where. Equip yourself with every available piece of information. Know as much about your prospect as possible. The more you know, the better you can service his needs.

Avoid wasting time—*make specific appointments!* Suggest another day if the prospect seems out-of-sorts. Don't push ahead with your proposition if he is in no mood to hear it. You'll be wasting time. Time and *timing* are important elements of good prospecting.

Check your file system and bring call-backs into focus. Know who you are going to see each day. Give attention to those customers who have given you a 'time-of-the-year' to see them. Send out a reminder card to them, place a telephone call to them and set an appointment. Your prospect file will be worthless unless you ACT on the information it contains.

SUMMARY OF IDEAS TO HELP YOU BECOME A MASTER PROSPECTOR

1. Don't let your sales volume drop because of a steady decline in customers. Boost sales dollars by enrolling new customers. Prospecting for new business is the life-blood of successful selling.

2. Time is the salesman's most important success factor. Too much time is spent on areas that could be dealt with in non-work hours. (Before nine in the morning and after five in the afternoon). Organize your time so that 'unproductive' periods can be turned into productive prospecting hours. The key: ORGANIZE YOUR DAY. BE A CLOCK WATCHER.

3. Establish a 'facts file', a system designed to keep your finger on the pulse of your business activities. It should include: sales trend cards, prospect file cards, marketing reports, activity reports, product facts, new development ideas, an appointment book.

4. Keep your file active and up-to-date. Keep an eye on call-back dates. Make systematic calls on all persons listed.

5. Your ability to be a successful prospector will depend on the following attributes: an alert mind; initiative; perseverance; organization; intuition.

6. Devise a workable rating system for your prospects: financial capacity to pay for your product or service; the need for your product; the incentives which could close the prospect; does the prospect have authority to purchase? Rate your prospects POOR—FAIR—EXCELLENT.

7. The five positive prospecting methods are: company leads, direct contact leads, advertising leads, directory leads, referred leads. Use them to build a steady-stream of new customers.

8. Setting an appointment with a prospect is the first step in the *action* of selling. It can be accomplished in any one of the following ways: requesting an appointment by phone; requesting an appointment by letter; a meeting time set by a friend; cold canvass.

9. Find the *right* man when requesting an interview. Selling to the wrong man wastes time, energy and money.

10. Appreciate the time of others. Be punctual. Don't overstay your welcome. Send a card of personal 'thanks' to secretaries, receptionists, sales managers or buyers who have taken time to listen to your proposition. Be courteous, charming and confident when requesting an interview.

HOW TO PLAN AND DRAMATICALLY OPEN A SALES PRESENTATION

FORMULA

9

Affirmative Ideas in This Chapter

- The Moment of Truth: Your Professional Responsibility
- How You Can Assure Selling Success
- Factors To Consider Prior To The Interview
- Order of Priority Planning
- Sales Call Schedule
- Example: Daily Route Schedule
- Planning Sales Goals
- Ascertaining Your Sales Worth Per Hour
- Yearly Sales Earnings And Hourly Dollar Values
- Know Who You Are Selling To
- 5 Logical Planning Steps
- Planning Is The Rule
- Meeting The Prospect
- Customer Personality Types
- 8 Customer Approaches
- Attitudes And Actions To Win Customers
- How To Raise The Importance of Your Visit
- Eliminate Tired Expressions From Your Greetings
- Use The 'Opening Teaser' Technique To Arouse Interest
- Entrepreneur Eliminates Resistance With Candy
- A Greek Bearing Gifts Wins New Customers
- Handling The Cold Call
- Building Confidence In The Mind of The Prospect
- Timing The Approach
- How To Eliminate First Call Nerves
- Fears Producing First Call Nerves
- Applying The AIDA Formula To Succeed In Selling
- Apply The Domino Principle To The AIDA Formula
- Domino Theory
- Dealing Effectively With Customer Buying Blocks
- Place The Prospect In The Picture Not Out of It
- Buying Blocks Chart
- Stress Values and Solve Problems
- 8 Sales Presentation Pointers
- Supporting Your Claims And Gaining Conviction For Them
- Proof of Claim Technique
- How To Build A Point System Into Your Presentation
- Visual Aids To Assist Your Presentation
- Point System Chart
- Summary of Ideas To Help You Plan And Open A Sales Presentation

182

9

THE MOMENT OF TRUTH: YOUR PROFESSIONAL RESPONSIBILITY

A responsible task lies ahead: your commitment to the preparation and presentation of your company message. The enormous amounts of time, energy and money spent by your company to develop its products will now depend on your expertise as a salesman to succeed in the market arena.

You are the man in the hot seat. Your company is relying on you to match goods and services to customers' needs and to provide reliable information on market trends. You are part of the company team. It is you who represents management in the field and carries its message to the buying public. Your important position requires that you plan and organize your sales presentations so that your company and its products receive the maximum benefits. To assist in the accomplishment of this aim, your company will support you with research, product planning, quality production methods, advertising and financial remuneration. The ball is now in your court. The *way* you handle your sales presentations will determine the success or failure of the product (or service) in your designated territory.

HOW YOU CAN ASSURE SELLING SUCCESS

Selling is a service function—never forget that. It means more (much more) than simply telling or showing your product to a customer. It means understanding the needs of the buyer and fulfilling those needs for him. When you understand the psychological and physiological aspects of the human personality you will be in a position to give your customers satisfactory service and build a strong bond of friendship with them.

The road to selling success is not linked to hard work alone. Devotion to duty, company loyalty, integrity, long hours of hard work have propelled many salesmen into executive positions and high pay. Just as many (if not more) salesmen have been left behind in the scramble for success because they left out one important ingredient: faithful *service* to their customers—giving them what they desire and need.

Plan to give service—*plus* service—not just to secure an order but to prove to the prospect that you are concerned with his welfare. That you want him to succeed through the use of your products or services. That your first concern (whether he buys or not) is to honestly appraise his needs and then, if it is possible, satisfy them. Additional services you can render your customers are:

- Satisfactory terms of payment.
- Speedy credit checking and approval.
- Prompt delivery.
- Special orders fulfilled to the customer's wishes.
- Special packaging consideration.
- Window and store displays and special promotions undertaken.
- Additional brochures and price lists supplied when requested.
- Customer service complaints handled quickly and satisfactorily.
- Damaged goods picked up and replaced promptly.
- Continuous checking with the customer to see that your goods are selling well and if not, to help him solve the problem.
- Sympathetic listening to the customer's problems and offering solutions to them.
- Appreciation of customer's time and orders given.
- A desire to 'help-out' when the customer is faced with difficulties.

FACTORS TO CONSIDER PRIOR TO THE INTERVIEW

In advance of the actual interview there are several factors to be considered and worked out. Some of these are:

- Preparation of a list of prospects to see. Number of calls per day to be made.
- An efficient route planned to cut down on wasted travel time.
- Appointment times set and confirmed.
- Time allotment schedule: travel time, sales presentations time, prospecting time.
- Display materials, brochures, price lists assembled.

- Analysis of customers to be visited and an 'approach and presentation' formula prepared for each.
- Sales target set.
- Review of product (or service) plus factors and technical data.
- Scheduling time for field reports and paper work.

The sales program must be planned well in advance and not left to the actual day of performance. Preparation of schedules and presentations takes the tension out of selling and helps to boost self confidence. Feelings of insecurity, doubt and failure are replaced by feelings of self-control, enthusiasm and success expectancy. Failure to plan your day in advance also results in confusion, loss of valuable work time and frustration. The salesman who goes about his work logically and with a sense of purpose, accomplishes what he sets out to accomplish. Without the proper organization of a work schedule, a salesman is like a dog chasing its tail.

ORDER OF PRIORITY PLANNING

Sort out and clarify which customers to call on first. Classify 'A' rated 'fair' and 'poor' rated customers into groups and areas so that you have an 'order of priority' for calls. Establish call times to be allocated to each.

This method will ensure that you call on customers and prospects in order of their buying potential to achieve the best possible sales results. The procedure cuts down on nonproductive selling time and helps you to reach sales goals.

SALES CALL SCHEDULE

Concentrate your time and efforts where they are most likely to pay off. By recording territory and customer information on your file cards you will be able to evaluate where to spend your time (and with whom) to bring the most profitable returns. Your cards will indicate current business and potential business. This accurate classification of accounts allows you to plan your work schedule to sell 'big' accounts first and then to develop other customers and prospects as time permits.

It is generally accepted that up to 80 per cent of profitable business (in most areas) is derived from approximately 20 per cent of the regular customer list. Since sales results closely relate to the efficient use of time and proper planning, it will pay you to concentrate your efforts on 'A' rated customers first and eliminate time wasters, talkers, alibi merchants, 'see me next weekers' and other nonprofitable types.

Once you have grouped your *current accounts* and your *potential accounts* and rated them, set a sales call schedule to take best advantage of your time. Plan to call on at least three 'excellent' rated prospects per day in addition to your regular calls. Concentrate your big guns on selling higher-priced items. It takes the same amount of effort to make big sales as it does to make small ones.

EXAMPLE

DAILY ROUTE SCHEDULE

Salesman .... Territory ....

Date .... Mileage ....

Calls priority	Regular customer	Rating	Prospect call	Rating	Time of arrival	Time of departure

Daily objectives: ....

Result: ....

Callbacks: ....

....

....

186

There are two sales call patterns. They are: *set calls* and *irregular* calls. Set or fixed calls are where customers are called on repeatedly at set times. Irregular calls are those made when the salesman feels inclined to do so.

Plan your daily call schedule along the lines suggested. The more carefully selected calls you make, the more interviews you obtain and the more efficiently you work. Thus, the more you achieve.

PLANNING SALES GOALS

The salesman's personal sales goals and those of the company he represents are one and the same: high productivity bringing high profits. It is the responsibility of the salesman to set a sales *plan of action* and to follow-through, systematically, until all sales goals are reached.

A sales manager judges his salesmen on their productivity. He's less concerned with alibis, more concerned with results. The salesman must, therefore, plan his day-to-day activities with great care and spend his time where it will return the highest rewards. Sales goals should include:

- Efficient management of time. A planned daily and weekly program.
- Customer classification. Prospect classification. (Programmed daily).
- Territory analysis: understanding of customers' needs, market potential, etc.
- Number of calls to be made each day on regular customers.
- Number of calls to be made on prospects.
- Number of sales to be made each day.
- Total (daily) sales target in dollars and cents.
- Detailed daily (weekly) reports filed with sales manager.

ASCERTAINING YOUR SALES WORTH PER HOUR

Every hour of every working day you are worth dollars and cents to your company and to yourself. But how much are you worth? And are you working in the most effective and profitable manner? The proper monetary value must be placed on your time so that you can readily see what your wasted time is costing you. As discussed in an earlier chapter, if you're spending approximately 36 per cent of your work day in face-to-face selling, then the other 64 per cent of your day is costing you money. The sales earning chart will give you an indication of the value of each hour corresponding to yearly earnings.

Total up actual selling time now spent (face-to-face calls) and review your day-to-day activities with the view to increasing your productivity and profits. Study:

- *Number of calls per day*
- *Sales-call ratio*
- *Time expenditure*

YEARLY SALES EARNINGS AND HOURLY DOLLAR VALUES

Yearly earnings	Hourly Values
$ 5,000	$ 2.60
6,000	3.12
7,000	3.64
8,000	4.16
9,000	4.68
10,000	5.20
11,000	5.72
12,000	6.24
13,000	6.76
14,000	7.28
15,000	7.80
20,000	10.40
25,000	13.00
30,000	15.60
35,000	18.20
40,000	20.80
45,000	23.40
50,000	26.00
55,000	28.60
60,000	31.20
65,000	33.80
70,000	36.40
75,000	39.00

KNOW WHO YOU ARE SELLING TO

You are now ready to plan your sales presentation in anticipation of meeting your customer face-to-face and having him sign an order. You must gather all available information about the customer and try to arrive at his basic needs. The big question is: WHAT IS THE CUSTOMER'S BUYING MOTIVE?

Every sales presentation must be prepared and presented with an arrangement of strong buying reasons that are easily understood by the buyer. There are many ways of securing information on a prospect. By personally checking his place of business, talking to other salesmen, sending him a questionnaire to fill out and return, which offers him some benefit for doing so, chatting to his secretary or company receptionist. Trade publications, directories, advertisements, brochures offer information that can be helpful when preparing the presentation. The extent of customer fact finding depends on what you are selling. If you are selling items for the customer's personal use you may not require too much information about him. If, however, you are selling to a company man, you will require both personal information and information about his company and their needs.

Information you should gather on each customer includes:

- His correct and full name.
- Job position and influence in the company.
- Family background. How many children and what are their names?
- Clubs, organizations, church affiliation.
- Sports played, hobbies, reading, music interests.
- Personality type: grouchy, pleasant, conceited, friendly, shrewd, honest, price conscious, etc.
- History of his company: who owns it?; what does it do?; is management conservative or progressive?
- What pleases the customer most? What are his immediate needs?

Whether your prospect owns his own company or is employed by one, the more information you have the better preparation you can do and the greater the chance of successfully concluding the sale.

If you require background information on a particular industry or profession, read trade, business or professional journals. This will give you an insight into the 'trading world' of your customers.

5 LOGICAL PLANNING STEPS

Every sales presentation should be constructed along scientific lines to produce maximum benefits. You are one mind influencing another mind. You cannot hope to 'influence' another person unless you know what will move him to action. You must discover your customer's wants, needs, desires, aspirations and objectives and relate your product's advantages to them. Until this is done, your sales presentations will be a hit-and-miss affair.

The five logical (and scientific) steps to follow when preparing a presentation are:

1. PRE-APPROACH.
2. APPROACH.
3. DEMONSTRATION.
4. SUM-UP.
5. CLOSE.

(1) *PRE-APPROACH*: The more you know about your prospect and his company the better you are able to plan your approach. And the more homework you do, the more confidence you will have in your ability to present your message. The more information assembled, the easier it will be to handle objections. Careful *advance planning* greatly enhances your chance of closing the sale satisfactorily.

At this point of your planning, decide on the approximate length of your presentation. Naturally, this will vary from customer to customer, but a basic presentation should be developed covering *all* aspects of the goods or services you are offering. Adjustments can be made as you proceed with the actual presentation. The pre-approach should include:

1. Length of presentation (include all points).
2. Grouping of *plus factors* to support each of the 5 buying motives.
3. Answers to anticipated questions and objections.

(2) *THE APPROACH*: the first 90 seconds of your meeting are crucial. You must check all aspects of your dress, grooming, personality. Your opening statement is important and should always be in harmony with your attitude. You must be alert, honest and friendly. Your first impression *must* be a good one. In planning your approach consider the following points:

1. APPEARANCE.
2. GENERAL ATTITUDE AND MANNER.
3. YOUR OPENING STATEMENT.
4. PROJECTION OF A WARM, FRIENDLY GREETING.
5. ESTABLISHING A RAPPORT WITH THE CLIENT.

(3) *DEMONSTRATION*: at this point you must turn curiosity into *want*. Ascertain what the prospect's buying motive is and build your plus factors (point system) around it. If there are several buying motives, tackle the most important motive first and build a point system around it, then move on to the next. If you have an item to demonstrate, get the customer involved in it. Let him hold it, try it, taste it, smell it or in some way *participate* in the demonstration. If you are quoting figures, write large numbers on a pad and get the customer to follow your additions, divisions, subtractions and multiplications. Other points to consider are:

1. GET THE CUSTOMER'S ATTENTION THROUGH INVOLVEMENT.
2. TALK ABOUT BENEFITS AND SHOW THEM.
3. ASSOCIATE PLUS FACTORS WITH BUYING MOTIVES.
4. TALK THE PROSPECT'S LANGUAGE SO HE UNDERSTANDS WHAT YOU'RE GETTING AT.

(4) *SUM-UP*: this is the final step prior to the actual close. It is a crucial moment and must be handled confidently. You have presented your case and supported your claims with facts. You have established that the benefits of your product or service outweigh the cost. You have been getting agreement on each point presented. Now, *quickly* sum-up the main points; go over the advantages and ask the prospect to agree with you that these points are to his advantage. Other points to consider and plan into this section of the presentation are:

1. LIST PLUS FACTORS IN ORDER OF IMPORTANCE.
2. GET AGREEMENT ON EACH POINT BEFORE MOVING TO THE NEXT.
3. BENEFITS MUST OUTWEIGH THE COST OF YOUR PRODUCT.

(5) *CLOSE*: immediately you have finished your 'sum-up', present a close question, get a 'yes' answer and proceed to write-up the order. If you have presented logical buying reasons then the buyer will act favorably. If you have not, then you must retreat and pick-up from the stage where you 'lost' your customer. (The close is covered in greater detail in chapter 10.)

PLANNING IS THE RULE

It's a *fixed* rule and one that should be taken seriously. Play through the interview in your mind. Write it out in longhand. Record it, play it back and make improvements. Get confident about it. Know that you can do it and do it *well*. Anticipate questions and objections. Write down a list of possible questions and objections and find suitable answers. Put yourself in the buyer's chair. What objections would you raise? What would impress you—motivate you to buy? What buying blocks would *you* present?

Pre-planning includes assembling all necessary brochures, price lists, samples and information that might be requested. Don't be caught empty handed—arrive at the interview fully prepared and equipped.

Add to your presentation a point system that lists the most important plus factors in relation to the buyer's motive. Your courteous, enthusiastic and confident approach will stem from your careful organization of your presentation. Other points worth considering are:

- Gather together facts about your product or service. Decide which facts to use to combat competition.

- Look for *key* benefits and build them into a point system.

- Don't use slang expressions or mutilate words.

- Become enthusiastic about your product or service.

- Get agreement on each point. Make sure the prospect understands you. Ask him if he understands. Don't proceed until each point is accepted.

- Back your statements with proof. Give them *support* and they become believable and acceptable.

MEETING THE PROSPECT

During the introduction the customer is judging you and making his mind up as to whether he likes or dislikes you and whether he will do business with you or not. Your opening performance must be effective: cheerful, natural, totally open and motivated by a desire to be of assistance.

During your introduction make sure that the prospect has clearly heard your name and the name of your company. Present your business card, smile, project the thought, 'I like this man.' Give a firm handshake. Repeat the prospect's name frequently throughout the presentation. Use background information you have gathered on the prospect.

CUSTOMER PERSONALITY TYPES

POSITIVE TYPE	NEGATIVE TYPE
Friendly	Disagreeable
Personable	Cold
Listener	Talks too much
Talker	Silent
Decision maker	Procrastinator
Reliable	Unreliable
Honest	Unscrupulous
Serious	Joker
Relaxed	Nervous
Knowledgeable	Ignorant
Competent	Bumbler
Tolerant	Prejudiced
Smiler	Grouchy
Forgiving	Grudge holder
Buyer	Shopper
Learner	Opinionated
Patient	Impatient
Courteous	Discourteous
Acceptor	Complainer
Controlled	Quick tempered
Interested	Disinterested
Enthusiastic	Dull
Realist	Dreamer
Organized	Disorganized
Quick payer	Slow payer
Easy to convince	Stubborn
Optimistic	Pessimistic
Socially refined	Uncouth
Appreciative	Selfish
Imaginative	Lack of imagination
Self assured	Fearful
Humble	Conceited
Strong will	Timid
Receptive	Unreceptive

Know as much as possible about his problems so that you can ask him intelligent questions and offer sensible solutions. Make sure your opening words have impact, convey what you mean and are persuasive upon delivery. Paint a 'mental' picture with sales points to help your prospect *visualize* how your product can benefit him. You are obligated to satisfy his needs, not to coerce him into anything. Put him at ease by speaking in a conversational and pleasant manner.

Your presentation should be smooth in its delivery. It shouldn't sound like a 'canned' presentation: memorized and given parrot fashion. Be *interesting,* be *exciting* in your delivery. Speak convincingly and with good grammar. And stop talking long enough to *listen* to what the prospect wants. Other pointers are:

- *INTRODUCE YOURSELF EFFECTIVELY* so that you gain the prospect's *total* attention. Hold his attention throughout the interview.
- *CREATE GENUINE INTEREST* as you proceed to unfold your message.
- *LISTEN ATTENTIVELY* to the customer's questions and objections so that you can answer them satisfactorily.
- *ASK QUESTIONS* to gain the information you require to build your presentation around buying motives.

8 CUSTOMER APPROACHES

Approaches must be attention-getting and interest-arousing. They must be undertaken with charm of manner, warmth, friendliness and devoid of irritating mannerisms likely to annoy the prospect. Shuffling walk, drooped and rounded shoulders, pasty complexion, limp handshake, mumbling, refusing eye contact are detractors that will spoil your chances of success in selling.

The following approaches will prove useful to you when you infuse your *own* personality into them and adapt them to fit the customer and the occasion.

1. *Profit approach.* To arouse the curiosity of the prospect begin your opening remarks with: 'Mr. Customer, would you like to increase your weekly profit margin by 6 per cent? Well, I can do that for you. My company has decided to reduce the profit margin on our electric range of stoves by 6 per cent and pass this saving on to the retailer.' This can be used in a variety of ways to suit the occasion and to fit in with special company promotions where price reduction applies.

2. *Showmanship approach.* A real eye-opening, dramatic approach is an instant attention and interest-arousing technique geared to win the prospect from the beginning. 'Mr. Customer, this watch face is shatter-proof and the case shockproof. Watch as I thrash it with this hammer. Here, Mr. Customer, you try it. Pound it and see its remarkable strength.'

3. *Counseling approach.* Every human being wants to solve personal problems. An offer to solve the prospect's problems will be wel-

comed. 'Mr. Customer, I read in the business review section of the paper yesterday that your company is having a staff-turnover problem. I've had 15 years in the employment hiring business and I can help solve your problem. I've devised a plan of action for you, without obligation, of course, and I'm sure you will be interested in hearing it.'

4. *Gift approach*. Everyone loves to receive a gift. An inexpensive advertising gift (or sample) presented to a prospect is an excellent technique to get him to *listen* to your message. 'Mr. Customer, my company has asked me to present you with this free gift and hopes that it will be an aid to your business. It's a combination wallet and diary with a special section for listing expenses. It carries a list of all holidays, a currency converter and a host of other informative facts I'm sure you will find useful.'

5. *Compliment approach*. This must be genuine and sincere or it will backfire. Take note of any new office decorations, window displays, store layouts. Compliment the prospect on them. 'Mr. Customer, my wife and I were window shopping on Sunday and we passed your store. We were so impressed with your unique display, I told my wife I'd pass along our congratulations. I expect you've had many such compliments. Mr. Customer, I wouldn't be surprised if your company wins the retail trader's window display prize this year.'

6. *Current affairs approach*. Take an important newspaper headline (when it pertains to business) and use it as a lead-in. Always maintain an affirmative attitude. Do not be pessimistic. 'Mr. Customer, that item in yesterday's paper about high interest rates affecting business. Quite a negative approach and one devoid of facts to substantiate their argument. The same situation came up last year. It had a reverse effect—people bought more. I'd like to hear your opinion on this.'

7. *Direct approach*. Can be used when cold canvassing. 'Mr. Customer, I'm here to solve mutual problems. I have a valuable product to sell. You are in business to sell valuable products. My visit this morning is to satisfy your need and in so doing you will benefit and so will I. Now I know that you aren't concerned with my problems in business and I don't expect you to be. But solving problems *is* my business—it's the business of every salesman and I'd like to be of service to you this morning. My advice is free, so is my friendship. I'd like to extend both to you.'

8. *Status building approach*. Used to build the prospect's ego and make him feel important. 'Mr. Customer, my company has imported this new compact adding machine from Japan. It has all the features of a full-size machine but it is a third the weight, size and cost of our standard model. I wanted you to be the first person to see it. My manager has asked me to record your comments as to it's sales potential.'

194

ATTITUDES AND ACTIONS
TO WIN CUSTOMERS

DO

SMILE: who could resist a warm, friendly smile? Breaks down the toughest prospect. SMILE and often.

USE HIS NAME: who can resist hearing the sound of his own name? When invited to do so, use the prospect's first name and *often*.

GET INTERESTED: show a genuine interest in your prospect. Don't be offhanded. Be concerned and your prospect will react in the affirmative.

LISTEN: stop talking long enough to LISTEN to the wants of your prospect or customer. People love a good listener. It builds goodwill.

SHOW RESPECT: it doesn't matter what position the prospect holds, show him respect as a human being. Don't look down on him, ignore his opinions. Make him feel important.

APPRECIATE HIM: we've talked about this friend-winning trait and it's worth repeating: it's human nature to appreciate the qualities of those who see good in us. Compliment the prospect when the occasion warrants it and extend genuine appreciation of his friendship and the business he gives you.

DON'T

BE COLD: being hard-hearted, lacking in warmth won't win you customers.

UNPLEASANT: rudeness doesn't pay. Don't use cutting remarks or be sarcastic. Don't be hard to get along with.

ARGUMENTATIVE: you may *think* you know it all, but chances are the other fellow is right *some* times. Stop arguing! You can't influence another person by shouting at him. Calm down and listen to the *other* point of view. There's a chance you might learn something by listening.

DISHONEST: you won't last long in the selling profession if you cannot be trusted. Integrity and honesty must be part of your character and a *large* part of it.

UNRELIABLE: another failure trait. When you give your word stick to it.

UNCOUTH: you can't win respect with slang expressions, smutty jokes or foul language. Check your tongue, it could lose you customers and your job.

HOW TO RAISE THE IMPORTANCE OF YOUR VISIT

An affirmative attitude, favorable to the salesman and his product, can be induced in the mind of the prospect if he is approached in a confident, courteous and dignified way. If the prospect is approached in a casual manner, he will think that the proposition is of little importance. You've got to gain and *hold* the prospect's attention from the moment you enter his premises to the time you leave. What you say, how you say it, the way you act must indicate the importance of your visit. You must show your prospect that you have an awareness of his needs and you are there to satisfy them. Three suggestions to follow during your presentation are:

1. Gain eye contact and hold the communication link.

2. Sit or stand easily and comfortably, not awkwardly.

3. Carry the conversation. Be affirmative in all statements.

ELIMINATE TIRED EXPRESSIONS FROM YOUR GREETINGS

Routine opening remarks by salesmen such as: 'How are you today?'; 'Nice day, isn't it?'; 'How's business?'; 'Lovely store you have.'; 'I'm here in response to your advertisement.'; etc., are tired phrases devoid of imagination. As a self power you must eliminate stock phrases from your speech, particularly from your opening remarks. Don't sound like an automated parrot. Use your thinking powers to create new and interesting greetings.

USE THE 'OPENING TEASER' TECHNIQUE TO AROUSE INTEREST

Supplanting stock phrases used in greetings with other clever phrases have the negative feature of themselves becoming stock statements. One way to overcome this problem is to eliminate using the customary opening interchange of niceties. A short question worded to arouse interest can be used to advantage.

This technique is called the 'opening teaser'. It works this way. The salesman shakes hands with his customer and opens with: 'I deposited 200 dollars in ideas into your cash register last week Mr. Brown.' The immediate response is a curious 'Oh?' There is no 'pat' answer but a purposeful one might be: 'Instead of devoting my time equally among other clients, I spent the entire week thinking about *your* sales problem and I've come up with some interesting ideas.'

Another 'teaser' opening is: 'Seeing you this morning has brought to mind a proposition that will be of mutual benefit.'

Devise your own opening teasers and write them on cards. The important thing is NEVER use them unless they fit the situation and the customer. They must seem 'off-the-cuff' not trite or insincere.

Never use slang expressions, vulgar or obscene words or crude jokes. Maintain a dignity about you. Whatever your opening remarks are they must be friendly, sincere and purposeful. Eliminate gossip and false stories. They will have an adverse psychological effect on the person they are delivered to. Be unique in your greetings. Use your imagination for all its worth and you'll find new material popping out of your mental computer. Ideas such as:

1. Using daily news headlines to open conversations.
2. Quoting from magazine editorials.
3. A cute situation you witnessed.
4. A message passed along.
5. Specific facts pertaining to changing business trends.
6. A statement relating to the customer's sports interests.
7. A newsy piece of information to bring a laugh. (Not gossip).
8. An offer of assistance in some way.
9. Bearing good tidings: price decrease, specials, gifts.
10. A sincere complimentary remark.

Make teasers and other opening techniques seem spontaneous. Change them frequently. Try a 'teaser' or 'opener' in your next greeting. Develop the art of clever openings and you will enhance your conversation ability both socially *and* in business.

ENTREPRENEUR ELIMINATES RESISTANCE WITH CANDY

Edmond Samuels, philosopher, author and manager of theatrical talent, is a well-known Australian who uses candy to help get his message across.

He uses it on the 'biggest' people and it works. During the introduction, Eddie takes two candies from his pocket and offers one to the prospect. 'Here, chew on this. You look far too tense. It's a pacifier. By the time I've gone you'll be in wonderful spirits,' he tells him. Eddie then unwraps his candy and pops it into his mouth. Both sit and chew through the conversation which follows.

'It's a great way to get the prospect to relax and listen,' Eddie told me. 'While he's chewing, he's got his mind centered on what I'm saying and not on a dozen different problems associated with his business or personal affairs.'

A GREEK BEARING GIFTS WINS NEW CUSTOMERS

Another friend uses a small polished stone called a 'pacifier' to give to new clients. He's a young Greek and an excellent salesman. The stones are collected as a hobby by his wife, hand polished and painted.

'I'm a Greek bearing a gift,' George tells his new customer. The opening remark brings a laugh and the tension is broken as George weaves a story about the usefulness of holding a stone pacifier to reduce tension.

'Everytime they pick up my pacifier they think of young George,' he mused. Good idea? Certainly is and one that came from the imagination of a clever-thinking salesman. Put your own imagination to work and create opening ideas to win new friends and bigger commissions.

HANDLING THE COLD CALL

You have entered the prospect's premises unannounced. The reception you receive will depend a great deal on the manner of your approach and your attitude toward the prospect. Self confidence and a smile can work wonders. Brashness of manner, sloppy appearance, hesitant speech and nervousness will bring a negative response.

Sell yourself as a person worth talking to. A person of substance, dignity and self confidence. If you feel that the prospect is in no mood to talk to you, request an appointment for another day.

Always use a straightforward approach when making a cold call. State your purpose in calling. Your main task is to quickly convince the prospect that it is well worth his time to listen to your proposition. You will have to capture his full attention, arouse his interest and create a desire to hear your message. Some additional pointers when making cold calls are:

- Offer the prospect an obvious benefit. (Why should he take time to listen to you?)

- Get to the point. Don't waste the prospect's time with inane chatter.

- Know what you are going to say in advance of the call.

- Arrive smiling and *leave* smiling, regardless of the outcome of your visit.

- Don't press the point if the prospect seems busy or in no mood to see you. Ask for a specific appointment time, thank the prospect and leave.

- Sell yourself, your product and your company in that order.

- Determine the prospect's needs and buying motives and present the advantages of your product to satisfy his buying motives.

BUILDING CONFIDENCE IN THE MIND OF THE PROSPECT

The professional sales representative, whether he is selling behind a counter, from a van, door to door or operating as an accounts executive, must instill confidence in the mind of the buyer. The more efficient and self confident the salesman is, the greater the customer confidence will be.

Appearance, behavior and sales skill are *plus factors* every salesman must develop. A smiling face, a word of appreciation, a pleasant disposition, a genuine desire to be of service, a thorough knowledge of product and company procedures, an ability to make people happy, will prove to be priceless ingredients when the salesman is canvassing for new customers.

TIMING THE APPROACH

Usually, the approach lasts about five minutes. During this 'breaking-the-ice' period, the salesman must aim at arresting the prospect's confidence, eliminating any suspicions he may have and establishing a common ground where a free-flow of ideas can pass between seller and buyer.

Rehearse your opening remarks. Be prepared to change your opening if it is not suitable to the occasion or for the person. Be flexible in this regard. Get down to essentials quickly. But give enough time to settle the mind of the prospect and relax any fears he may have about you. Don't move into the mainstream of the presentation until you are convinced that the buyer is ready for it, otherwise you will not obtain your objectives. Build a rapport with the prospect by getting him to tell you the problems associated with his business.

HOW TO ELIMINATE FIRST CALL NERVES

First call nerves hit the best of salesmen. The 'pro' learns to control them and to use the energy at his command wisely. 'Nerves' are the result of fear, due to an uncontrolled imagination. The salesman lacks confidence in his presentation and his ability to be convincing. He fears objections which *possibly* could arise and this throws his performance into an embarrassing chaos.

A prospect is not a monster to be feared. He is just as eager to buy the right products or services as you are to sell them. Overcome the fear of sales failure by checking your 'runaway' imagination. Allow your imaginative powers to work affirmatively instead of negatively.

Approach the prospect with the confidence of a real professional who is ready to render honest service. You have nothing to fear or to apologize for *if* you have prepared your presentation and *know* that you are offering the prospect a fair and sound proposition.

FEARS PRODUCING FIRST CALL NERVES

- FEAR OF CRITICISM.
- FEAR OF REJECTION.
- FEAR OF JOB LOSS.
- FEAR OF LOSING CUS-TOMERS.
- FEAR OF CUSTOMER COMPLAINTS.
- FEAR OF MAKING WRONG DECISIONS.

- FEAR OF NOT MAKING SALES.
- FEAR OF ILL HEALTH.
- FEAR OF NOT BEING LIKED.
- FEAR OF COMPETITION.
- FEAR OF CUSTOMER OBJECTIONS.
- FEAR OF MEMORY LOSS.

APPLYING THE AIDA FORMULA TO SUCCEED IN SELLING

The AIDA formula is a recognized system of selling used by professional salesmen world-wide. Every sales presentation should be structured according to its principle. It is a step-by-step method of opening, building and closing a sales presentation. The letters AIDA stand for:

> Attention
> Interest
> Desire
> Action

We have already discussed getting the *attention* of the prospect and holding it throughout the presentation. Once this has been done, the prospect must become *interested* in your proposition. To become interested is to become involved, to participate, to become curious and to want to know more. From this point a *desire* can be aroused which spurs the prospect on to think about purchasing your product or service. You've made the proposition sound convincing and you've promised to satisfy a need which now has motivated the prospect to *action*. He *wants* to buy.

By stressing the values of your product or service, by presenting its uses and applications, by making your proposition sound thoroughly convincing, by your acts of courtesy, enthusiasm, confidence and *service*, by working through the AIDA formula and effectively handling buying blocks, you are in a position to logically and honestly secure a firm order and complete your objective.

While it is easy to state the formulas for successful selling, putting them across convincingly and psychologically requires a great deal of skill. Careful preparation, knowledge of the person you wish to sell to, discovering the buying motive, presenting incentives, fulfilling desires and easing the prospect through the AIDA system are the factors that determine whether the sale is made or lost. Practise using the AIDA formula. Keep the 'steps' in your mind and play through them. The more you understand the strategy, psychology and principles of dealing with people, the more successful (and richer) salesman you will become.

APPLY THE DOMINO PRINCIPLE TO THE AIDA FORMULA

The Pentagon calls it the Domino Theory. (Relating to the fall of one country after another to the Communists.) Line up a number of dominos or blocks and tip the first one. It will fall and tip the second, the second the third and so on until the last one is knocked down. When the lead domino falls, *all* fall, one after another. The AIDA formula works the same way, if you apply the domino principle to it.

Begin with ATTENTION. Knock it down first. That is, gain the total attention of the prospect and once you have it move to creating INTEREST. Once interest has been established move (automatically) to knock down DESIRE. Desire will knock down ACTION. You've now succeeded in opening the sale and building it scientifically to a successful conclusion.

This could be called a cybernetic principle in action: do the right thing at the beginning and the end result takes care of itself. Applying principle correctly, stirs creativity and challenge instead of attracting fear, anxiety and frustration into your work.

DEALING EFFECTIVELY WITH CUSTOMER BUYING BLOCKS

Having secured an interview, the next step is to prepare for a possible 'buying block'. Physically getting in to see a prospect does not guarantee a sale will be made. The salesman must 'ease in' to the prospect's mental presence. The full attention of the buyer is needed

DOMINO THEORY

```
┌─────┐ ┌─────┐ ┌─────┐ ┌─────┐
│  1  │ │  2  │ │  3  │ │  4  │
│     │ │     │ │     │ │     │
│Atten│ │Inte-│ │Desi-│ │Act- │
│tion │ │rest │ │re   │ │ion  │
└─────┘ └─────┘ └─────┘ └─────┘
```

before the salesman can effectively communicate his message and motivate the prospect to act on it.

Since you will have to deal with buying blocks every time you face a prospect, it will be helpful to understand the reasons why they are raised and what you can do to counter them. Buying blocks are different to presentation objections. They center on *you* the man in the hot seat, the person facing the prospect. The salesman must spot them quickly and deal with them effectively at the beginning of the presentation. Study the chart on buying blocks and devise ways of combating them should they confront you at your next interview.

PLACE YOUR PROSPECT IN THE PICTURE NOT OUT OF IT

Place the prospect in the picture, not outside it. Allow him to try your product or if this is not possible, to imagine himself using it. Paint word pictures: 'Can't you see yourself, Mr. Customer, on that cruise ship, basking in that warm tropical sun by the ship's pool, sipping a tall drink? Sounds pretty inviting doesn't it?'

Use your imagination to *involve* the prospect in your presentation. If you are selling an automobile, get him behind the wheel. If you're selling a boat, get him *on* it. You can increase the customer's desire for your product by glamorizing your appeals, by mental image building and by active participation.

BUYING BLOCKS CHART

1. INSTINCT

There is a natural impulse on the part of most people to be suspicious of others. It is only natural that the prospect is slightly suspicious of the salesman who calls on him for the first time. He thinks: 'Who is this man and what does he want?' Disarm the prospect mentally by being totally 'open' in your approach. You have nothing to hide or to be ashamed of. Present your *real* self and boldly (but charmingly) present your proposition.

2. HABIT

People are ruled by habits. They dislike changing their routine. They've been doing things the same way for many years and they are quite content to continue in this manner. Some buyers set specific days and times for sales interviews. Others refuse to grant interviews unless a definite appointment is made. Some buyers restrict their business to companies they know and seldom make purchases from salesmen they haven't checked out or previously done business with. Discover the habit patterns of those you want to do business with. Don't try to buck them.

3. FIRST IMPRESSIONS

Possibly *the* most important aspect of winning sales. Your overall appearance and manner create a definite image and this image wins or loses sales for you. Create a dynamic first impression. The way you talk, walk, dress, listen and respond are vitally important to your success.

4. PREJUDICE

Look for signs of prejudice in a buyer: politics, religion, countries, peoples, things. Some people have closed their eyes and ears to the facts of life. They see and hear *only* those things they want to see and hear. Steer clear of arguments on controversial matters. If you suspect a customer is prejudiced against you, quietly and without malice, ask him why and seek to correct the situation.

5. EMOTIONAL DISTURBANCE

A major factor in winning sales. Every human being, no matter how exalted his position in life, experiences personal problems. Unhappiness within the family and home environment brings on emotional disturbance which eventually affects an individual's business life. Gain an understanding of 'causes' of negative personality traits in your customers. Discover their mood patterns and deal with them (tolerantly and sympathetically).

STRESS VALUES AND SOLVE PROBLEMS

Stress the values of your product or service by presenting its uses and applications, by making comparisons of the benefits derived. Talk benefits: service, long life, low maintenance, profitable use, pleasurable use, pride of ownership, etc. Look for obvious problems your customers and prospects may be encountering and find solutions to them through your product or service.

There are literally hundreds of problems that confront trades, business and professional men: cost, delivery, display, advertising, marketing, image, time, staff, packaging, waste, service, competition, declining market, producing methods, etc. *Your sales presentation must stress values and solve problems.* Through careful listening and subtle questioning find the *values* the prospect is seeking and the *problems* he wishes to solve. If your attitude is sincere and your presentation professionally carried out, you can expect an affirmative result and a highly satisfied client.

---

8 SALES PRESENTATION POINTERS

1. HOLD INTEREST.
2. AROUSE CURIOSITY.
3. SUPPLY LOGICAL BUY-ING REASONS.
4. LEAD—PERSUADE—NEVER PRESSURE.
5. SUPPORT CLAIMS.
6. USE AFFIRMATIVE SUG-GESTION.
7. USE AFFIRMATIVE REPETITION.
8. DON'T OVERSELL.

SUPPORTING YOUR CLAIMS AND GAINING CONVICTION FOR THEM

Your proposal must not only *sound* convincing it must *be* convincing to the point where your prospect accepts your claims. Your attitude and manner must be straightforward if you want your prospect to feel secure and confident in his decision to purchase your product. If you are out to deceive your prospect, he will see through your falseness and reject your proposition.

Every time you make a claim for your product support it with *proof* that what you say is *accurate*. Evidence to support your claim is vital if you want to secure conviction. Making rash claims for your product without ample evidence that what you say is true, results in loss of confidence by the prospect in your proposition. Apply the technique of *affirmative suggestion* and *affirmative support*.

Affirmative suggestion is the affirmative claim you make for your product. Affirmative support is the backup statement or proof of your claim. Here is an example using an automobile as the product being sold.

AFFIRMATIVE SUGGESTION	AFFIRMATIVE SUPPORT
Best value of all makes of cars.	Comes with 16 'no cost' extras and sells for $23 less than competitor models.
Lower initial cost saves you money.	Bank the saving at 6 per cent and buy yourself a present after one year.
Good investment.	Biggest resale value as shown in latest copy of Car Journal and US Auto Club magazine.
Best looking car on the road.	Winner of the 'Auto Design Award' this year and praised by 16 international automotive writers.
Easiest model to drive.	Our new power steering unit has been tested by 20 internationally-famous race drivers and they attested to this fact. Their names are listed on our brochure.
Finance is no problem with us.	We now carry our own hire-purchase system and have yet to reject a customer's credit application.

HOW TO BUILD A POINT SYSTEM INTO YOUR PRESENTATION

A point system is a number of major plus factors which act as *incentives* for the prospect to say 'yes, I'll buy it.' Your point system must match buying motives.

Gather your plus factors and group them according to buying motives. Use only those factors that are important to the prospect's buying reasons. Don't bring confusion to the presentation by presenting too many points for the prospect to consider. Five main points should be sufficient. Others can be grouped together as 'added advantages' and presented as a group: 'There are eight other advantages in addition to the five I've mentioned, Mr. Customer. They're on the brochure and I'll be happy to go through them with you if you wish.'

The buying motives should be established (if it is not known prior to the interview) at the point of *interest* building. If the motive isn't obvious, then ask a series of questions to establish it. As soon as you have the motive(s), mentally select the plus factors to match the motive(s) and proceed to present them to build interest and establish a desire for your proposition.

This strategy is effective in most cold calls or where your objective is to secure an appointment for a formal presentation. The buying reasons can be established at this point and a presentation planned to support them.

VISUAL AIDS TO ASSIST YOUR PRESENTATION

- Presentation books.
- Newspaper reviews, articles.
- Photographs.
- Maps.
- Blackboard.
- Slides.
- Product components.

- Scrap books.
- Reprints of facts and figures.
- Flip charts.
- Mock-ups.
- Flannel Boards.
- Films.
- Flash cards.

POINT SYSTEM CHART

PRODUCT: electric drill
CUSTOMER: tradesman
BUYING MOTIVES: gain and fear
NUMBER OF POINTS: 5
ADDITIONAL POINTS IF REQUIRED: 5

BUYING MOTIVE	POINT	PLUS FACTOR (Incentives to the Motives)
Gain—time saved.	1	Takes little effort. Light weight, portable, convenient to carry from job to job.
Gain—money saving.	2	Costs cents a day to run. Guarantee gives 2 years free service.
Fear—safety of user.	3	Special cover-guard protects the user from injury. Has perfect safety record.
Gain—money saving.	4	All metal construction cannot be broken. Takes great deal of punishment. Heavy duty casing protects motor. Special design requires minimum of servicing.
Gain—money saving.	5	Multi-purpose saves buying other equipment. Can be used for sanding, buffing, polishing as well as drilling and 5 other uses.

SUMMARY OF IDEAS TO HELP YOU PLAN AND OPEN
A SALES PRESENTATION

1. Your important position as a company sales representative requires that you plan and organize every aspect of your company message. The manner in which you handle your presentation determines the success or failure of your company's product in the territory under your command. PLAN —EXECUTE.

2. Selling is a service function. You must understand the needs of your customers and satisfy those needs. Render service *plus*—willingly.

3. Classify customers into buying groups. Concentrate your efforts where they are most likely to bring the greatest return. Follow a daily route schedule and reduce wasted time. You are judged on your productivity level. Total actual selling time and figure your hourly earning rate. If you aren't working to peak efficiency find out why and change your routine.

4. Obtain every piece of information available on your client prior to meeting him. Get his name, job position, personality type, etc. The more you know, the better service you can offer and the more sales you will close.

5. Follow the 5 logical and scientific steps when preparing your presentation: *pre-approach, approach, demonstration, sum-up, close.* Play through the interview in your mind, refine it. Get confident about it. Your self confidence is built

on solid preparation; of knowing what you are going to say and do. The first 90 seconds of meeting the prospect are crucial. You must present yourself in a dramatic and confident way.

6. Eliminate tired or slang expressions from your greetings and presentations. Gain eye contact, carry the conversation and hold a communication link. Use 'teaser' openings. Make them sound spontaneous not 'canned'.

7. Always support your product claims. It isn't enough to say 'it's the best.' You must state why and on what authority the claim is made. Use the technique of *affirmative* statement backed by *affirmative support*. This brings conviction to your message and confidence in the mind of the buyer.

8. Place your prospect in the picture, not out of it. Let him touch, taste, smell, hear or see the product you want him to buy. And remember, selling to the male buyer sometimes requires a different approach to selling to the female customer—responses are different. Both groups have buying blocks you must surmount. Study the buying blocks chart and acquaint yourself with the various traits and idiosyncrasies of buyers.

9. Every sales presentation must be structured around the AIDA formula. Use the Domino Principle and you will bring success to your sales closes. Build a point system (plus factors) into your presentation.

10. The point system must correspond to the buying motives. Match them. Tell the customer what he wants to hear, what he wants to know. Fulfill his needs.

HOW TO PSYCHOLOGICALLY CLOSE A SALE

Affirmative Ideas in this Chapter

- The Technique of Closing Sales
- Cut Down Buying Decision Confusion
- Give The Customer What He Wants
- Handling The Interjector
- Get A Commitment At Each Step With 'Feeler' Questions
- How To Identify Psychological Buying Signals
- Buying Signals
- Don't Expect The Prospect To Do Your Job For You
- Ask Close Questions
- 10 Trial Close Questions
- Handling The Group Sales Situation
- Use 'Feelers' To Determine The Mood of Your Audience
- 10 Successful Closing Formulas
- The Button-Up
- The Written Order
- When To Stop Selling
- Eliminate High Pressure From Your Closing Techniques
- Reasons Why Salesmen Fail To Close
- Polishing Your Sales Presentations
- Check Your Performance And Analyze Sales Failures
- Personal Sales Analysis Chart
- Summary of Ideas To Help You Psychologically Close Sales

10

THE TECHNIQUE OF CLOSING SALES

Presented in this chapter are tested closing techniques designed to bring your sales presentations to a successful and profitable close. To these techniques you will add variations to suit your own personality and style of selling. You will give preference to some formulas and reject others. The important objective (whatever the technique used) is to *close* sales.

The most important closing technique involves knowing what problem, need, want, desire or fulfillment is sought and then directing your presentation (and closing remarks) to satisfy whatever it is the prospect requires. Sell incentives; sell benefits; sell needs and you will successfully close sales.

CUT DOWN BUYING DECISION CONFUSION

Some salesmen contribute to the indecisiveness of their customers when it comes time for them to buy. This happens with frequency where the customer is given a multiplicity of similar items to choose from instead of a few choices.

Eliminate confusion from the decision-making process. Don't confuse customers with too many choices or alternatives. Help the customer to come to a quick and accurate decision by offering a choice of two or three items (or alternatives of color, size and price).

GIVE THE CUSTOMER WHAT HE WANTS

Never attempt to palm-off items, bribe with false price reductions or trick customers into purchasing unwanted merchandise. Practise honesty in selling. If you cannot give the customer what he wants or what he can make use of then direct him to those who can. I'm sure you would feel badly if another salesman managed to trick you into buying items you couldn't afford or use.

HANDLING THE INTERJECTOR

Where you are confronted by a husband and wife team (or customer and friend who comes along to assist in the buying selection), take care not to arouse hostility in either person. Subtly guide the conversation along the lines you want it to take and direct your remarks more to the 'decision maker' of the pair.

Carefully study the buying 'atmosphere'—the *mood* of the husband and wife team. Get *both* to agree on the value of the plus factors you present. Avoid arguments. Do not irritate customers with sarcastic remarks, not being attentive to their needs or by displaying impatience when they raise objections and questions. Never allow customer remarks to upset you. Remember: *it's not what's said that causes emotional damage, it's your reaction to what's said.* Whenever a customer is rude or contradicts something you know to be correct say: 'Perhaps you're right. Let's move to this next important point . . .'

GET A COMMITMENT AT EACH STEP WITH 'FEELER' QUESTIONS

As your presentation progresses through the AIDA formula, encourage your prospect to commit himself to a 'yes' answer each time you present a plus factor. Ask: 'Would you not agree, Mr. Customer, that this particular model constructed of steel, is strong enough to do the job?' A series of 'yes' answers to your questions leads the prospect to say 'yes' when you ask him to sign the order.

Other 'feeler' questions that can be used are:

- 'I'm sure you see the value in this particular model. Do you, Mr. Customer?'
- 'Does that sound reasonable to you?'
- 'Would I be correct in saying that this policy will give you the security you need?'
- 'You're the type of person who likes to make up his own mind, is that right?'
- 'Now that you've had a chance to compare models, this one offers more than the others, is that not so?'
- 'You're going to select the best value for money, right?'
- 'And don't you agree, that this service agreement is more than fair?'
- 'You're looking for a comfortable, well cut, quality, but reasonably priced suit. Is this true?'
- 'I believe you're really impressed with this color. Is this correct?'

HOW TO IDENTIFY PSYCHOLOGICAL BUYING SIGNALS

There is a precise psychological moment when a prospect is ready to buy. Leading up to this time there are indicators or 'buying signals' given by the prospect and these must be identified and acted upon. Many of these indicators are physical actions; others come in the form of objections or questions. The alert salesman watches for them and takes immediate action to close the sale.

Observe any change in attitude on the part of the prospect. If his attention increases, he asks questions indicating he wants to buy, if he leans forward in his chair, smiles, loses his tenseness, ceases to raise objections, then any of these actions could indicate that the prospect is ready to say 'yes, I'll buy.'

Buying signals are likely to come at any time during the presentation. They may come at the time of the approach. ('Mr. Salesman, you're just the man I want to see, I need to reorder 12 tape recorders.') The 'yes' may come after you have successfully handled an objection or after you have presented a plus factor that matches a buying motive.

Do not make the mistake of not attempting to close until you have completed your entire presentation. If the opportunity arises to close the sale, close it. (It is never too early to test the prospect's readiness to buy.)

Avoid high pressure closing techniques. It isn't a question of them not working—some do—it *is* a question of future customer relations and the image you are establishing of yourself and your company. A well prepared presentation offering definite benefits and presented in a friendly, courteous and professional manner, will bring the results desired without having to resort to trick methods. Getting the signed order is your job. That's what you are paid to do; paid to do it in an honest and ethical way.

BUYING SIGNALS

SPOKEN WORDS: listen for *key* words which indicate a prospect is ready to buy. He may ask details about price, delivery, availability of special orders, colors and sizes available. Words such as 'if' are often an indication: 'What *if* I take the small size.' 'And' and 'but' give indications of genuine interest: '*And* can you assure delivery on time?'; '*But* can I get this in another color?'

VOICE: nervousness reveals itself in the voice. If the prospect's voice comes across with a slight quiver, it indicates that he is frightened by your proposal and would like to 'ease' out of the situation before you attempt to close him. A slight raising of the voice and a quickened speaking pace oftens indicates excitement for your proposition and the prospect is anxious to buy it. A lowered speaking tone and slower delivery of words can sometimes mean the opposite.

EYES: these are the mirror of the soul and they cannot hide a person's inner feelings. Watch the prospect's eyes for tell-tale signs of acceptance or rejection of your proposal. Half-closing of the eyes or 'squinting' means the prospect is skeptical. A sudden wide opening of the eyes means he is convinced or 'yes that sounds interesting.'

HEAD: held high means the prospect wants to be convinced of the point you are making. Head down indicates that he is weighing the proposition and the statements and claims made. Head angled to one side indicates that he is contemplating a decision or weighing the pros and cons before making up his mind. An abrupt nod sometimes indicates that the prospect has reached his decision and is willing to proceed with the deal.

FOREHEAD: when a prospect frowns, wrinkles his brow, he is weighing your statements or rejecting them. A raised eyebrow often means that he is ready to buy.

HANDS: closed or tightly clasped, means that the prospect is tense and on guard. Relaxed, open, hanging loose means that his mind is open and he is interested.

DON'T EXPECT THE PROSPECT TO DO YOUR JOB FOR YOU

The close is the climax of the presentation and should move smoothly without conscious volition on the part of the salesman. The object of the professional sales presentation is to create in the prospect's mind sufficient desire for the proposition. If the salesman has planned his presentation and obtained from the prospect agreement on each sales point, then he will have little difficulty making an affirmative close.

Precise psychological moments will arise when the prospect is ready to buy. This is the time to 'close' by using a trial close question. If the question is properly phrased and delivered in an easy (without-pressure) manner the prospect *has* to make a decision.

Don't lose control of the presentation by expecting the prospect to close for you. Some prospects fear making a decision to buy, others want to be persuaded, others want to be *asked* for their business. Don't be guilty of being timid when it comes to asking for an order. A positive attitude will overcome any fear of asking a prospect to buy.

Keep your presentation talk to a minimum. Eliminate meaningless points, side talk or distractions of any kind. Continually push the YOU FACTOR, covering all major benefits. A prospect will *want* to buy if he can be shown that he will benefit from ownership of a product. Persuade him. Motivate him with strong buying reasons and it will be difficult for him to refuse your proposal. You cannot *make* a prospect buy. But you can make him *want* to buy.

ASK CLOSE QUESTIONS

Make it easier for the prospect to say 'yes' than 'no'. Present trial 'close' questions which lead to a 'yes'. Yes-building questions nearly always lead to an affirmative close. Don't regard a negative reply to a trial close as final. This is the point where you must take up the challenge and use psychology to win the prospect back to your court. Back off and present another selling point for which you seek agreement. Then try another trial close.

Worth remembering, is that a customer's 'no' rarely ever means 'no' as a final decision. Quite often it means: 'No, I haven't quite understood the message.'; 'No, I'm not convinced that this particular item suits my purpose.' Don't take 'no' for an answer—a *final* answer. Most closing difficulties come from the procrastinators. It's easier for them to get off the hook by saying 'no' instead of 'yes'. Whenever a negative reply is given to your close question, use it as an invitation to *continue* with the presentation, not to quit.

10 TRIAL CLOSE QUESTIONS

1. 'Will this be a cash sale or on your account?'

2. 'When would you require delivery if we were to conclude the arrangement today?'

3. 'Would you require an assortment of colors or prefer all white?'

4. 'Are there specific instructions you would like me to note on the purchase order?'

5. 'I know you will be satisfied with this item. I'll direct it for immediate delivery if you'll give me your full name, address and telephone number.'

6. 'You've agreed to the advantages and I'm sure you'd like the set in your home as soon as possible, is that right?'

7. 'If we were to deliver the policy to your office would that be satisfactory or would you prefer me to visit your home after work?'

8. 'I know you'll appreciate that this home could be sold by another salesman even while we're discussing it. I'm sure you'd be disappointed at missing out because of waiting too long before deciding. Let's safeguard your interests by presenting an offer today.'

9. 'We must take action now, Mr. Customer, if you wish to beat the price increase. If you place the order now, you'll save 50 dollars. That's quite a saving isn't it?'

10. 'May I have your business card and with your permission I'll take down the necessary particulars.'

HANDLING THE GROUP SALES SITUATION

Always concentrate on the key decision maker when addressing a board of directors or committee. This does not mean that you should ignore others in the group. Spread your message by holding their eye contact and talking *to* them not *at* them. If you have an opportunity of visiting members prior to giving your presentation, try to discover the 'attitude' each holds toward your company and product. Find those who are 'on side' and get them to state why they support your proposition.

Get your personality beaming. Project affirmative statements, specific benefits, values which are likely to influence a decision your way. Don't ask questions likely to embarrass members of the group. Enunciate and articulate and eliminate word whiskers (ums and ahs) from your speech. Project your voice so that you can be heard by those in the rear seats. Group your audience so that each person has a clear view of you and can see every aspect of your demonstration.

USE 'FEELERS' TO DETERMINE THE MOOD OF YOUR AUDIENCE

To determine in which direction the sale is headed, tactfully ask questions at the right time. This could be during the presentation and *or* at the conclusion of it. 'Gentlemen, are there any questions on the first part of my proposition you'd like to ask before I begin phase two?'

Get your audience involved in what you are saying and doing. Talk to each by name in a friendly manner. 'Mr. Smith, perhaps you have a point you'd like me to clarify.' Answers to questions often uncover sales objections. Before moving on to another point make sure that the audience is in agreement or accepts the answers you give. Always come back to a point of *customer benefit*. When a negative objection cannot be countered, retreat to a previously agreed upon benefit. 'There's no denying, Mr. Jones, that our pump does not have an extra valve in this section. However, you did agree with the point I made earlier, that a second valve, while beneficial, is not absolutely necessary and does increase the cost of this unit by 43 dollars. I submit to you gentlemen, that the extra cost is not warranted, particularly since our service department hasn't had a single case of valve breakdown.' Keep pushing buying motive benefits such as: extra profits, less overheads, greater customer satisfaction, reliability, better servicing facilities.

10 SUCCESSFUL CLOSING FORMULAS

Study the various methods given and develop them to suit your own style of selling (and personality). The most effective closing techniques are usually the simplest. Therefore, keep your closing actions simple, direct and positive. Here are 10 basic closing suggestions.

CLOSING FORMULA 1: *POSITIVE ASSUMPTION*

Always *assume* that your prospect is going to buy and that the only details to be worked out are those concerning price, delivery, quantity and specifications of size and color. Positive assumption must be backed by confidence in your sales ability. Believe in your ability to sell and to move others to action. *Expect* to close because your product or service is something *worth buying.*

CLOSING FORMULA 2: *POSITIVE SUGGESTION*

Suggest the size of the order you would like your prospect to place. Give him solid reasons why he should buy the amount suggested. Place the thought in his mind that it is better to be 'well stocked' with a fast moving item than to be without it and thus lose out on extra profits. Use positive suggestion to close and to increase your sales volume.

CLOSING FORMULA 3: *AMBITION APPEAL*

Show where your product or service can guarantee the fulfillment of your prospect's ambition: advancement in job, business, creative accomplishment, financial gain, etc. Appeal to his ego drive.

CLOSING FORMULA 4: *MINOR DECISION*

The procrastinator doesn't want to make a *major* decision. Accommodate this wish and lead him to make *minor* decisions instead. Offer a choice between two minor alternatives such as, models, colors, dates of delivery, terms of payment, etc. Getting the prospect to make minor decisions leads him to a 'yes' answer when trial closes or the final close question is presented.

CLOSING FORMULA 5: *FOLLOW THE LEADER*

Everyone wants to experience success in life. Suggest to your prospect that your proposition has made others successful in their business and or personal lives. Suggest that he too can become successful through the purchase and use of your product or service. Where possible, show prospects testimonial letters and a list of names of those who have purchased from you.

CLOSING FORMULA 6: *THE INDUCEMENT*

Where an extra 'push' is needed to close a prospect, use an inducement: genuine price reduction, free gift, special service, some benefit not ordinarily given. The idea is to get the prospect to say 'yes' *now,* instead of waiting.

CLOSING FORMULA 7: *EGO INFLATER*

Pass a genuine compliment indicating your respect for the prospect's wisdom, knowledge, position and decision making ability. 'Mr. Brown, a man in your respected position is very much aware of this valuable offer. You're ability to make a quick decision is unquestioned. I'm sure this will be the case now.'

CLOSING FORMULA 8: *REVERSE SELL*

Must be carefully used without deflating the prospect's ego or insulting him. Suggest that the proposition is beyond his present ambition, price range, quality level or that he may not have the necessary requirements to qualify. 'I'm sure this policy would be of great benefit and I can see you would like to have the security of it, but I really cannot put my signature to it until my company gives its approval. I wouldn't want you to be disappointed if I cannot get them to approve your application. However, if you'll sign it and include a check for the premium, I'll do my best to have it passed as quickly as possible.'

The two most important factors in buying are, *desire* for gain and *fear* of loss. Both these aspects enter the 'reverse sell' technique. When you plant the idea in the mind of the prospect that he isn't in a position to buy your valuable product or service, the prospect dwells on the loss factor and this (psychologically) induces him to buy. Hold this technique in reserve. A danger exists that a prospect might 'sense' what you are doing and seize upon the opportunity to agree with you and leave it at that.

CLOSING FORMULA 9: *THE TIP-OFF*

Let the prospect in on a trade secret: price rise, change of model, deleted number, slight imperfection. Give the prospect an 'incentive' to buy: while stocks last, while existing price holds. 'Mr. Brown, this item will be deleted from our catologue in November. It's been one of the best sellers you've had from us. I suggest that you buy the remainder of the stock at a price and you'll be the only retailer in the city to carry it.' Another 'close' using this technique could be: 'Mr. Customer, we've imported this range from Sweden and found a slight imperfection in the lining. It isn't noticeable, nor does it affect the construction of the garment. I'm willing to reduce our price if you take the total order. You'll save quite a lot and have an exclusive on this line.'

CLOSING FORMULA 10: *ASK FOR THE ORDER*

This is a straight-forward technique. Don't be frightened to come right out and ask for the order. 'Well, Mr. Customer, let's make a decision. I'd suggest you order ten gross.'

THE BUTTON-UP

A close is not something that is stuck onto the end of a presentation. It is a natural conclusion to the proposition being presented. If the customer has been handled correctly (and honestly) and is satisfied with the terms and conditions of the proposal then there is little likelihood of the sale being cancelled.

Customers *do* change their minds. And often they are entitled to do so because salesmen are not always truthful in claims made for their products or services. High pressure selling is one of the biggest reasons for cancellations. Customers coerced into buying products that do not live up to salesmen's claims should not be expected to follow-through and accept delivery and make payment for such goods.

It is generally accepted that up to 12 hours after a customer has signed an order to purchase goods or services a danger period exists. If the customer has doubts or hasn't quite understood the terms and conditions of the purchase or suspects that he has made a wrong decision, then cancellation is likely.

Use the 'button-up' method to reassure customers that they have made a wise buying decision. Summarize all sales points. Make sure that the terms are understood. Be certain that your customers are happy with the arrangements decided upon. Leave *no* doubts whatsoever. BUTTON-UP your sales and you'll reduce (to a minimum) customer cancellations.

THE WRITTEN ORDER

The first rule is to write *legibly*. Poor handwriting results in mistakes being made when orders are being prepared and dispatched by the shipping department. Print the customer's name, address and order requirements. Request a business card and attach it to the order so that the correct name and address can be checked without delay.

Special instructions, terms of payment, etc., should be initialed by the customer to avoid possible disagreement. Listen to the customer's special requests and do not agree to things you know your company cannot supply.

Personally check to see that your company follows-through with customers' special requests: special delivery instructions, terms of payment, size, color, number, special packaging, etc. Customer satisfaction is of prime importance, particularly if repeat business is expected.

Points to remember when writing the order are:

- Print, do not write instructions. Use a ball point pen and make sure carbon copies are clear.
- Include full name, address and telephone number of customer. Attach customer's business card to the order form.
- Be certain that special delivery instructions are clear. If goods cannot be delivered after a certain hour then state this on the order.
- Include the customer's account number, sales tax number and terms of payment: net 7 days, net 30 days, C.O.D., etc., on all orders.
- Use product identification codes where applicable. Make sure that sizes and colors are correctly stated.
- Have all orders signed in full by the customer and special instructions initialed.
- Check and recheck your written order. Leave nothing to chance or memory. Write *accurate* orders. You'll save time and money.

WHEN TO STOP SELLING

The presentation should be stopped at the first indication of a buying decision on the part of the prospect. This is the *precise* time to ask for a signature to the order. Regardless of whether this decision comes at the beginning, during the middle or at the end of the presentation, make it a firm rule to close the sale by asking for the order. Overselling is dangerous and must be eliminated from your selling practice.

To continue reassuring the prospect that he has done the right thing after he has said 'yes' gives him time to reconsider his move and to wonder why you are trying so hard to 'sell' him. This brings doubts to his mind and a loss of confidence in your story. It can have an adverse effect, to the point of losing the sale.

ELIMINATE HIGH PRESSURE FROM YOUR CLOSING TECHNIQUES

High key selling makes a nervous prospect even more so. Don't frighten him half-to-death by throwing a mental hammerlock on him and attempting to pressure him into buying. If this is your practise then perhaps there is something wrong with your proposition (dishonest?) and something *very* wrong with your style of presentation.

Without sounding contradictory, there are times when certain customer types (the procrastinators) need a slight nudging. They want you to make a decision for them. Where your proposition is right for the prospect (will fulfill a need), then certainly *lead* and *persuade* the prospect to place his signature on the order.

REASONS WHY SALESMEN FAIL TO CLOSE
They fail to prepare and organize a sound sales presentation.
They fail to think affirmatively about the outcome.
They fail to get all pertinent details on the prospect and his needs.
They fail to work through the AIDA formula.
They fail to overcome the buying blocks.
They fail to effectively handle objections.
They fail to put excitement into their presentations.
They fail to match plus factors to buying motives.
They fail to build a strong 'point system' into their messages.
They fail to ask the prospect to buy.

POLISHING YOUR SALES PRESENTATIONS

Do not rest on your laurels. Keep polishing your presentations. Try new methods, different approaches, a new line of questioning. Personalize your closing techniques. This 'polishing' is a continuous study of selling procedures, human psychology, general knowledge and product knowledge.

Monitor the presentations of other salesmen. Judge their ability to open and close a sale. Learn from their mistakes and their 'strengths.' Keep the learning process active and strive to improve every day.

CHECK YOUR PERFORMANCE AND ANALYZE SALES FAILURES

Conduct a post mortem on presentations and attempt to discover where you went wrong. By uncovering clues to 'sales failures' performance improvement comes about. Remember: selling is a percentages game. You cannot hope to sell *every* prospect. Not every prospect you meet wants, needs or could possibly use your product or service. Therefore, you are not to blame for *all* sales turn-backs.

The best way to discover your sales effectiveness is to answer the questions listed in the Personal Sales Analysis Chart.

PERSONAL SALES ANALYSIS CHART

Your Action	Yes	No

THE APPROACH

	Yes	No
Did you plan and organize your presentation?	☐	☐
Did you gather information on the prospect?	☐	☐
Did you know his name prior to the interview?	☐	☐
Did you create a dynamic first impression?	☐	☐
Did you clearly identify yourself, your product and company and present your business card?	☐	☐
Did you gain and hold the prospect's attention?	☐	☐
Did you find the prospect's buying motive(s)?	☐	☐
Did you ask questions to select + factors?	☐	☐

Subtotal:

THE PRESENTATION

	Yes	No
Did you bring all samples, brochures, price lists?	☐	☐
Did you supply incentives to match buying motives?	☐	☐
Did you place the prospect 'in the product picture?'	☐	☐
Did you listen to his wants?	☐	☐
Did you overcome buying blocks?	☐	☐
Did you get agreement on each point presented?	☐	☐
Did you build interest, create a desire for your item?	☐	☐
Did you invite questions?	☐	☐
Did you have full product knowledge?	☐	☐
Did you show how your product can be used?	☐	☐
Were you honest?	☐	☐

Subtotal:

THE CLOSE

	Yes	No
Did you restate advantages?	☐	☐
Did you sum up your main points?	☐	☐
Did you use trial closes? (Ask for the order).	☐	☐
Did you motivate the prospect to buy and sign him?	☐	☐
Did you leave the door open for a return visit?	☐	☐
Did you do a 'button-up' and leave the prospect knowing *exactly* what he purchased?	☐	☐

Total 'Yes' and 'No':

SUMMARY OF IDEAS TO HELP YOU TO
PSYCHOLOGICALLY CLOSE SALES

1. Find and sell to the *right* man—the person who has the authority to make a decision.

2. Select the buying motives (major ones first then secondary ones) and induce buying action with YOU FACTOR benefits. Sell the customer what he wants, not what you want to get rid of.

3. Get the prospect to agree on each point. Present 'feeler' questions. A series of 'yes' answers will lead to a 'yes' close.

4. Get the prospect actively involved in your presentation. Get him to visualize himself using the product. Satisfy his emotional needs by covering ALL product or service benefits.

5. Watch for psychological buying signals. Fast analysis of feedback information helps you to close quickly.

6. Handle objections (or customers' friends interjections) smoothly. Don't argue or irritate them. Your job is to sell, not to make enemies. Use caution when dealing with group situations. Don't ask questions likely to embarrass members of the group.

7. Get your own personality into shape. Look bright. Be enthusiastic. Smile at your prospects and make them feel happy. Your enthusiasm will ignite their enthusiasm and they'll want to buy your proposal.

8. Use the technique of *positive assumption*—taking for granted the prospect is going to buy. Be confident when using this approach. Show your order book at the beginning and start writing the order at the first sign of buyer acceptance. Follow the other successful closing formulas and apply them to suit your own style of selling and personality.

9. Don't talk too much or oversell after the customer has agreed to your proposition. Thank the customer and leave promptly after writing the order. Don't use high pressure close methods.

10. Use trial close questions and ask for the order. Don't be timid about it. Button-up your sales to reduce cancellations.

BOOK THREE

In the years I've spent in various countries tracking down success, the most significant thing I've learned about achievement is this: IT'S A DO-IT-YOURSELF OPERATION. My biggest achievements and most satisfying creative accomplishments have been brought about by my own efforts. My most frustrating experiences and set-backs have been the result of relying on the promises of others. Waiting for other people to bring you success is the most time-wasting, self-defeating and foolhardy practice I know.

HOW TO HANDLE
OBJECTIONS—NEGOTIATE
COMPLAINTS
AND CANCELLATIONS

FORMULA

11

Affirmative Ideas in this Chapter

- The Psychology of Harmonious Human Relationships
- How To Produce Customer Goodwill And Become An Outstanding Salesman
- A Magic Technique For Avoiding Customer Complaints—Objections—Cancellations
- Apply The Golden Rule To All Transactions
- The Practical Method of Handling All Complaints—Listen
- How To Keep Customers Happy
- How To Establish Better Public Relations
- Politeness Pays Off
- Apply The Principle of Co-Operative Effort But Avoid Customer Domination
- Negotiate And Avoid Pride And Sales Loss
- You Can't Win Arguments By Arguing
- Make Objections Work In Your Favor—Capitalize Them
- Separate Trifling Objections From Real Ones
- Use Strategy When Countering Objections
- Turn Objections Into Questions To Reduce Their Sting
- How To Use The Indirect Denial Technique
- How To Use The Figuring Technique To Rationalize Your Claims
- Handling Price Complaints And Objections
- How To Justify Price
- Handle Price Objections Positively
- Handling The Bargain Buyer
- Record And Analyze Standard Objections
- Objections Guide
- When To Bypass An Objection
- Anticipate An Objection And Kill It Before It Kills Your Sale
- Handling Cancellations
- The Rewards of Effective Complaint And Objection Handling
- Standard Customer Objections Chart
- Summary of Ideas To Help You Negotiate Complaints And Objections

226

11

THE PSYCHOLOGY OF HARMONIOUS HUMAN RELATIONSHIPS

Human relationships make or break salesmen. They play too big a part in the business of selling to be treated casually or ignored. Every salesman worthy of the name will study the various ways and means of dealing with people in a friendly, harmonious, satisfactory and just way. To get the most out of selling (financial and creative satisfaction), salesmen have got to like and get along well with people so that people will like and get along well with them.

Resentments, prejudices, hates, bigotry, jealousy and envy have no place in the consciousness of the professional salesman. It is not possible to love others while harboring inner feelings of hate. The formula to achieve better and more harmonious human relationships is twofold:

1. LOVE THYSELF.
2. EXTEND THIS LOVE TO OTHERS.

Love thyself does not mean to think of yourself as superior to others or to adopt a conceited manner. It means to recognize the glories and beauties within you. To respect the powers, attributes and aspects of Infinite Life which surround you, guide you and are part of you. This is your path to success. It's your path to freedom of fear, frustration and want. It's your passport to happiness, health, spiritual freedom and creative achievement. It's a positive step toward getting people to like you and to respond to you as you want them to respond.

Extend this love to others and your life will take on new wonders, joys and victories. There is a *law of attraction* that will supply you with as many friends and customers as you wish to have. Your *new* self (positive, tolerant, compassionate, poised) will attract others of a similar nature and yet others who will wish to *be* like you and capture your technique of radiating love, peace, prosperity and goodwill.

HOW TO PRODUCE CUSTOMER GOODWILL AND BECOME AN OUTSTANDING SALESMAN

Your business is to help people in *their* business. Your business will begin to boom when you adopt a 'giving' attitude: when you sincerely desire to help others without thought of 'taking' something from them. Your attitude must be full of right thought, right expression and right action. When it is, people will flock to buy from you because you will have built a reputation of honesty and forthrightness. Your customers will express their appreciation of your efforts on their behalf by buying *more* from you. New customers will be attracted to you by the *law of universal attraction*. You cannot fail when you adopt an attitude of 'giving'; of contributing to the success of others.

Your primary thought in selling must be *service*. You must look for ways to help your customers make money or save money; to experience happiness, creative fulfillment and satisfaction through your transactions. You will be an outstanding success as a salesman if your personal and business relationships are in accord with these principles.

A MAGIC TECHNIQUE FOR AVOIDING CUSTOMER COMPLAINTS—OBJECTIONS—CANCELLATIONS

Simply stated, this technique requires that you take immediate action to *stop taking advantage of your customers*. Cease attempting to 'load' customers with merchandise you know they cannot resell or receive satisfaction from.

Complaints, objections, cancellations are due to customer dissatisfaction and annoyance. When you satisfy a customer's need you leave no room for complaints, objections or cancellations. Good business, right business, honest business *always* prospers. Dishonesty in selling always has and always will attract problem situations. Using 'trick' methods to sell customers shoddy, worthless merchandise is short term selling. Give fair and just value and service. Never take advantage of a customer in any way whatsoever. This means of preventing possible problems from arising, will win you the respect of your customers.

APPLY THE GOLDEN RULE TO ALL TRANSACTIONS

Do not unto others what you would not have them do unto you. Treat your customers as you wish other salesmen to treat you. Would you appreciate being landed with a contract producing hardship? Practise the golden rule. Treat your customers *exactly* as you would like them to treat you if the tables were reversed.

It's far better to close all avenues of possible complaints, objections and cancellations before they arise. Psychological selling is not tricking others into doing what you want them to do. It's assisting them to arrive at a sensible, logical and worthwhile buying decision. Begin every sale with the thought: *I will tell this prospect what I myself would want to be told if I were the buyer. I will not do to him what I would not want done to myself if the positions were reversed.*

THE PRACTICAL METHOD OF HANDLING ALL COMPLAINTS—LISTEN

Customers complain for a variety of reasons: price too high, service arrangements poor, faulty manufacture of merchandise, rudeness of salesman, objectionable and false advertising claims. Whatever the complaint, there is *one* sensible way of handling it: listen and reserve judgement until you have the true details and know what satisfaction the customer desires.

If you react too quickly and jump to conclusions you are in for a battle royal with your customer. Your *manner* is the key to successful complaint handling. An unsympathetic attitude is often taken as 'personal antagonism' by the person making the complaint. This brings an antagonistic response.

Hear-out the other person's complaint. Demonstrating your superiority and ridiculing your opponent's view are *not* ways to build customer satisfaction. Give due consideration to the point of view of the person making the complaint. Your attempt to sincerely help the customer solve his problem is the most practical method of handling complaints and the best way to retain his business.

HOW TO KEEP CUSTOMERS HAPPY

One of the most effective ways of keeping customers happy (and ensuring repeat business) is to keep in touch with them and give attention to their queries and complaints. Make a courtesy call (or telephone) about two weeks after making the sale. Ask the customer if he is totally satisfied with your product (or service) and if there is a service you can perform for him. Never forget a customer after you have sold him goods or services. Keep in touch and your customer will not forget you when it comes time to reorder.

HOW TO ESTABLISH BETTER PUBLIC RELATIONS

Greater emphasis is being placed on public relations in selling. Influencing others through improved customer relations is not a method of getting something for nothing. It *does* mean rendering personal services to your customers: helping them without undue thought of personal gain. *Salesmanship is servemanship.* A few thoughts given to the other man's problems will return dividends in the long run. Public relations in business also means:

- To go the 'extra mile' without selfish motives.
- To examine all viewpoints carefully.
- To be as objective as possible, not letting personal emotions 'color' thinking or affect decision making.
- To keep an open mind free of prejudice.
- To do the utmost to satisfy customer complaints.

229

POLITENESS PAYS OFF

Courtesy costs the giver nothing. It certainly does 'pay' when dealing with irate customers. Don't irritate customers with an aggressive, impolite attitude when they confront you with complaints, objections or cancellations. Be friendly, charming and polite and put them at ease. Melt their icy approach with a smile.

If you approach your customers with a warm smile and indicate that you are genuinely interested in helping to solve their problems you will succeed in reducing their hostile attitudes and be in a better position to deal with their complaints sensibly and calmly. A friendly, helpful, *smiling* salesman will get better results than an argumentative one. Remember: politeness can change the hostile outlook of a customer who has a complaint. Rudeness makes the customer feel that you and your company owe him something.

APPLY THE PRINCIPLE OF CO-OPERATIVE EFFORT BUT AVOID CUSTOMER DOMINATION

Co-operative effort means to employ the principle of 'give and take'. It means to show understanding, tolerance and compassion for the other person's position. It also means to genuinely help the other person by selling him goods and services which enhance some aspect of his life and live up to all promises and claims made about them.

To co-operate with a customer does not mean that you should accept undue abuse from him or allow him to mentally blackmail you into conducting the transaction *his* way, benefiting *him* alone. Do not become a 'yes' man, agreeing to things you know are wrong and not to the advantage of yourself or your company. You cannot win respect of others by practising appeasement or allowing the other person to dominate your views and unjustly influence your decisions and actions.

NEGOTIATE AND AVOID PRIDE AND SALES LOSS

Being dogmatic and insisting that the customer bear the brunt of a mistake (regardless of who is at fault) is the quickest way to lose the customer's goodwill and hope of future business.

Understand the customer's point of view. Calmly reason with him when he is upset. Call for the facts. Prepare a solution, but only after you fully understand the circumstances associated with the problem. Offer an alternative solution—negotiate a satisfactory compromise. This gives the customer a chance to withdraw from the subject with honor.

Many customers will fight an issue because of so-called 'principle'. The only way out of this situation is to allow them to save face through a compromise. Regardless of who is at fault, never criticize. People make mistakes and change their minds every day of the week. However, these actions can be minimized by making sure that customers are properly sold in the beginning. When a co-operative attitude exists between salesman and customer, satisfaction on both sides is gained and an harmonious business relationship established.

YOU CAN'T WIN ARGUMENTS BY ARGUING

Some salesmen find it difficult to apologize or say, 'I'm sorry you've had so much trouble with our product. I'll do everything in my power to make matters right.' They'd rather argue with customers.

Tactfulness wins arguments. Apply the principle of diplomacy and avoid shouting matches with irate customers. You cannot hope to pacify a customer if you become involved in an argument with him. The more you argue, the stronger is his conviction that he is right and you are wrong. When you feel like blowing your top in a confrontation with a customer, stop talking and listen—give yourself time to cool off. You'll reduce tension by 50 per cent and chances are, you'll find that the customer reduces his vocal steam and aggressiveness. This technique is effective when tempers flare and the situation looks like getting out of control. The idea is to reply to the customer's negative approach with a positive one. Stop talking, start listening and view the situation from the other person's point of view. A well chosen statement such as: 'Yes, you have a valid point there,' will help to pacify the customer. *Enforced silence* brings greater self-control and allows you time to think creatively and rationally *and* to arrive at a suitable solution.

MAKE OBJECTIONS WORK IN YOUR FAVOR—CAPITALIZE THEM

Most objections raised by a prospect mean one thing—the salesman hasn't made his proposal clear. The prospect is not convinced that what is offered by the salesman is of real benefit to him. When this occurs, it is inevitable that objections and excuses will be presented to release the prospect from any obligation to purchase.

Capitalize the objection—reverse it so that it becomes a reason *for* buying instead of a reason for not buying. Restate the claim, support it with benefit factors which act as *incentives* to motivate the prospect to buy. Satisfy the prospect that his objection is not valid when compared to the reasons why he *should* make a decision to buy. If you 'capitalize' correctly, you can often close at this point.

SEPARATE TRIFLING OBJECTIONS FROM REAL ONES

Learn to separate trifling objections and excuses from important ones. Genuine objections are often raised after the prospect has made a thoughtful consideration of the salesman's proposal. When it is obvious that the prospect has valid reasons for *not* buying and the proposal is of little benefit to him, no attempt should be made to pressure the prospect into buying. Do not label valid objections excuses. Sometimes valid objections are raised in terms of the benefit factors. (Benefits haven't been matched to buying motives). Treat these as valid questions and proceed to identify YOU FACTOR benefits with the prospect's buying motive.

When trifling objections are raised as a stalling tactic, don't waste time countering them. It will only lead to others being raised. Find the *true* reason why the prospect doesn't want to buy. Deal with this reason and supply substantial answers to counter the objection.

When a prospect raises objections he is asking for reasons to be convinced. Too many objections mean that a salesman isn't making his prospect aware of personal benefits. The buying reasons must be strong motivating factors to convince the prospect that he is doing the right thing.

USE STRATEGY WHEN COUNTERING OBJECTIONS

Handle objections as skilfully as you would play a game of chess. Counter each objection with a strong buying reason. State your case in concise, easy-to-understand terms. Supply the necessary information (product knowledge), give comparative information to minimize objections. Look for the psychological reasons behind objections. Not all objections speak for themselves. Many of them have to be interpreted. In other words, people do not always mean what they say and often color their statements or objections because they have a personal axe to grind or a prejudice of some kind against the salesman, his company or product.

Deliberate misrepresentation can sometimes occur when the person raising the objection attempts to influence the emotions of the seller by being derogatory about his company or product. This attitude may be taken when a person cannot find a legitimate reason for saying 'no', so he makes one up: 'I'm sorry, I've used your product and it just doesn't live up to its advertised claims.'

The expert objection handler must use a subtle questioning technique to discover the *real* problem and then solve it. Logic and scientific thinking methods can overcome the trickiest objections. *Seek* out, *think* out and *work* out the best possible answers to false objections.

TURN OBJECTIONS INTO QUESTIONS TO REDUCE THEIR STING

Invite the prospect to raise questions as you proceed with your presentation. Inform him that you welcome questions as they will help to clarify the proposal step-by-step. This places you in the position of being a *question answerer* not an *objection defender*. The psychological theory behind this technique is: the prospect will heed your advice and present mild questions rather than strong objections. Thus, the sting is taken out of the prospect's negative response or reluctance to buy.

HOW TO USE THE INDIRECT DENIAL TECHNIQUE

This is a tactful way of denying the prospect's objection without offending him. Instead of contradicting him with a flat, 'I'm afraid you're wrong,' response, indirectly side-step the objection by using: 'yes, I'm sure you're right, Mr. Customer, but consider this . . .'

The *yes-but* or 'indirect denial' technique enables you to outflank the prospect's line of defense and divert his attention to points that are likely to influence a buying decision.

HOW TO USE THE FIGURING TECHNIQUE TO RATIONALIZE YOUR CLAIMS

Use the 'figuring' technique as a motivating factor when dealing with price objections. Always sell 'quality' vs 'inferior-made' goods. Use a pad and felt pen to illustrate your points.

(+) *ADD UP* customer benefits in relation to quality.
(÷) *DIVIDE* higher cost of item by longer life.
(×) *MULTIPLY* customer satisfaction by number of benefits.
(−) *SUBTRACT* disappointments arising from inferior merchandise.

HANDLING PRICE COMPLAINTS AND OBJECTIONS

Price complaints relate to 'value' received. If the price you are asking is *just* and constitutes fair value for monies received then you will have no difficulty in handling complaints of this nature. Your answer to price complaints must center on relative values: cost vs quality of manufacture and performance. Examine competitor merchandise and compare cost and quality to your own items. There must be a valid reason given why your merchandise or service is priced as it is. Draft a list of reasons substantiating your company's pricing structure.

As a rule of thumb, ask yourself whether you would be prepared to pay the same price if the situation were reversed. If you feel quite satisfied with the price of your merchandise and *know* that it is worth every penny, then everything will be in proper order. Should a complaint arise, you will be ready to (honestly) justify the price charged and therefore, satisfy the customer's objection.

HOW TO JUSTIFY PRICE

Reduce 'price' into small units, especially if the item is high priced and can be used over a long period of time. A $1,000 machine sounds expensive compared to a $300 one. But when the more costly machine is broken down into costs per day a different picture is produced. You can (logically) *prove* that your higher cost item will be less expensive in the long run than a less expensive, economy-built one. The advantages must outweigh the initial cost: quality construction, longer life, trouble-free service, added features of operation, greater resale value, etc.

Stress the exclusive features, the *advantages* and *differences* associated with your item. The more important differences you can present, the less price comparison will be made. Support your claims with evidence: testimonial letters, longer guarantee, facts, figures, newspaper reports of performance, etc.

Turn the 'high price' objection into an *asset* rather than a liability. Stress prestige, profit and savings over a longer period of use. Make no apology for quality—there is no substitute for it.

HANDLE PRICE OBJECTIONS POSITIVELY

The question of price is likely to crop up in nearly every sales presentation. Rather than it become a problem turn it into a challenge and handle it positively. While there is no rule when price should be introduced (it depends on what you are selling and to whom), it will be to your advantage to hold the price factor until near the conclusion of your presentation. No sense talking about cost until the customer knows what he is getting. After you've stressed the advantages and the customer is in agreement with you that the item is 'excellent', subtly mention the cost and deal with the price question at this point if it is raised.

Sometimes the prospect will demand a quote or price and refuse to let you proceed until you tell him. In this instance, it is better to quote the price and then proceed with benefit factors.

HANDLING THE BARGAIN BUYER

When competitors under-cut or reduce prices, find the reasons why and counter them with logical explanations such as: company is over-stocked; discontinued item; lack of consumer acceptance; too many faults; servicing difficulties, etc. When you know *why* competitors are reducing prices you are in a position to use the reasons 'why' as a genuine counter to, 'I can buy a different brand cheaper.'

A customer buying shoddy merchandise because the price is 'right' might think that he is getting a bargain. When it is pointed out that it will cost him money in the long run because of poor service, costly replacement, the 'value' aspect is turned around and the prospect's thoughts are then centered on quality, satisfaction, value. Most people like to *identify* with the best. Tactfully point out that 'inferior' goods or services do not identify with or present a good image. *Quality reflects good taste—Quality saves money over a long period of use—Quality brings satisfaction of use.*

RECORD AND ANALYZE STANDARD OBJECTIONS

Make a list of every conceivable objection prospects could raise. Find suitable answers and list them alongside each objection. Analyze past sales. What were the most frequent questions raised? What questions did you fail to answer which lost you the sale? You will find that there are five or six main objections common to all sales made or lost. Be 'aware' at what point in your presentation objections or questions are raised. Keep your 'objections guide' up to date. It will prove to be a valuable sales aid.

OBJECTION GUIDE

1. Make a list of objections you've already encountered.
2. Find logical answers to your list of objections.
3. List testimonial evidence gained from *satisfied* customers.
4. Study competitor products and services and list the advantages of your product (service) over those of your competitors: price, packaging, quality of manufacture, etc.

WHEN TO BYPASS AN OBJECTION

When a prospect is adamant about his point of view or objection and proceeds to argue his case, it is wise to concede his 'point of fact' and bypass the objection. This compliments the prospect's judgement, gives him a sense of authority in the situation and boosts his ego. It costs you little and in the long run gains you a great deal of goodwill and possibly a successful close.

Bypassing the objection allows you to continue with your presentation without hostility building up in the prospect's mind. Instead of bruising his ego you've boosted it. You've made him respect you, thus turning the objection into a psychological advantage.

ANTICIPATE AN OBJECTION AND KILL IT BEFORE IT KILLS YOUR SALE

Learn to 'feel out' or intuitively sense when a prospect is about to raise an objection and knock it on the head. As an example: 'Now, Mr. Customer, I know what you're going to ask: "why is it 20 per cent higher than X Brand?" Well, there's a very good reason and it's this . . .'

Anticipate objections. Quickly counter them and kill them off before they 'build-up' in the mind of the prospect and become major obstacles. In a majority of instances, the prospect will accept your answer with little or no argument, because you answer his query before it is raised. You have turned the objection back on your prospect as a valid reason why he should say 'yes'. This technique can be used two or three times throughout the presentation with a slight rephrasing of words: 'Now, here's another point, I'm sure you'd like me to clarify, Mr. Roberts.'

Soften this technique by using a smile *and* the prospect's name. If used sincerely, this technique will hold the attention and interest of the prospect and result in fewer major objections being raised.

HANDLING CANCELLATIONS

They can be a nightmare to the inexperienced salesman or a 'challenge' to the professional. Cancellations are part and parcel of selling and while they can be reduced to a minimum they cannot be totally eliminated.

Customers are apt to change their minds. This occurs when the salesman has not properly closed and buttoned-up his sale. It's like catching the horse and then leaving the gate open. You've left an easy way out for the customer.

Where the reason for cancelling an order is a valid one, very little argument should be given. If a contract has been entered into by a prospect and he finds that he cannot pay for the goods or services he has committed himself for, it is better to release him. Attempting to force the sale loses goodwill in addition to further valuable selling time. If the prospect has accepted goods or services, used them and then desires to cancel for reasons which are not valid, then the final action to be taken should be left to the discretion of management.

It is my belief, that forcing a customer to accept goods or services he does not want (where his cancellation reasons are valid), is poor policy. The amount of time and effort it takes to follow-up and resell the customer and possibly *insist* that he complete his obligation, is 'lost' time which could be spent selling a new prospect.

Whatever the reasons for cancelling an order, the salesman must listen to them. All cancellations are not motivated by stupidity or dishonesty. Quickly find the real reason for the cancellation and if it can be countered and clarified (so that the customer is happy), that time will have been well spent. Always keep in mind your company's good will and public image. Remember: *a satisfied customer once, is a buyer twice.*

THE REWARDS OF EFFECTIVE COMPLAINT AND OBJECTION HANDLING

The ability to think and deal with customers' complaints and objections in a fair and satisfactory way is not an innate quality. It has to be cultivated through practise. With the importance of human relations in selling, the prime ability to get along with people and satisfy their needs must be developed.

It takes skill to single out facts, questions and objections and a great deal of patience to handle difficult customer situations. A salesman's ability to act in a most prudent manner is a valuable human relations skill. Customer satisfaction and repeat business are the rewards.

STANDARD CUSTOMER OBJECTIONS CHART

OBJECTION	POSSIBLE ANSWERS
Your price is too high:	
Your product is not in demand:	
I've used your product and I don't like it:	
I've found your service to be unsatisfactory:	
I cannot afford your proposal:	
I'm not interested:	
See me next week:	
I've never heard of your company or product:	
A friend bought it and didn't like it:	
I'm satisfied with the product I'm already using:	
I wouldn't buy it at any price:	
Your product hasn't been on the market long enough:	
Your credit arrangements aren't suitable:	
I've had a better offer from your competitor:	
You haven't given me a good reason why I should buy:	
It's not dependable:	
I don't like your range of colors:	
Insurance is a waste of money and a poor investment:	
Your shipments are never on time:	
My customers are always complaining about your product:	
Your claims are farfetched:	
What proof can you give me that it's the best?:	
I'm over budget now, see me next year:	
I want to look around first:	
I have no room to display your product:	

SUMMARY OF IDEAS TO HELP YOU NEGOTIATE
COMPLAINTS AND OBJECTIONS

1. Human relationships make or break salesmen. Learn to like and get along well with your customers and they'll like and get along well with you. Your business is to help people in their business to succeed. Adopt an attitude of 'giving'.

2. Stop taking advantage of your customers. Sell them only those items and services you know will be of advantage to them. Do not 'load' a customer with unwanted merchandise or shoddy items. Apply the golden rule: *do not unto others what you would not have them do unto you*. Treat customers with respect and you'll have outstanding success as a salesman.

3. The practical method of handling complaints is to *listen* before you act. Get the message, then solve the problem in a fair and just way.

4. Greater emphasis is being placed on public relations in business. Be sincere, honest, as objective as possible, keep an open mind and do your utmost to satisfy the customer. Remember: politeness pays off. Don't irritate your customer by arguing with him. Don't be dogmatic. Co-operate, be friendly and SMILE!

5. Make objections work in your favor—*capitalize them*. Reverse them so that they become reasons for buying. Learn to separate trifling objections from real ones. When a prospect raises objections he is requesting reasons to be convinced. Present logical reasons and convince him that he is doing the right thing by saying 'yes' to your proposal.

6. Use strategy when countering objections. State your case, support it with proof and testimonial evidence. Use questions to elicit the *real* reasons a prospect is resisting your proposition.

7. Take the sting out of objections by inviting the prospect to ask questions as you proceed with your presentation. Become a 'question answerer' instead of an 'objection defender.'

8. Use the 'indirect denial' technique to avoid offending customers. The 'yes-but' formula enables you to outflank the prospect's line of defense and divert his attention to the major reasons why he *should* buy.

9. Justify price by talking: value, quality, longer life, less service costs, prestige of ownership, etc. Bargain hunters can be handled by pointing out that inferior goods cost more in the long run. Quality brings satisfaction.

10. Make a list of standard objections and work out suitable answers to them. Make sure your reasons are *valid* when handling objections. You must be convincing.

HOW TO USE THE SUCCESS
SECRETS OF THE
PROFESSIONAL MOTIVATORS

❖

Affirmative Ideas in this Chapter

- Proof Positive These Techniques Work
- Keep A Journal And Involve Yourself In Action Thoughts
- Keep A Notebook Handy At All Times
- How To Keep Track of Important Ideas (At Odd Hours)
- Million Dollar Ideas of Raymond Loewy
- Super Salesman Turned Dream Into Millions
- Far-Sighted Ideas Man Sold New Car Concept And Made Millions
- Great Motivator Saved Nation From Collapse
- How To Become A Millionaire Salesman At 27
- She Turned Employment Agency Idea And $100 Overdraft Into Millions
- You'll Never Succeed As A Procrastinator Famous Greek Told
- Detractors Laughed But The World Chewed—And Paid Millions For It
- Stop Being A Slave To Opinions of Others—You'll Succeed Faster
- Do One Thing At A Time—Organize Advises Super Car Salesman
- Sell 365 Days A Year Advises Sales Consultant
- Top Insurance Man Writes $8 Million A Year Selling 365 Days
- Professional Advice From A Great Audience Communicator-Motivator
- Personal Integrity Paid For The House That Jack Built
- The 3 Best Money-Making Words In A Salesman's Vocabulary
- Clothing Sales Tycoon Offers 4 Success Formulas
- How To Increase Sales With Vivid Imagining Technique
- Selling Tips From A $600 A Week Car Salesman
- Success Secret of 'People Conscious' Mayor
- Secret of Billy Graham's Dynamic Motivating Ability
- An Effective Technique For Improving Sales
- How To Make Big Sales And Get Rich
- Practical Tips To Increase Sales And Commissions
- Summary of Ideas To Help You Use The Success Secrets of The Professional Motivators

12

PROOF POSITIVE THESE TECHNIQUES WORK

A book such as this is the end result of years of experience in working with others and in researching the success techniques of countless sales professionals and communication and motivation experts. In this chapter, I have assembled a number of stories concerning successful people I have known, worked with or researched. You will notice that the formulas for success presented by these master communicators have already been expressed—in one way or another—in earlier chapters. The ingredients for 'getting ahead' in life are *workable*. Others have used them and succeeded in their chosen fields and so can you.

All the basic essentials of successful salesmanship are contained in these pages. These techniques can work wonders in your life if you will accept and use them. Life rewards those who help themselves . . . *According to their deeds, accordingly he will repay.*—Isa. 58:10.

KEEP A JOURNAL AND INVOLVE YOURSELF IN ACTION THOUGHTS

Many famous writers have followed the practice of keeping a journal. It's not important that your journal be a literary masterpiece. No one has to read it but you. The purpose of keeping a record of your day-to-day thoughts, ideas and useful information is to get your consciousness engrossed in powerful thoughts. Thoughts designed to inspire you to success in your life-work.

Purchase a loose-leaf notebook and begin writing down (every day) plans for developing your career, selected thoughts and ideas on all aspects of selling and marketing and human relations. Make a note of your progress. Recording your progress is one way of strengthening your personal commitment to your aims and ideals. It will also help to discipline your pattern of thinking—keeping your mind centered on things that are important to your sales success.

KEEP A NOTEBOOK HANDY AT ALL TIMES

A former Governor-General of Australia, Lord Casey, an inveterate diarist, would like to see the practice spread. 'Keep a notebook and pencil in your pocket and write the things you want to remember to do or things that you have been told to do,' he suggests. 'I learnt this lesson when I was quite young and have practised it all my life—a most useful habit,' advises the Governor-General.

Nothing is more fleeting than a clever idea. A notebook is the place to store 'bright ideas' where they can be studied at a later date and then, if practical, used to advantage.

Keep a collection of sales strategy ideas and use them to improve your performance. Observe, listen and note ideas worthy of use. Good ideas are worth money to you if you *act* on them.

HOW TO KEEP TRACK OF IMPORTANT IDEAS (AT ODD HOURS)

Bill James, a sales professional earning $55,000 a year selling insurance in Los Angeles, told me that he uses the early hours of the morning (when he cannot sleep) to advantage. Here's his technique for keeping track of important ideas:

'I like my sales life. It takes up a lot of my thinking. I'm a poor sleeper, so instead of tossing and turning half the night, I concentrate on solving a particular problem that may have arisen during the day or I plan in my mind a sales presentation I want to give. I keep a pad and pencil alongside my bed and if I have an important idea I want to remember, I scribble down a few key words which remind me of the thought in the morning. Then I act on it.'

Use the James technique for plotting sales strategy and keeping tabs on useful ideas when they pop into your mind at odd hours of the night. Ideas are useful—but only if you put them to work.

MILLION DOLLAR IDEAS OF RAYMOND LOEWY

Industrial designer Raymond Loewy turned simple ideas into millions of dollars when he streamlined industrial and commercial products and services. His modern ideas transformed popular taste in industry and commerce by linking quality, safety, efficiency and beauty.

He decorated dugouts in World War I, streamlined railway engines, toothbrushes and automobiles. His fancy-designed Studebaker car gave it a new image of speed and elegance. His Schick double-head razor showed that even mundane items could be dressed-up and given buyer appeal.

Loewy's new methods of sales promotion and layouts for large stores won him the title of 'the great packager.' He meticulously supervized every detail from the erection of the outer walls to the careful wrapping of each product to be sold. As a forward-thinking designer, he had many imitators but few equals. His secret: *develop workable and appealing ideas and act on them.*

SUPER SALESMAN TURNED DREAM INTO MILLIONS

As a boy, Eric McIllree developed a fondness for aircraft and motor cars. He dreamed of being a part of Australia's growing transport scheme—a *big* part. His dream was formulated into a specific goal, pushed relentlessly through five failures and finally succeeded after 30 years of 'gut-tearing' frustration and hard work.

While in his teens, McIllree entered the motor wholesale business and tried to rent cars as a side-line. The venture wasn't too successful. A quick air trip from Sydney to Canberra in 1935 convinced him of the futility of business men driving long distances by car. Fly-drive was the answer, he felt. In 1938 he parked his first fleet of rental cars at Sydney airport. The venture didn't succeed.

Determination and a belief in his boyhood dream motivated him to try again in 1946. Again, the operation failed to take on. In 1954 two more attempts to introduce his 'fly-drive' idea proved unsuccessful. Finally, in 1955, he planned an 'all-out' attempt to make his idea pay off.

McIllree registered the names Hertz and Avis in Australia and then went to the US to speak to both company managements to set a deal with one. Avis was impressed with his idea of a nationwide airport tie-up and he arrived back in Australia with their deal. He gave back the Hertz name for a fee of one dollar with the proviso that the company not enter the Australian market for three years. This grace period allowed him to establish Avis free of major competition.

McIllree's success secret: *a big idea, determination to see it through and confidence in his ability to make it work.*

FAR-SIGHTED IDEAS MAN SOLD NEW CAR CONCEPT AND MADE MILLIONS

A lot of people thought Henry Ford had been in the sun 'a little too long' when he announced plans to build a great automobile priced so low it would be bought by millions of people. 'Nonsense! It can't be done,' his critics said. But Henry Ford had other ideas—big ones. And he lived to see a new production technique (designed by William Knudsen) turn out a never-ending stream of Model T's.

243

Ford wasn't wrong in his estimation of how many cars he thought he could sell. Between 1908 and 1927 the model T became one of the best selling cars in automotive history. The company sold more than 15 million of them. In 1921, the Model T represented 67 per cent of all cars built in the US.

Henry Ford ruthlessly sacked many of his key men. This and other ill-timed and emotionally-arrived-at decisions came close to undoing one of America's most powerful companies. But none will deny the Ford creative genius—the ability to inspire and gain the support of others to design and produce an outstanding automobile. The secret of Ford's power over others: *an ability to communicate ideas in a dynamic way and to incite others to peak performance in carrying them out. A man of strong vision, self confidence and initiative.*

GREAT MOTIVATOR SAVED NATION FROM COLLAPSE

Hitler was pounding London with bombs. Europe was falling to the German dictator. British morale kept sinking lower with each report of Hitler's advance. Winston Churchill, that doyen of British leaders, rallied his people with eloquent and courage-inspiring speeches. Churchill was an outstanding salesman. His ability to communicate personal concepts and motivate others to accept and act upon them is legendary. Churchill understood the *technique* of persuasion and he used it throughout his career to get his way with others. His secret: *bulldog tenacity of purpose.* Who can forget his stirring challenge to others:

'Never give in! Never give in!
Never, never, never! In nothing
great or small, large or petty—
never give in except to convictions
of honour and good sense.'

HOW TO BECOME A MILLIONAIRE SALESMAN AT 27

Young Gary's first job was as a bottle washer in a resort hotel at Surfers Paradise, Queensland. He was 17, hard working and ambitious. After working his way up to assistant manager, he decided to head for Sydney and open a carpet cleaning company.

He bought scraps of carpet from carpet layers he met on cleaning jobs and resold them. Sensing a real opportunity was at hand to establish himself in the cut-price carpet business, Gary opened his first retail shop with one roll of damaged carpet. He displayed it outside his store and sold it the same day. He bought more damaged rolls and sold them at less than half the normal cost.

Today, he sells more than $1 million worth of new and damaged carpets a year from his chain of five stores. His secret: *find a consumer need and supply it. Gamble on your own ability to succeed. Be ambitious and pursue your aims and objectives.*

244

SHE TURNED EMPLOYMENT AGENCY IDEA AND $100 OVERDRAFT INTO MILLIONS

In 1946 in London, Marjorie decided she would open an employment agency and offer *service plus* to people seeking jobs. Obtaining a $100 bank overdraft she established an employment agency bearing her name. Today, she has offices in Britain, America and Australia and her ideas and efforts have made her a millionairess.

Her success didn't arrive overnight, she encountered many setbacks. But failures to Marjorie are the very foundations on which success is built. She turned failures into successes. 'Analyze them and avoid making the same mistakes twice,' she advises. And that's the secret of Marjorie's success: *learn from failure. Never brood over it. Keep going, regardless of the adversity facing you.*

YOU'LL NEVER SUCCEED AS A PROCRASTINATOR FAMOUS GREEK TOLD

'Make a definite decision and act on it!' This advice was given to a poor Greek boy named Demosthenes who had a strong desire to be a public speaker despite the fact that he was a stammerer. His friends laughed at him for desiring such an unreachable goal. But Demosthenes acted on the advice, made a decision to become a fluent and dynamic speaker and then set about correcting his speech defect. He eventually mastered the handicap and became one of the great orators of the world.

The secret of Demosthenes success: *decide on a goal and act. Have firm belief in a successful outcome. Persist until you win.*

DETRACTORS LAUGHED BUT THE WORLD CHEWED— AND PAID MILLIONS FOR IT

Business associates laughed at the decision of William Wrigley Jr., to devote his entire business career to the manufacture and sale of inexpensive chewing gum. Wrigley knew that there was a definite market for his product and he decided he would capture it. His decision—against the advice of others—brought him financial returns of millions of dollars a year.

Wrigley's success secret: *a definite goal, the courage to decide and act.*

STOP BEING A SLAVE TO OPINIONS OF OTHERS— YOU'LL SUCCEED FASTER

You cannot hope to succeed in life if you allow others to dictate how you should think and act. Stop being a slave to other people's opinions. You may as well sign your life over to them. If your critics say, 'it can't be done,' ignore them and follow your own inner feelings and beliefs.

An Australian sales manager friend, told me that he listens to the opinions of those who offer them, smiles, thanks them and then does exactly what his inner thoughts dictate. 'If I'm wrong in making any particular decision then I don't have to spend time running around telling all those who gave me the poor advice that it was their fault.' Good thinking and a success formula worth following.

DO ONE THING AT A TIME—ORGANIZE ADVISES SUPER CAR SALESMAN

'Get organized and do one thing at a time,' is the advice of master salesman Bob Morgan. 'Correct use of time involves detailed planning of your day, your week, your month and year. The more you keep track of time, making every minute productive, the greater will be your success in selling,' he says.

Bob Morgan should know. He's been selling real estate in California for 16 years and his annual income exceeds $75,000. I've seen his daily work schedule file and it sometimes runs to two and three pages of 'things' to do and appointments to keep. Bob measures his time against successful results. He analyzes the outcome of each day and tries to improve his work system to produce better results in the shortest possible time.

Make the best use of your working time. Specify a routine group of tasks and discipline yourself to follow-through on each one. Give yourself deadlines for accomplishing each task. Unlimited opportunity is open to the salesman to serve more effectively by achieving more effective use of his time through careful planning.

SELL 365 DAYS A YEAR ADVISES SALES CONSULTANT

Charles B. Roth, an American sales consultant and author of several books on the art of selling, stresses the importance of salesmen selling 'all the time.' In his book, *Selling 365 Days A Year*,[1] Roth points out that all champion salesmen 'think' selling 365 days a year. They never miss an opportunity to close a prospect. The greater part of their day is spent selling, thinking of selling or planning sales presentations. This all-consuming interest in their career is the secret of their success.

In analyzing your future in selling, it is wise to consider assets that develop your sales ability and then acquire them as quickly as possible. Following the advice of professionals such as Charles Roth, can accelerate your advancement to the 'champion' class.

It's already been pointed out, the growing need for highly trained personable, psychology-oriented sales professionals. To this list of credentials add the Charles Roth* idea of being alert *365 days a year* to sales opportunities. When they present themselves, act on them!

TOP INSURANCE MAN WRITES $8 MILLION A YEAR SELLING 365 DAYS

Wes Wyatt's home base is Stillwater, Oklahoma, a town of 40,000, yet his insurance agency writes a total of $20 million worth of insurance a year. Wes personally writes $8 million of the total amount and credits his success to 'hard work.'

* *Selling 365 Days A Year*, Charles B. Roth. Prentice Hall, Inc.

Wes likes to set goals and achieve them as quickly as possible. This is the reason he works 16 hours a day, six days a week. 'I am able to make as much money as I am willing to work for,' he says. The secret: *a positive attitude, a desire to achieve success through hard work. Sell all the time.*

PROFESSIONAL ADVICE FROM A GREAT AUDIENCE COMMUNICATOR-MOTIVATOR

Eddie Cantor, as a young boy, used to run errands for the housewives who lived in the same block of tenements on the lower East Side of New York. The money he earned he saved for his education.

It didn't take him long to notice that the women never sent him to the shop next door but always to one several blocks distant. Eddy wondered why they patronized this particular grocer. He soon found the reason. This storekeeper always added a little extra. Instead of 12 bagels, he gave 13. Instead of six ounces of coffee, he gave seven ounces. Eddy thought the grocer was making a mistake and drew his attention to it.

The grocer told the boy that 'giving a little extra' was the secret of his success. Eddy never forgot the lesson. Years later, at the height of his theatrical career, Eddie Cantor gave a great deal of his time to charity organizations. The famous entertainer is gone now, but his good deeds live on.

Learn to 'give a little extra' both professionally and personally. The *extra* time spent with your family will give them a feeling of being wanted and loved. The *extra* help or service rendered to customers will make all the difference to your sales figures. Give—*a little extra* and often. Your life and the lives of others will be richer because of it.

PERSONAL INTEGRITY PAID FOR THE HOUSE THAT JACK BUILT

Jack Ferrie, a canny young Scotsman worked for me in Toronto for several years. He was the advertising manager of several newspapers I published. He built a reputation of absolute honesty, integrity and loyalty and it returned him respect, admiration, added income and a house he'd dreamed of owning.

Customers liked Jack because they knew they could count on him to serve their best interests. His reputation as a person of honesty motivated prospects to do business with him. Dedicated to hard work, his professional sales attributes helped to raise his weekly salary high into the three figures category. The secret of Jack's sales success: *following the habit of rendering more service, better service and honest service than he was paid to render. Showing absolute loyalty to his company.*

THE 3 BEST MONEY-MAKING WORDS IN A SALESMAN'S VOCABULARY

I worked with my friend Charles Pilleau on a specialty sales program in Los Angeles. A salesman who learned his craft in Australia, Chuck, as he likes to be called, is in his early sixties. He'd outsell two good salesmen half his age.

Chuck uses three magic words throughout his sales presentations and seldom has difficulty in closing prospects. 'I discovered, very early in my career, the three most important words in a salesman's vocabulary,' he told me. 'They are, the prospect's name, which should be liberally sprinkled throughout the presentation and "I'll help", which must be clearly stated at the beginning and throughout the sales message.'

Walk into a man's place of business and offer to help him solve his problems and he'll welcome you with open arms. Individuals spend fortunes going to other individuals seeking either personal or business help: doctors, psychiatrists, dentists, accountants, travel agents, business consultants, employment agents, plumbers, mechanics, electricians, carpenters, etc. The list is endless. Get into the business of *helping* people and let them know that you are a professional sales adviser and counselor.

Chuck makes sure he gets on a first name basis with prospects as quickly as possible. He uses charm and a sincere, friendly manner to help them solve their problems. 'The sound of a person's first name is magic to his ears and when it is used frequently throughout a conversation it cultivates a friendly atmosphere.' The secret of Charles Pilleau's sales success: *use the prospect's name frequently and tell him you're going to help him.*

CLOTHING SALES TYCOON OFFERS 4 SUCCESS FORMULAS

Sydney's exuberant entrepreneur of menswear, Reuben F. Scarf, believes a salesman's success depends on how well he *organizes his life,* his *degree of self esteem, ambition* and *love for what he is doing.* 'I have discovered, that for a man to have success, he must have self esteem, ambition and really love what he is doing,' he says.

Reuben Scarf used his four success pointers to leap-frog from small-town draper to tycoon menswear manufacturer and retailer with an annual turnover in millions. His success secret: *organize your life; raise self esteem values; have ambitious aims and objectives and love your work.*

HOW TO INCREASE SALES WITH VIVID IMAGINING TECHNIQUE

Vivid imagining is simply imagining yourself in various sales situations, then finding suitable ways to handle them (in your mind) until you are confident you can handle similar *real* situations.

Selling is a series of *situations* encountered by the buyer and the seller. If you know how to handle *typical* (sometimes difficult) customer situations then you *close* more sales.

See yourself face-to-face with the prospect and imagine him throwing strong objections against your sales points. Work out the best possible answers to them. Rehearse the entire presentation in your mind and visualize the client reacting favorably to your planned and confidently-handled presentation. Vividly imagine the prospect smiling, thanking you and signing the order form.

SELLING TIPS FROM A $600 A WEEK CAR SALESMAN

Harry J. Jones has been selling automobiles for 23 years. He's learnt a lot about customer buying motives, about communication and motivation and he's used this knowledge to raise his commission earnings from $23 a week to a present average of $600 a week. How does he sell so many cars every week? 'By knowing what *best* suits the needs of my customers and supplying it,' he told me.

'I get a lot of repeat business and a great many referrals. I make sure that I never place a customer in a car that doesn't fit his pocket book, his ego or his particular preference. I dig for that buying reason. I'm more investigator than salesman and when I get my answers, I go to work to supply the customer with an automobile I *know* will satisfy him.' Harry follows-up a couple of weeks after the sale is made to make sure the customer is pleased with the car he's bought. If any servicing difficulties arise, Harry is on the job ironing them out.

Harry J. Jones has a secret selling tip and it's this: *investigate the needs of customers and satisfy them. Follow-through after the sale has been made to ensure complete customer satisfaction.*

SUCCESS SECRET OF 'PEOPLE CONSCIOUS' MAYOR

I count Samuel Yorty in the top ten American political motivators. Having personally studied his methods of persuasion, it is easy to see why the former Los Angeles Mayor is so successful in his current law practice. His basic strategy and psychology for handling people is this: he welcomes objections; he listens carefully to them; he agrees in part with them; he attempts to find a satisfactory solution to them.

Many politicians I have met and worked for (and there have been many), have had a common failing: they talk too much and listen too little. An individual with a personal problem or complaint, wishes to register it with the proper authority and get satisfactory action to cure it. The politician (or salesman) who runs from complaints and objections, who won't listen to them and cannot be concerned with finding ways to correct them, is asking for a short-lived political (or sales) career.

I've watched Sam Yorty handle objections and make the objector feel ten feet tall. He has empathy. He gets *interested* in the attitudes, ideas, wants and needs of those he comes in contact with. I commend this practice to all salesmen. Take a genuine interest in your customers. Listen to their complaints. Make them feel 'ten feet tall.' Refrain from bruising egos. You're in the business of winning and influencing people. You've got to get things done *through* people. Remember, you're in a people business. Don't spend priceless energy in small and pointless struggles with people. Promote your personal growth by developing empathy—like people and show it. The Sam Yorty success secret: *get closer to the people who can make you a success. Spend more time listening to others so as to understand their needs. Practise good listening.*

SECRET OF BILLY GRAHAM'S DYNAMIC MOTIVATING ABILITY

Dr. Billy Graham, in my opinion, is the greatest communicator-motivator in the world today. The vast audiences he draws to hear his power-packed religious messages attests to this claim. No theatrical, sports or political identity has the charisma to attract to a single meeting, as many people as Billy Graham draws to his crusades. His speaking appeal is unrivalled.

I've watched Dr. Graham at work on the lecture platform. The 'feelings' which emanate from his entire being are 'electric'. He dramatizes his message vocally, physically and emotionally to communicate to his audiences and to motivate them to action.

During personal conversations with Billy Graham, I've noticed a holding back of this 'magic' energy. Billy knows how to *conserve energy,* to release it when and where it will count.

There's another secret to the success of Billy Graham: *he sincerely believes in everything he says.* He believes the course of an individual's life can be changed through the acceptance of the truths in the bible and he's devoted his life to spreading this belief.

Two lessons for salesmen: *check the flow of energy. Release it when it will pay-off most. Don't burn yourself out on matters of little importance.* And *believe—sincerely believe—in the message you are presenting. Be truthful and act according to the golden rule.*

AN EFFECTIVE TECHNIQUE FOR IMPROVING SALES

A young office supplies salesman approached me following a sales seminar I gave for his company. 'I am worried, my sales aren't very high and my company is considering replacing me unless I can increase business in my territory,' he told me.

I suggested that he sit quietly before retiring and repeat the following statement for approximately five minutes: 'Tomorrow I will attract more sales. Each prospect I call on will readily see the advantages of my product and buy from me.'

This statement eliminated the conflict that had blocked his progress. It engaged the support of his conscious and subconscious mind and after a few weeks, he experienced wonderful results. This young salesman now tops his weekly sales target and his sales manager is satisfied with his performance.

The secret: *unify the conscious and subconscious and indoctrinate your consciousness with thoughts of success.*

HOW TO MAKE BIG SALES AND GET RICH

Each new prospect you approach, hold the thought: 'I will assist this man to greater wealth. *His* good, will be *my* good.' Thought power is greater than any atomic power created by man. Your thoughts govern all your affairs. You cannot escape from the effects of your innermost thoughts. Your thoughts control your actions. What you decree in thought will come to pass at some time in your life. Your fortune begins with your thought. Your thought and your feeling create your destiny—your success or failure.

Let your thoughts flow from the standpoint of truth. You will rise in consciousness and enrich your life in many wonderful and profitable ways. *The key to every man is his thought,* said Emerson. The *key* to your happiness and prosperity as a sales professional is: *impregnate your subconscious with thoughts of success, wealth and creative accomplishment.*

PRACTICAL TIPS
TO INCREASE SALES AND COMMISSIONS

- Never make a statement which you do not believe to be true. BE HONEST in all your dealings with others. Do not lie.

- Develop a sales philosophy which others admire.

- If you cannot serve a customer without being rude, impatient and selfish, you have no right transacting business with him.

- Treat customers as friends, not as victims of trickery.

- Modern-day selling is highly scientific in its approach and method. Practical training in the techniques of psychological selling should be undertaken by *all* individuals desiring a place in the professional selling ranks.

- You cannot hope to make financial gain out of stupid actions. *Think* before you act and you won't regret your actions.

- Every thought you release from your mind becomes a foundation stone on which your future is built. Create strong, morally uplifting thoughts and you will build a solid career for yourself.

- You cannot get something for nothing in this life. The person who tries attracts failure.

- Even if you have a legitimate alibi to offer—don't! You'll develop the habit of making excuses and eventually convince yourself that making excuses is far easier than finding ways to succeed.

- Take pride in the things you do. Put yourself on a merit system and reward yourself for jobs well done. Give yourself something to live-up to. Set your sights high and persist until you win.

SUMMARY OF IDEAS TO HELP YOU USE THE SUCCESS SECRETS OF THE PROFESSIONAL MOTIVATORS

1. Keep a notebook and pencil handy at all times to record ideas as they 'pop' into your mind. Purchase a loose-leaf notebook and use it as a journal. Record the progress of your career.

2. Develop workable ideas and act on them. The secret of Henry Ford's success was an ability to communicate his ideas to others and then motivate them to carry them out.

3. Follow the advice of Winston Churchill: *Never give in!* Never, never, never! Gamble on your own ability to succeed.

4. Learn from your failures. Keep going, regardless of adversity. Decide on your goal and act with confidence. Remember: you must make decisions. You cannot succeed as a procrastinator.

5. Organize your day, your week, your year. Do one thing at a time. Put into practise the Charles Roth suggestion: *sell all the time.* Never miss an opportunity to close a deal.

6. Eddie Cantor took the advice of his neighborhood grocer and always gave 'a little extra' without thought of reward. Jack Ferrie followed the habit of rendering 'more service' than being paid for and greatly enhanced his selling success.

7. Charles Pilleau uses the 3 best money-making words in a salesman's vocabulary: the customer's *name* and 'I'll help!' Reuben Scarf's million dollar success is the result of: organizing his life, raising his self esteem, having ambitious objectives and loving his work.

8. Harry Jones has been selling automobiles for 23 years and he earns $600 a week by investigating and satisfying the needs of his customers.

9. Attorney and former Mayor of Los Angeles, Sam Yorty, takes a genuine interest in people. He listens to their problems and attempts to find a satisfactory solution to them. Get closer to your customers and help to solve their problems. As an adviser, it is your duty to understand the needs of your clients.

10. Unify your conscious and subconscious mind. Clear your consciousness of negative concepts. Think affirmatively! You will increase sales and commissions when you *think* wealth, *think* creative accomplishment, *think* success.

HOW TO GIVE EFFECTIVE PUBLIC SPEECHES AND GROUP PRESENTATIONS

Affirmative Ideas in this Chapter

- What Public Speaking Ability Can Achieve For You
- Get Your Message Clear
- How To Prepare A Formal Speech
- Don't Procrastinate—Get Moving And Write
- Don't Underestimate Your Audience
- Apply The AIDA Formula To Speech Making
- Keep Your Message To One Central Theme
- Shot Gun Your Message And Let Ideas Fall Where They May
- What To Do With Hands
- Gain Eye Contact And Hold It
- Make Nervousness Work For You Not Against You
- Gestures And Bodily Movements
- Ideas To Help Get Your Message Across
- Why It's Important To Sell Yourself And Your Ideas At Sales Meetings
- Effective Attitudes And Actions At Sales Meetings And Conferences
- Selling To Groups
- Identify And Tag Your Audience
- Establish A Friendly Atmosphere
- Points Worth Following
- Arrive Early And Check Your Surroundings
- Put Yourself On An Equal Footing With Your Audience
- Salesmanship Is Showmanship—Perform Dramatically
- Showman's Formula For Repeat Bookings
- The Question And Answer Period
- How To Handle Rude Interjectors
- Make Your Visual Demonstration Interesting
- Practise In Front of A Mirror And Refine Your Performance
- Summary of Ideas To Help You Give Effective Public Speeches And Group Presentations

13

WHAT PUBLIC SPEAKING ABILITY CAN ACHIEVE FOR YOU

It is generally recognized by business leaders that good oral communication is the first and foremost ability which should be developed by every individual aspiring to enter the professional selling ranks. The ability to speak effectively has a close connection with success. Oratory skill builds self confidence and involves the proficient speaker in leadership activities. Study and practise the art of public speaking. It will considerably increase your success potential.

Having performed as a professional motivational speaker for many years, I highly recommend the cultivation of an individualistic speaking style. If you're going to own *self power,* you've got to get people to *listen* to you and to *act* as you want them to act. Using a fluid inventory of phrases in a powerful way compels others to be conscious of you and to treat you with respect. Therefore, devote as much time as possible to the development of an effective, individualistic and pleasing speaking style.

The techniques presented in this chapter will be of triple value to you. They will:

1. Illustrate ways of getting others to listen and take notice of you.
2. Present formulas you may use to gather your thoughts and communicate them logically and with dramatic clarity and appeal.
3. Change the thinking and buying habits of others through a mental communion with them.

255

GET YOUR MESSAGE CLEAR

Unless you understand what you are speaking about you cannot expect your audience to get the message. Know exactly what you want to say, in what order and how you want to say it. What is the theme of your message? What proposals are you making? What do you want your audience to do at the conclusion of your speech? What decisions do you want them to make? What changes do you wish to bring about? What do you propose as a solution to the problems under discussion?

HOW TO PREPARE A FORMAL SPEECH

It is common practice with professional speakers to fully write out the message in long hand. This helps to set the *theme* firmly in the mind of the speaker. Preparation is the key: the more planning you do, the more secure you will feel at the time of the presentation. The steps to follow are:

1. *Know your subject*: research every aspect of your subject. Obtain reference books, magazine articles, newspaper clippings, etc. Become an expert on the subject of your lecture. The more you know, the easier it will be to handle questions and answers. Research takes time and is sometimes boring, but it's essential to a good speech presentation.

2. *Know your time allotment*: if you have been given 10 minutes or one hour, do not go beyond your time. Finish a few minutes under your time. You will soon lose the interest of your audience if you tax their patience. When writing your speech, time it and cut it to allow a five minute spread for audience reaction.

3. *Write it out and reduce it to cards*: write it out in long hand. Cut it to time, then type it out. Read it and make further cuts. Now reduce it to headings and important sentences you wish to quote word-for-word. Type these on 3 x 5 or 5 x 7 index cards. Write additional main points or subtopics on a separate card and keep this card handy in case you need to elaborate on them during the question and answer period.

4. *Write opening and closing sentences*: review them daily and add new thoughts or ideas as they occur to you. Your opening must be powerful: pose a question, make a statement, give an example, present an anecdote. Get the attention of your audience with an 'audience-builder' opening. Your close must offer a 'pay-off' for your audience. What are you suggesting they do? What solutions are you offering? Make your audience feel your talk is well worth listening to.

5. *Know your audience*: know who they are, what they represent, how many will be in attendance and in what age range? If possible, get to know the names of those in attendance. If appropriate, use these names during your talk.

6. *Prepare for salty questions*: prepare a list of possible questions and prepare suitable answers. Chances are you'll be asked 'curly' questions; to avoid embarrassment, you should be ready to handle them without flustering or mumbling your way through an inappropriate answer.

DON'T PROCRASTINATE—GET MOVING AND WRITE

One of the hardest things for a writer to do is to get his opening lines on paper. Make a speech prepare itself. Jot down random thoughts and then put them into sequence. Use a quote, make a statement or pose a question to 'hook' your speech to. It helps to write down a few lines describing your personal feelings on the subject to be presented. Weave a central theme out of this. Now write an opening statement and a closing statement. Drop your random thoughts between the two and you have a 'first draft' ready to be developed and polished.

Some speakers I know prepare a 10 point outline of the subject matter in terms of their own convictions. Each point is then used as a subtopic and the speech is built around the 10 subtopics.

DON'T UNDERESTIMATE YOUR AUDIENCE

Speakers too often communicate their messages at about the third-grade level. This reflects a lack of understanding of the nature of the audience. Don't talk down or above the heads of your listeners. You'll insult them and lose their interest in you and your message. Four simple rules will help you avoid this:

1. *Don't* overestimate the *knowledge* of your audience.
2. *Don't* underestimate the *intelligence* of your audience.
3. *Don't* talk to your audience as if you blame them personally for the problems you are discussing.
4. *Don't* leave your audience hanging. Offer some solution to to the problems under discussion. Make your speech 'pay-off' with a pay-off suggestion.

APPLY THE AIDA FORMULA TO SPEECH MAKING

Attention, interest, desire and *action* must be incorporated in your presentation if you desire to work scientifically at speech making. It is important to gain the attention of your audience before you proceed with your message. Get *with* your audience as quickly as possible. Communicate your personality—warmth, charm, wit—and 'sense' the reaction of the audience to you. Don't begin too 'high key' or you have little to build-up to. Start gradually, easily, naturally. When you have gained the attention of your group, swing into the main body of your message and proceed to build interest. As you build a strong rapport with your audience, create a desire within their minds to accept your points of view. Build to a climax and offer a 'pay-off', causing your audience to *act* on your suggestions.

A public lecture must not waste the time of the audience. The speaker has an obligation to his audience and it is encompassed in the following:

- TO INFORM.
- TO AROUSE INTEREST.
- TO ENTERTAIN.
- TO PROSPER.
- TO UPLIFT.
- TO BENEFIT.

KEEP YOUR MESSAGE TO ONE CENTRAL THEME

Theme your message. That is, build it around a central idea and use repetition to support your main point. State your theme early in your speech and keep restating it. Drive your points home one after another, each point supporting the last and generally backing up your main idea.

All support or subtopics must relate to your central theme. Do not stray from your main topic. Your job is not to throw your audience into confusion, it's to get them to fully understand and sympathize with your theme. As you talk to (not at) your audience, you will 'feel' their acceptance or rejection of your ideas. The more facts, good ideas, related anecdotes, stories you can use to support your central theme, the more interesting your speech will be and the more interested your audience will become.

SHOT GUN YOUR MESSAGE AND LET IDEAS FALL WHERE THEY MAY

My own personal oratory style at a public lecture is to talk on a central theme which I build into my title: *Grow Rich With Your Million Dollar Mind; Learn To Laugh and You've Got The Problem Licked; Wake Up And Live,* are a few of the titles I use. Following a dramatic or humorous opening statement I plunge right into the main body of my material and pound the audience with repetition of a dozen or so subtopics. This technique moves the speech along at a fast clip, keeps the audience mentally stimulated and holds their attention throughout the presentation.

Select your own style of approach and delivery. The important factors to remember are: you have an obligation to your audience *not* to bore them; you must communicate your message in easy-to-understand language and in such a way that your audience is moved to *act* on your suggestions.

WHAT TO DO WITH HANDS

Hands can be a problem for the nervous speaker. He doesn't quite know what to do with them. Placing them behind your back is not a good idea. It doesn't create a dynamic visual image. Place them by your side. When you feel at ease with your audience then use them, casually at first, to emphasize an important point. Don't place hands in suit pockets. Apart from creating unsightly bulges, it is indicative of your nervousness.

GAIN EYE CONTACT AND HOLD IT

Look *at* your audience, not over their heads or at their feet. In an attempt to overcome nervousness and shyness, some speakers avoid an eye-to-eye confrontation with their listeners.

When speaking to a group, looking at them is the best source of feedback. The listeners' faces will give you the information you need to adjust your delivery pace, volume and message content. You will discover whether your audience is bored, excited, antagonized or happily enjoying your message.

MAKE NERVOUSNESS WORK FOR YOU NOT AGAINST YOU

Stage nerves plague most performers. Nervousness can contribute to your performance if you do not allow it to take charge and reduce you to a shivering, knee-knocking, clammy-palmed weakling. Control nervous energy by taking charge of your thoughts and disciplining your mind to concentrate *only* on what you must say and do. Force yourself to look at your audience. Concentrate on 'winning' them. Eliminate all thoughts of a negative nature.

Take deep breaths as you rise and walk to the speakers position. Hold the thought: 'With sheer boldness, I conquer.' Let go . . . r e l a x ! And *smile*. It will help to relax your audience.

GESTURES AND BODILY MOVEMENTS

Don't use gestures and bodily movements unless you have reason to do so. Uncoordinated waving of the hands and unnecessary body movement are distracting and tend to irritate an audience.

IDEAS TO HELP GET YOUR MESSAGE ACROSS

- Fully understand your own points of view and be ready to be challenged on them.
- Use emotional appeals to sway your audience and convince them of what you are saying.
- Be credible. Don't make outlandish statements. Support your statements with proof.
- Watch for feedback signs of: boredom, antagonism, confusion, etc.
- Ask your audience to take action. Give them reasons *why* they should take action and *how* to go about it.
- Remember the value of repetition. Hold to a central theme and use subtopics or support ideas to establish your theme.
- Remember, a speech is a vehicle to communicate ideas and motivate others to action through your ideas and suggestions.
- Control (nervous) thoughts and change them to affirmative ideas. Self-motivate confidence and control.
- Speak up; enunciate and articulate so that your audience catches every word. Avoid using slang expressions, incorrect grammar.
- Develop a natural speech rhythm, a fluency of words, an expressive flow of ideas.

Gestures must be used to emphasize a particular point or to draw the eye attention of the audience to you. Bodily movements can be used to enhance your dramatic performance but they must be skilfully blended with the flow of dialogue. Gestures and bodily movements must be used to enhance your performance—not detract from it. A simple rule to follow is: if you feel uncomfortable making a movement of any kind, stop making it.

Avoid slouching against the lectern (desk, table, chair) or standing crane-like with your weight on one leg. Place feet about 18 inches apart with one foot slightly ahead of the other. Stand comfortably and well balanced. Don't stand rigidly at attention. Move the weight from one foot to the other and relax the knees to release body tension.

WHY IT'S IMPORTANT TO SELL YOURSELF AND YOUR IDEAS AT SALES MEETINGS

Sales meetings offer the alert salesman a chance to project a favorable image and to communicate his ideas to senior management who are often present. Greatly enhanced job security can result from an impressive oral and visual performance given by a salesman at a sales meeting or conference. Sales meetings give the sales manager (and other executives) an opportunity to appraise their salesmen in terms of product knowledge, general attitude, territory knowledge, projected image qualities and sales potential.

A salesman's organizational ability, self confidence level, speaking skill and his ability to communicate and motivate others via speech, dress, attitude and actions, are on display at the company sales meeting. An unfavorable impression is to be avoided at all costs.

EFFECTIVE ATTITUDES AND ACTIONS AT SALES MEETINGS AND CONFERENCES

Creating a favorable image at sales meetings, seminars and conferences is essential. Do not allow fellow salesmen to interject comments (humorous or otherwise) while you are speaking. *Keep firm control.* You cannot hope to communicate effectively to an audience of jokesters. Some salesmen approach a sales meeting with the idea of 'gagging it up'. Sales meetings are fact-finding and problem solving sessions to help improve efficiency. They should be attended with the express purpose of gaining company, product, marketing and territory information.

Avoid referring, in a disparaging way, to customers, company officials or fellow salesmen. Avoid all negatives: criticism, arguments, personality clashes, pessimism. Be a 'pepper-upper', an optimistic thinker, a speaker of affirmatives: ideas, concepts, opinions, suggestions, praise. This does not mean that you cannot disagree with the opinions or suggestions of others, but do not attack them for their views or shout them down.

Avoid referring to a fellow salesman by his first name or nickname. Use his full name: 'John Green's suggestion offers a workable solution to the problem.' A certain formality (without stuffiness) will help to uplift the general tone of the meeting. Other rules of etiquette to follow are:

- Be punctual for meetings. Arrive early.
- File reports with your sales manager at least two days prior to the meeting.
- Do not become involved in arguments or name calling.
- Come prepared with notes, specific ideas, requests and suggestions.
- Dress correctly. (Button your jacket. Keep hands out of pockets).
- Don't smoke. Eliminate annoying habits: fiddling with glasses, avoiding eye contact with audience, etc. Don't mumble.
- Stand still unless you have reason for moving.
- Carry yourself as a gentleman.
- Extend gratitude to those who have helped you.
- Don't ramble. Make your point. Don't go beyond your alloted time.

SELLING TO GROUPS

Quite often, salesmen find themselves selling to groups of buyers. The procedure of selling to a group is the same as selling to an individual. Whether it be an individual or an audience of 100, the speaker must gain *attention,* create *interest,* build a *desire* and motivate an *action.* Planning the presentation is essential. It might be useful to use graphs, charts, point of sale material, films, slides or other equipment as sales aids.

IDENTIFY AND TAG YOUR AUDIENCE

Know your audience. Pinning name tags on each buyer helps you to address individuals by name and thus 'personalize' your presentation. Gather as much information as possible: buyer's name, position, company, market he's selling to, needs, etc.

ESTABLISH A FRIENDLY ATMOSPHERE

Put your audience at ease. Avoid a too formal atmosphere. Your aim is to motivate your audience to buy. A friendly, relaxed atmosphere will help you to accomplish this aim. Introduce yourself and ask each participant to shake hands with the person sitting next to him, if the group is not from the same company.

Work with individuals within the group. Talk directly to each person. Use the person's name: 'This feature will be of particular interest to John Brown of Walker and Company and to those selling to a medium income group.'

POINTS WORTH FOLLOWING

Adjust vocal delivery to suit the conditions of the room and the size of your audience. A small room does not require the same volume of voice as a large auditorium seating hundreds of people. Never shout—*project* your voice. If using a microphone stand back from it about 12 inches to avoid 'popping.' Gauge audience reaction and adjust your performance accordingly. Eliminate word whiskers (ums and ahs). Present logical ideas in sequence, one idea building to the next. Give your audience something to 'think' about. What holds attention determines action. Involve your audience in selected ideas. Hold forth a promise that your proposal will meet one or more of their needs.

ARRIVE EARLY AND CHECK YOUR SURROUNDINGS

Arrive at your place of presentation early and familiarize yourself with the surroundings. What are your requirements: blackboard, table, lectern, special seating arrangement, microphone, electrical outlets? Give yourself plenty of time to set-up and test equipment you may wish to use. Careful preparation helps to guarantee a smooth-running show.

PUT YOURSELF ON AN EQUAL FOOTING WITH YOUR AUDIENCE

Your audience will appraise your performance in order to arrive at a decision of whether to buy or *not* to buy. Therefore, the first 90 seconds are important in establishing yourself as a distinctive personality. Raise the level of your consciousness; place a 'value' on your abilities. You have the power to conquer and win. The only defeat you will experience is the *fear* of defeat which denies you the right to perform confidently. Eliminate fear of failure. Place yourself as an 'equal' with your audience (or higher) and have faith in your power to win their confidence.

SALESMANSHIP IS SHOWMANSHIP—PERFORM DRAMATICALLY

Showmanship is the ability to present, in a dramatic and highly effective way, your product or service to a group or an individual and to generate enough 'excitement' to win orders.

It doesn't mean 'spieling' or high pressuring or jumping up and down or shouting or brow-beating a prospect or audience. Showmanship is the ability to *hold the attention* of an audience and to get them totally involved in your performance. Your presentation must deliver 'impact'. It must receive an *enthusiastic* response from your audience and capture their interest and imagination.

Watch how a professional stage performer captures attention, generates interest, builds a desire and finally 'wins' his audience. Good actors and entertainers can keep an audience of hundreds spellbound for hours. If you're a good performer you should be able to 'hold' the attention of your prospect or group of prospects for 30 minutes or so. Here's how:

- *Set* the stage.
- *Open* dramatically.
- *Hold* attention.
- *Build* interest.
- *Create* a desire for more.
- *Capture* audience imagination so they'll respond in the way you want them to respond.

SHOWMAN'S FORMULA FOR REPEAT BOOKINGS

Canadian comedy star, Jackie Kahane, told me the secret of getting an audience to request 'more'. 'Always leave 'em smiling.' I interviewed Mr. Kahane on my television Tonight Show in Sydney and he credits this formula as an extremely effective one. It's appropriate advice for all salesmen.

People love to be happy. A 'smiling' buyer is more likely to want to do business with you a second time than one you've left in a sour frame of mind. Leave a customer happy (regardless of whether he has bought from you or not). Bring a smile to his face with a clever or flattering remark: 'You've made my day, Mr. Brown. I always enjoy talking to you. You're one of my favorite customers.' Naturally, your closing remarks must be sincere. A customer can easily detect falseness. Use the Kahane technique: *leave 'em smiling.*

THE QUESTION AND ANSWER PERIOD

Having presented your message, the objective during the question and answer period is to clarify points your audience may not be clear on, to handle objections and to offer solutions to any problems presented.

Allow persons asking questions to finish without cutting them off. Make certain you fully understand questions or objections before replying to them. Keep your answers short and to the point. Ask the questioner if your answer satisfies his query. If it doesn't, clarify it before moving to the next question.

Give your answers in a cheerful, positive and confident manner. Handle objections in the same way. Be a good listener. Show respect for the other person's point of view and if necessary sympathize with his position. And remember the magic value of a smile. It works wonders when confronted by a stoney-faced audience.

HOW TO HANDLE RUDE INTERJECTORS

You may be confronted by people who will test their own power and try to reduce your level of confidence. Don't be shattered by these thoughtless, rude and ignorant individuals. Regardless of what they say, maintain your dignity and composure and face up to them. Ask, 'Did you have a question dealing with the subject under discussion or are you making a personal statement? Would you qualify it for me, please?'

Where an individual is deliberately being rude, turn to him and with politeness say, 'I'm sure your intention is not to be impolite.' And then ignore the person and continue with your message. Don't allow your audience to gain sympathy for the person interjecting. *You* must be the one to gain the sympathy of your audience. Be polite and charming. Retain control. Charm of manner has won many a battle.

MAKE YOUR VISUAL DEMONSTRATION INTERESTING

The objective of a visual demonstration is to show what the product can do—to explain its function and point out its benefits. Begin by telling your audience what you intend to show them before actually demonstrating it. Keep this brief. Use demonstration aids or visual sales tools to retain the interest of your audience. If possible, recruit members of your audience to hold the product or to test it. The more audience involvement you foster, the more your prospects are likely to remember product or service facts.

When demonstrating the product, don't talk benefits, *show them*. Point them out one by one. Uses, features and benefits, when shown, greatly increase buyer receptivity. Your audience can actually *see* the benefits with their own eyes and there can be no doubt that the claims you are making for your product are accurate. *Seeing is believing.*

PRACTISE IN FRONT OF A MIRROR AND REFINE YOUR PERFORMANCE

Set up your product and display material on a table in front of a large mirror and practise your demonstration. Enlist the aid of a member of your family or a friend to ask questions and present objections. Refine your performance. Get it flowing smoothly. Remember your basic aims:

● To *communicate* your ideas effectively and persuasively.

● To *show* rather than to talk about benefits.

● To *clarify* questions and handle objections to the satisfaction of the audience.

SUMMARY OF IDEAS TO HELP YOU GIVE EFFECTIVE PUBLIC SPEECHES AND GROUP PRESENTATIONS

1. Oral communication is necessary to a salesman's success. Oratory skill builds self confidence and involves the proficient speaker in leadership activities. Study public speaking techniques and you will increase your success potential.

2. Make sure *you* understand the message you are to give to others. What do you want to convey and how will you convey it to bring the response you seek?

3. Carefully prepare your speech. Know your subject. Know your surroundings. Anticipate likely questions and prepare suitable answers. Write your opening and closing sentences. Add new thoughts and ideas each day.

4. Use the AIDA formula to establish a rapport with your audience. Don't underestimate their intelligence or over-estimate their knowledge of the subject under discussion.

5. Keep your message to a central theme and add subtopics to support your central idea. Use facts, anecdotes, examples, personal stories to make your presentation interesting. You have an obligation not to bore your audience.

6. Stage nerves plague the best performers. Discipline your thoughts and *concentrate* on delivering your message. Let go . . . relax! And smile. It will help to relax your audience.

7. Don't use gestures and bodily movements unless you have reason to do so. Keep hands out of pockets. Let them hang loosely and comfortably at your sides. Retain eye contact with your audience.

8. Sales meetings offer the alert salesman an opportunity to project a favorable image and to communicate his ideas to senior management who are sometimes present. Be punctual for meetings. File reports with your sales manager at least two days prior to the meeting. Dress correctly. Speak clearly. Keep your message brief. Present it with enthusiasm.

9. Group sales presentations aren't as difficult as you might imagine. Know your audience. 'Tag' them so you can refer to individuals by name. Establish a friendly atmosphere—an informal one. Talk directly *to* your audience, not *at* them. Adjust your performance to suit the room and the size of the audience. Put yourself on an equal footing with those present. Use showmanship to present a dramatic and interesting story. Don't spiel or shout your message. Watch for valuable feedback information.

10. When a member of your audience is deliberately being rude, gain the sympathy of your audience. Be polite, charming and retain control of the situation. Answer questions in a cheerful and positive manner.

11. Visually demonstrate your product. Show *how* it works. Describe and demonstrate plus factors that make your product worthy of purchase. *Seeing is believing.*

HOW TO PSYCHOLOGICALLY HANDLE CONSUMERS IN THE RETAIL SALES FIELD

FORMULA

14

Affirmative Ideas in this Chapter

- The Changing Face of Retailing
- From Australia To Spain The Methods of Retail Marketing Are Similar
- A New Approach To Consumer Selling Attitudes
- The Role of The Retail Salesperson
- The Retail Seller Characteristics
- If You Can't Help Don't Hinder
- The Art of Friendly Persuasion
- Apply Standard Sales Techniques To Retail Selling
- Greeting The Customer
- Your Personality Is The Key To Your Success
- Leave Your Personal Problems At Home
- Advice of Famous Psychologist On Balanced Human Relationships
- The Retail Sales Presentation—Clarify The Situation
- Building Interest
- Creating Desire
- Closing The Sale
- Handling Complaints And Exchanges
- Dealing With The Slow Customer
- Selling Substitute Brands
- How To Trade-Up For A Larger Sales Volume
- Study Personality Types
- Don't Take Customers' Product Knowledge For Granted
- Know Your Merchandise
- Be Aware of Store Promotions And Advertising
- Uphold Your Store Policy And Image
- Retail Sales Ability Chart
- Summary of Ideas To Help You Psychologically Handle Consumers In The Retail Sales Field

14

THE CHANGING FACE OF RETAILING

The first retail traders were small shop owners who specialized in certain lines or carried a variety of goods such as hardware lines, eating utensils, food items, clothing, etc. Department stores came into being in Europe during the early 1800's. Since that time, the face of retailing has changed drastically. New sales and marketing methods have been developed, new packaging and displaying of merchandise have been glamorized and the actual sales techniques of sales clerks geared to 'psychologically' deal with the new breed of consumer.

Products themselves have undergone drastic changes. New items appear in showrooms and on store shelves every day, replacing outmoded ones. Examples include: automatic washing machines, dishwashers, television sets and recorders, electric toothbrushes, razors, typewriters, calculators, carving knives, coffee makers, blankets and an endless list of other innovations for the consumer.

New types of retailers have sprung up: chain stores, supermarkets, self-serve stores, fast-food outlets, party plan merchandisers, franchise-operated outlets, mail order distributors, etc. Huge suburban shopping complexes are challenging the downtown storekeepers for a slice of the consumer dollar. Millions of dollars a year are spent by manufacturers and retailers to advertise and attract a buying-conscious public.

Manufacturing, marketing, retailing innovations (for the most part) have helped *change* the buying patterns of millions of peoples around the world. People today *think* differently, *act* differently, *dress* dif-

269

ferently and *spend* differently to those of 30 years ago. It's an ever-changing market place.

FROM AUSTRALIA TO SPAIN THE METHODS OF RETAIL MARKETING ARE SIMILAR

During a trip to 14 countries and 33 major cities recently, I couldn't help but notice a sameness of sales and marketing procedures in all but two of the cities visited (Istanbul and Tangier). In Melbourne, Los Angeles, Toronto, London, Paris, Madrid, Barcelona, Rome, Zurich, Geneva, Tokyo, Nice, Cannes and a host of other cities, retailers are selling internationally known brands of merchandise. The techniques used to promote, display and market goods are remarkably similar.

Chain-stores have sprung up at an amazing rate throughout the world. Supermarkets, self-serve stores, franchise outlets are evident everywhere. Giant department stores in London, Paris, Los Angeles, Sydney, Rome, Madrid, Geneva, have a *sameness* about them. Only the languages and accents are different.

Galeries Lafayette in Paris, El Coite Ingles in Madrid, Harrods and Selfridges in London, Eatons and Simpsons in Toronto, Broadway Stores in Los Angeles, David Jones' in Sydney, Myers in Melbourne have much in common: retail volumes run into millions, goods are attractively packaged and displayed, a wider variety of merchandise is offered, an extended range of imported goods is available and *all* use sophisticated promotional techniques to entice consumers into their stores.

A NEW APPROACH TO CONSUMER SELLING ATTITUDES

The one aspect of retailing which hasn't changed much over the years is the attitude of *some* sales individuals. Lack of product knowledge, customer disinterest, slow and impersonal service, cases of abruptness and discourtesy cost retail managements millions of dollars each year in lost business. Staff trainers do their best to eliminate such attitudes and actions, however, some people lack the *desire* to change their ways.

Change is the key word in all areas of retail selling and marketing today. The population explosion, rapid transport systems, faster and better communication links, a youth-oriented market and space-age products are dictating a new approach to consumer selling methods. Retail sales personnel must be better educated, more product-oriented, give more personable and personalized service, improve their appearance and know how to *psychologically* sell goods to customers. This new breed of retail salesperson is sought by store managements everywhere.

THE ROLE OF THE RETAIL SALESPERSON

The inside salesperson's role in selling is changing from that of a sales clerk handling money and packaging customers' goods, to a vital member of a marketing-management team; a team that begins its planning with customers' *needs* in mind. Fair value, helpful service, honest trading practices have been catchwords in retail selling for years. Today, consumers are demanding more than 'lip service' to these offers—they want *assurances* that they are part of every retailer's policy.

The modern-day retail salesperson must act as a professional consultant to his customers. He must be aware of how they feel toward the merchandise offered, why they require certain goods and services, what objections they have toward them. This knowledge and the expert use of it, allows the seller to speak the buyer's language and thus places him in a position to efficiently *serve* and *satisfy* the buyer's needs.

THE RETAIL SELLER CHARACTERISTICS

If you are really anxious to get ahead in retail selling (move into a management position), you can and you will if you put forth the necessary effort to develop the characteristics listed. They are:

Ambitious	Personable
Dependable	Loyal
Sincere	Helpful
Thorough	Knowledgeable
Tactful	Courteous
Cheerful	Cooperative
Understanding	Patient
Uncomplaining	Trustworthy
Anxious to improve	Realistic attitudes
Hard worker	Effective persuader
Pleasant communicator	Tolerant listener
Poised and self-assured	Memory for details and faces

IF YOU CAN'T HELP DON'T HINDER

If you cannot satisfy the needs of a customer still give him the same attention you extend to a buyer. After all, that same customer may return tomorrow or next week and buy; unless of course, you've been rude, abrupt or disinterested in him during his first visit.

A salesperson's attitude and manner go a long way toward building customer goodwill. Always be motivated by a desire to *help* others. Do not allow yourself to be drawn into heated arguments, regardless of who is at fault. Arguing will not solve an irate customer's problem. Note the philosophy of Voltaire on this subject: *We cannot always oblige, but we can always speak obligingly.*

THE ART OF FRIENDLY PERSUASION

The art of persuasion (motivation) is closely related to getting along with people. Customers will not buy from a salesperson who is unfriendly, ill-mannered or disinterested in offering friendly service.

271

They *will* buy from a person who shows genuine interest in servicing their needs, who approaches with a warm smile, a charming and polite manner.

Persuasion is at the heart of decision making. Regardless of how independent of thought a person is, he is susceptible to the gentle and friendly art of persuasion. The inside salesperson must develop the ability to communicate and *persuade*. In many instances, customers look to the salesperson to make a decision on their behalf. If this is not done, the customer decides *against* making a purchase and leaves to buy from another store. The inside seller must be aware of this type of buyer and act accordingly.

The art of persuasion does not mean pressuring customers to buy. Distasteful selling methods are not condoned by responsible retail managements. The salesperson desiring to succeed in retail selling is faced with the challenge of being able to persuade customers to buy without undue pressure being applied. A customer-oriented problem solver who has a sincere desire to serve and to please customers, will avoid falling into the trap of 'slick' selling.

The word *persuade* implies an *influencing* of a person to an action or belief by an overt appeal to his reason or emotions; a subtle leading to a course of action so that the decision seems finally to come from him (her).

APPLY STANDARD SALES TECHNIQUES TO RETAIL SELLING

The same techniques that specialty (outside) salesmen use apply to retail (inside) salespeople. The major difference between these two classifications is that the retail seller works indoors where the customer comes to him, whereas company sales representatives go outside to call on prospects. The fundamental principles of salesmanship apply to all fields of selling. The AIDA formula should be used as the basic structure of the presentation. The approach, actual body of the presentation and the close are used to firmly establish a rapport with the customer and to effectively communicate the sales message. The ideal presentation should follow the concept that your purpose is to service the needs of customers and sell goods for your store.

The four phases of retail selling are:

1. The customer approach (greeting).

2. Qualification of buyer's need.

3. Establishment of buying motive(s).

4. Sales message including point system supporting buying motive(s).

GREETING THE CUSTOMER

Your first job is to sell yourself. Create a pleasant impression by smiling, quietly asking the prospect if you can be of service to him (her). The warmth of your smile and sincere opening remarks help to overcome the customer's fear of being sold something he does not want. You can do much to relax the mind of the customer by your friendly approach.

Rudeness or abruptness on your part is a barrier to establishing a rapport with customers. Ask questions to discover the prospective customer's buying motive.

Three standard opening remarks are:

1. 'Good morning (afternoon) madam (sir). May I help you?

2. 'Hello. May I be of service?'

3. 'Good morning (afternoon) my name is Miss Simpson. I'd like to be of service. Is there something I can show you?'

When greeting a customer an important point to remember is this: it's not *what* you say, but *how* you say it that counts. Your attitude toward your customer can be 'sensed' and if the customer feels that you are not sincere in your greeting or desire to be of service, you will have difficulty establishing a suitable rapport.

YOUR PERSONALITY IS THE KEY TO YOUR SUCCESS

If your personality is agreeable you will find it *easier* to communicate your message to people and *easier* to persuade them to act on it. A friendly attitude toward those you must do business with is a key factor in determining the degree of success you will have with them. The right attitude (affirmative) is a strong motivating force within itself. Correct attitude breeds correct action. Correct attitude and action attracts success.

Your personality is a reflection of your inner thoughts and feelings. You express your affirmative or negative state of mind through your eyes, the muscles of your face, your posture, your walk, your handshake, your voice quality. A bright, sparkling, enthusiastic and happy personality is a product of a bright, sparkling, enthusiastic and happy state of mind. Change your (negative) attitudes and you'll change your (negative) personality. You'll win the applause of customers and put yourself in line for promotion.

LEAVE YOUR PERSONAL PROBLEMS AT HOME

People have problems, but salespeople in particular cannot afford to let them intrude into a sales situation. Change negative attitudes before greeting a customer. When you're serving a customer your personality is on display. A negative personality works against you.

Cleanse your consciousness and discipline your thinking and feeling. Project happy thoughts and peaceful feelings. A smile will do much to make your day an easier and happier one—you'll get along *better* with people. Smile—you'll attract happy smiling customers—*birds of a feather flock together.*

ADVICE OF FAMOUS PSYCHOLOGIST ON BALANCED HUMAN RELATIONSHIPS

William James, the father of American psychology, said: 'The greatest discovery in my generation is that human beings can change their lives by changing their attitudes of mind.' During his time, James taught the principle of adjusting mental attitudes to correspond with the life-style desired. Personality development, career success, health and happiness, better human relationships are possible when you feed your subconscious mind with concepts of harmony, joy, beauty, power, enthusiasm and success.

The salesperson must learn to get along with *all* types of people. Harmonious human relationships are an end result of being able to get along with yourself. If you are emotionally upset by personal problems, unable to function in a calm and rational manner, then busy your mind with happy thoughts.

THE RETAIL SALES PRESENTATION—CLARIFY THE SITUATION

Many retail customers are vague as to what they actually want. If you find yourself up against a 'vague' customer, ask questions to clarify the situation. Ask 'clarification' questions such as:

'Are you buying this for yourself or another?'
'Is there a particular color you have in mind?'
'Are you familiar with the various brand names?'
'What price bracket do you wish to stay within?'
'Is quality an important factor?'
'Did you notice this particular item in our advertising?'
'Is this the style you are considering?'
'Do you know your exact size?'
'Would you like me to measure your size?'
'Are you thinking of matching this item with anything else?'
'Is appearance or comfort the major factor?'

BUILDING INTEREST

When you have established the *exact* need of the customer through clarification questioning, your next move is to quickly satisfy the need. Build interest in the item under inspection by placing the customer 'in the product picture'—establishing *self* interest. Use interest-building sentences such as:

'This is the latest design and it would look very smart on you.'
'Can you image this new razor cutting your shaving time by a third?'
'You will have many enjoyable weekends with this fast runabout.'
'The mirror will reflect how perfect this suit looks on you, sir.'
'This stove fulfills all your cooking requirements. I'm sure you see that it will compliment your kitchen.'
'Excuse me for saying so, but your choice of color is excellent. It enhances your complexion.'

Hold the interest of your customer by further questioning and getting him to agree with your point building as you elaborate on the product's plus factors. Remember: supply plus factors that act as incentives to the buying motive. Never attempt to indoctrinate a customer with points that are of little interest to him. To do this is to build a case *against* yourself.

CREATING DESIRE

With maximum interest being held, create a definite desire for the item under consideration by allowing the customer to see it at close range, to touch it, try it and evaluate it. Help the customer to understand how the product works, what it can do. Convince him that this is the answer to his needs. Confidently advise him that this item will bring the satisfaction he desires. Stress the value of the item and point out its long life expectancy, its guarantee and service advantages. Point out the features, show the advantages and stress the benefits.

CLOSING THE SALE

When you 'sense' the precise psychological time to close the sale, stop showing the merchandise and go into a trial close. Use trial-close questions:

'I can see you favor the green over the yellow, is that so?'
'Will this be cash or charge?'
'Would you like us to deliver the item?'
'We could arrange credit for you.'
'It would be wise to purchase now, stocks are low.'
'This new item is imported and there could be a later price increase.'
'I know you'll be happy with it. Shall I have it wrapped?'
'A very wise choice, madam (sir). I'll write a receipt for you.'
'A small deposit would hold it or would you rather buy it today?'

HANDLING COMPLAINTS AND EXCHANGES

The same principles of objection handling discussed in chapter 11 apply to retail selling. The rule is to sincerely try to help the customer solve his problem. Do not irritate the customer by attempting to prove him wrong. The success of your store depends on satisfied, *repeat* customers.

Exchanges of merchandise should be handled according to store policy. Most stores have return-exchange departments and this removes the salesperson from possible embarrassing situations. Here are several steps which can be taken to handle possible customer complaints.

1. Ask the customer to give you all details of the complaint.

2. Listen to the complaint without interrupting the customer.

3. Acknowledge the customer's right to complain.

4. Repeat the complaint to the customer to make sure you have the details right.

5. If the complaint is justified, acknowledge this and take steps to correct it. If the customer is wrong, do not attempt to prove it. Ask the customer, in view of the circumstances, what he would like you to do. If necessary call your immediate superior for a ruling.

DEALING WITH THE SLOW CUSTOMER

Not all customers make snap judgements when making purchases. Some are slow at making a purchasing decision and ask questions with annoying repetition. To deal with this type of customer try these steps:

1. Be patient. Do not lose self control. Smile—you'll close the sale, eventually.

2. Reduce the number of alternatives by showing one or two models or colors. The greater the number of items to choose from, the longer and more confusing the decision-making process will be.

3. Move the customer along one step at a time. Make sure that he fully understands each point before moving on to the next or he'll want to go back and clarify earlier points.

4. Keep firing 'close' questions at him.

5. You may have to make a decision for him. If so, be positive: 'This model fits your requirements, Mr. Jones. I'll have it packed for you.'

SELLING SUBSTITUTE BRANDS

Many customers will resent your mentioning a substitute brand if you are out-of-stock of the brand requested. Offer to order the requested brand and then add: 'We do have an excellent alternative to the brand you requested, I'd like to show you its outstanding advantages.'

Place the substitute item before the customer as quickly as possible and explain its features. If there is a definite price advantage point this out. Eliminate any impression that you are trying to pressure the prospect into buying the item because it is the only one you stock. Your product knowledge and sales ability will often lead the customer to accept your suggestion of another brand and he will be quite happy doing so. Your aim is to please and satisfy. You, as the salesperson, are the expert. Play your role confidently and with a desire to help your customer receive the best possible value. You will build a steady-stream of *repeat* customers if you follow this sales philosophy.

HOW TO TRADE-UP FOR A LARGER SALES VOLUME

Begin your demonstration using a medium price item. This enables you to introduce a higher price item as a comparison and then show (as a third comparison) a low price model. Point out the additional benefits of the top-of-the-line model and the disadvantages of the low price unit. Get the customer to agree that the best and most satisfactory purchase would be the unit costing more, but *worth* more because it has the in-built features to accomplish more. Always talk quality—*sell* quality and value.

If a customer has his mind set on a low cost item, he will make this plain. Without undue 'pressure' suggest the customer look at the features of the *new* and *better-built,* value-for-money unit. Most people will buy quality once they have been given a reason to do so and can see the obvious advantages.

STUDY PERSONALITY TYPES

Study the 'personality type' of each customer. What type of person is he (she)? What are his (her) dislikes? What approach will get through to this customer?

Analyze the customer's manner of speaking, degree of self confidence, attitude, dress and grooming. The salesperson must be ready to handle any one of a number of personality types. The first step is to adjust your own manner to that of the prospect (unless the prospect's manner is negative). Train yourself to make accurate character and personality assessments of people.

DON'T TAKE CUSTOMERS' PRODUCT KNOWLEDGE FOR GRANTED

Some salespersons expect customers to know all there is to know about the products they desire to buy. This is an unrealistic attitude to adopt and one that causes a great deal of customer irritation. Other 'assumptions' on the part of untrained, unprofessional retail salespersons are:

- The customer knows what he wants. (*Not always.* Some have a vague idea and need to be made aware of their wants by the salesperson).

- The customer knows the difference between quality and inferior workmanship. (*Wrong.* Not *all* people can immediately tell the difference. The salesperson must point out and sell quality features).

- A customer bought it once, he'll buy it again. (*Wrong.* He bought it once and may never buy it again because it didn't do what it was supposed to do. Make sure you match the product to the customer's need).

- The customer will always buy the best and most expensive. (*Wrong.* Many customers will buy on price alone. They have to be *sold* on expensive features. They must be *convinced* that the extra charge is real value for money and better in the long run).

KNOW YOUR MERCHANDISE

Once you have been assigned to a particular department, take steps to familiarize yourself with the merchandise you will be selling. This will take many hours of homework. Select brochures, service manuals or company promotion materials on each item and study them. Evenings and weekends are best suited to study as you will be free from distractions. Purchase a loose-leaf notebook and make your own set of notes on each item: price, size, color range, product plus factors (benefits), etc. Know the advantages of one item over another. Pick out the important points of each item. Speak to the various company sales representatives when they visit the buyer of your department. Discuss the various merits of each item with your department head. Customers will expect you to know *all* there is to know about the items you sell.

There are three types of benefits associated with products. They are:

1. *Hidden benefits*: durability, value for money, special working parts, etc.

2. *Obvious benefits*: beauty, advantages of use, special packaging, guarantee, etc.

3. *Exclusive benefits*: patented working parts, features not used on competitor products, etc.

BE AWARE OF STORE PROMOTIONS AND ADVERTISING

Always read your store advertisements. If tearsheets aren't available, cut the advertisement from the newspaper and keep it for reference. You may find that some customers haven't read the ads and are not aware of specials being offered. Additional sales often can be made by telling customers of 'today's special' and alerting them to the benefits of buying 'today'.

I've encountered store employees who were unaware of special promotions planned until the actual day of performance. Having conducted many in-store promotions as well as staff training sessions, I have discovered that the problem arises through a communication break-down between management and sales staff. Quite often, I've arrived at a large department store to be greeted with: 'Oh, yes, it was scheduled for today. I'd forgotten.'

A close liaison with the advertising department will put you in the picture so to speak of upcoming store promotions and special advertising campaigns.

UPHOLD YOUR STORE POLICY AND IMAGE

The retail salesperson has an important duty to perform and a large responsibility on his shoulders. Customers look on the salesperson as representing store policy and image. Regardless of how attractive a store is, how smartly its merchandise is displayed, it will not enjoy maximum success unless its sales staff are attentive, professional in attitude, smartly dressed and well groomed, courteous and helpful.

Think of the 'image' management is building. Endorse it and help to build it. Your responsibility as a professional salesperson is to treat your customers as you would wish to be treated were the situation reversed.

RETAIL SALES ABILITY CHART

QUESTION	YOUR ANSWER	CORRECT ANSWER
1. Your customer asks you a question and you are not sure of the answer. What would you do?		Be honest. Say, 'I haven't the answer. If you'll wait a moment, I'll ask my section manager.'
2. When your customer has a complaint do you attempt to interrupt and make a quick decision to get him out of the store?		Never. Hear the customer out. You cannot make any rational decision until you know the full complaint.
3. Do you use the term 'I think this will fit your need?'		Do not use 'negatives' (I think) in your sales message. You must *know*. You're being paid to know. *'This is ideal for your purpose'* is positive.
4. When explaining a new product do you take the customer along step by step or miss points because you think he's getting the message?		Adjust your talking speed and take each point step-by-step. Make sure your customer understands each point before moving on to the next.
5. Is it better to talk or listen when dealing with a snap decision buyer?		Listen! He'll tell you exactly what he wants and you'll save his and your time.
6. If a customer doesn't buy and says he'll 'shop around' do you thank him and leave it at that, hoping he'll return?		Thank him, yes. But give him your card and tell him you'll place the item aside and if he doesn't find what he's looking for elsewhere, he'll be sure of this item on his return.
7. Are certain words important to your sales message or is it O.K. to describe an item as best as you can?		Descriptive words which add emotional appeal and positive sounding words are best.
8. Is it better to let the customer decide on a decision to buy or should that be done by the salesperson?		Lead the customer to a buying decision by asking close questions. Take the initiative.

SUMMARY OF IDEAS TO HELP YOU PSYCHO-LOGICALLY HANDLE CONSUMERS IN THE RETAIL SALES FIELD

1. Consumer buying patterns are constantly changing. Study buying habits and adjust to changes.

2. Change is the key word in all areas of retail selling. The salesperson's attitude must also change. Improve attitudes and actions. Learn to deal with customers psychologically —to interpret their motives and to satisfy their needs.

3. The art of friendly persuasion (motivation) is the secret of selling success. Develop the ability to *influence* the buying decisions of your customers. Persuade them—never pressure them into buying.

4. Apply the AIDA formula to retail selling. Listen to customers' needs. Set about satisfying their needs.

5. Get your personality shining. Leave your problems at home. Follow the advice of the late William James: adjust your attitudes to correspond with the life-style you want. Remember: *like attracts like*. An affirmative attitude attracts affirmative conditions.

6. Ask the customer 'clarifying' questions. The more information you have, the more efficiently you can service the wants of the buyer.

7. Satisfied customers are nearly always repeat customers. If you have complaints to handle, don't irritate customers by arguing with them. Call your superior if you cannot solve the problem yourself.

7a. Sell substitute items if you are not carrying the item requested. 'Trade-up' by demonstrating a medium price item, then introducing a higher price item as a comparison of value.

8. Study personality types. Get to know how to effectively deal with each type. Don't take customers' product knowledge for granted. YOU are the expert on product benefits and customers will rely on you for advice.

9. Be aware of store promotions and advertising specials. Keep a copy of advertisements handy and refer to them when serving customers. Check with your department supervisor and with the store advertising department to learn of special promotions. Mention upcoming promotions to your customers.

10. Uphold your store policy and image. Your store needs your support to promote a successful image with the public.

THE ROLE OF THE
SALES MANAGER

FORMULA

15

Affirmative Ideas in this Chapter

- The Leadership Process
- Professional Skills Required of The Sales Manager
- Explore Your Role As A Sales Manager
- Change The Concept of The Role You Are Playing
- Set Personal Standards And Stick To Them
- 3 Steps To Advancement
- How To Win The Support of Subordinates
- Applying The 5 Basic Management Functions
- How To Make Effective Use of Your Time As A Manager
- Successful Formulas To Increase Your Skills As A Sales Manager
- How Customer Relations Conscious Are You?
- Business Letter Writing
- Punctuation
- Letter Writing Points To Follow
- Develop A Personal Writing Style
- For Reference And Accuracy in Writing
- Letter Forms
- Eliminate These Bridging Cliches
- Sample: Letter Layout—Modified Noma Form
- The Purpose of Sales Meetings
- Best Times And Venues For Sales Meetings
- Guest Speakers
- Inviting Participation
- The Think Tank
- Keep A Record of Think Tank Sessions
- Limit The Size of Think Tank Groups
- Establish A Pressure-Free Environmental Climate
- Develop Lateral Thinking Habits
- Training Is Important To The Success of A Sales Team
- Leave Training To The Professionals
- Special Skills Development
- Explore New Ways of Doing Things Advises Canadian Trainer
- Former Insurance Salesman Explores New Teaching Methods
- Use The Ogden Formulas For Greater Success
- How To Hire Sales Staff And Profit By It
- Interview Questions Worth Asking
- The Reasons For High Staff Turnover
- How To Spot Time Wasters
- Duties-Functions-Characteristics of The Sales Manager
- Summary of Ideas To Help You Become An Effective Sales Manager

15

THE LEADERSHIP PROCESS

A sales manager must have the ability to recruit, organize and motivate a successful sales team. He must determine the best qualities of each recruit and then give each one the opportunity to maximize those qualities for the benefit of the company. Through formal training sessions, personal coaching and persuasion, the sales manager will mold his salesmen into a dynamic team carrying out company policy and achieving sales targets.

No sales manager should limit anyone's opportunities for growth by arbitrarily deciding that some men have the capacity to grow while others have not. He must learn to develop *all* men under him to the degree of their individual capacity. All men have the capacity to grow to some degree if they are encouraged to develop and exploit those qualities in which they are initially strong.

PROFESSIONAL SKILLS REQUIRED OF THE SALES MANAGER

Today's sales manager is a highly skilled communicator-motivator very much concerned with planning, organizing, problem-solving, sales target and goals-setting. He must be a responsible individual capable of leading others to outstanding achievement.

The sales manager is judged on the sales figures he can generate. Superiors also judge him on the soundness of his decisions, the manner in which he handles his sales team, his dependability, organizational ability, appearance, manner of speaking and accuracy of sales forecasting. Punctuality, trustworthiness and observance of company policy are other evaluations made by senior management of the sales manager.

EXPLORE YOUR ROLE AS A SALES MANAGER

Can you communicate? Do you *really* work hard? Can you adapt to change? Can you tell what's important? Are you respected as a leader by your sales team? Do you know what your management obligations are? These and other important job qualification questions need analyzing and answering by every sales manager desiring to function effectively, dynamically and profitably.

A sales manager must understand the functions of retailing, marketing, advertising, packaging, the science of buying, pricing strategy and territory planning and development. He must be concerned with the financial aspect of his company's operations. The balance sheet, the profit and loss statement, the advertising appropriation, the production budget and the sales budget must be analyzed to gain an overall view of his company's progress.

The sales budget should come under close scrutiny of the sales manager. He must check all data that goes into its preparation. To do this, he will require some knowledge of finance and a great deal of judgement regarding sales potential for the budget period.

One of the obligations of the sales manager is to regard every man under him as a potential sales manager. This obligation is a challenge as it tests his judgement of human beings and his unselfish concern for the advancement of those who earn it.

He is a leader and a friend to his sales staff. He guides and motivates them to reach sales targets. He is a person of moral courage, honest business practices and personal integrity. He has a pleasant personality, enthusiasm for his work and a thorough knowledge of his company's products and policies.

CHANGE THE CONCEPT OF THE ROLE YOU ARE PLAYING

Sales managers can reach a higher level of job satisfaction and increase effectiveness at the same time by changing the concept of the role they play.

See your job, not as managing a department or type of business, but as managing *people*. You are in a people business and people are necessary to the success of your business. The importance of getting along with others and getting them to do the job that has to be done should be noted and *set* as a number one aim. The more effectively you can motivate subordinates to perform as you want them to perform, the more successful you, your department and your company can become. And the greater the job satisfaction will be of those participating.

SET PERSONAL STANDARDS AND STICK TO THEM

The sales manager must be regarded as a 'pro' by his sales team. Being a 'professional' in a management position is more than doing only what you are being paid to do. Professionalism is a state of mind. A way of thinking and acting that clearly shows the professional as an individual who isn't afraid to make decisions, to take on extra responsibility, to get tough when the situation demands it and to offer praise when warranted.

A professional sales manager is a leader—a *true* leader. He is a person with a strong sense of morality. He does not abuse his authority. He is scrupulously honest in all of his business and personal dealings. His word is his bond. Honesty and integrity are a way of life for the 'pro' manager. He is aggressive, ambitious, but not abrasive, hard to get along with or dogmatic in his viewpoints. He knows that guesswork is outdated when it comes to solving problems and making important decisions. He applies reason, calls for the facts, weighs the pros and cons and makes judgements after carefully considering *all* angles of the problem.

3 STEPS TO ADVANCEMENT

Regardless of how excellent a performer you are as a sales manager, you will not be in line for advancement unless your superiors like you. Dedicated service, personal efficiency and good relationships with senior executives (and subordinates) are almost a *guarantee* of job advancement.

The sales manager who works at establishing good subordinate-superior relationships takes a positive step forward in personal efficiency and job satisfaction. The necessary elements to establish with others are:

1. MUTUAL APPROVAL.

2. MUTUAL RESPECT.

3. MUTUAL MOTIVATION.

HOW TO WIN THE SUPPORT OF SUBORDINATES

● Give subordinates every opportunity to develop their own potential.

● Allow subordinates the opportunity of planning and deciding on courses of action to take. Get them involved in decision making.

● Make them feel important. Give them a sense of job security.

● Invite them to present new ideas. Give them credit for their ideas.

APPLYING THE 5 BASIC MANAGEMENT FUNCTIONS

The basis of sound management is the application of positive principles. The sales manager must be profit-oriented in his thinking. He must avoid making hasty, irrational and unproductive decisions.

He must concentrate his energies on the accomplishment of planned goals. Management success is 90 per cent system—made up of:

1. A detailed analysis of the job to be done.
2. Objectives set and decisions made.
3. An action plan to accomplish objectives (eliminating obsolete methods).
4. Delegation of jobs to be completed by subordinates.
5. Supervision and follow-through to see that plans are accomplished.

HOW TO MAKE EFFECTIVE USE OF YOUR TIME AS A MANAGER

Success, in many cases, is a direct result of how well an individual uses his time. Many sales managers never overcome the frustrating thought that they have more work than they can efficiently handle or have time to accomplish.

Personal planning is the answer—learning how to get the *most* out of a work day regardless of the time spent. Here are several suggestions for making maximum use of your time:

- Plan (on paper) each day's activities. Stick to your plan.
- Decide which tasks are most important. Work on these first.
- Keep to a time schedule. Learn to value time.
- Avoid procrastination. It's a time waster. Make decisions. ACT!
- Don't take on too many tasks in any one day.
- Don't force yourself to go beyond a tolerable work period.
- Work at a steady pace. Avoid stress and strain. Learn to relax.
- When tension creeps up, stop and stretch your limbs.
- Take charge of paper work. A cluttered desk is a sign of inefficiency.
- Work to a system and discipline yourself to adhere to it for maximum benefit.

SUCCESSFUL FORMULAS TO INCREASE YOUR SKILLS AS A SALES MANAGER

There are certain attributes which the sales manager will do well to acquire. In addition to those (qualities) already written about, the following will help to increase your effectiveness as a manager:

SEPARATE THE IMPORTANT FROM THE UNIMPORTANT: distinguish between the important and the unimportant and have the courage to tackle tasks that may be unpleasant. Take on jobs in order of priority and stay with them until they are completed. Do not leave a string of uncompleted letters, phone calls, appointments, meetings, jobs. Self management of your time (energies and abilities) is your key to management success.

ADAPT TO CHANGE: every sales manager must be ready to change attitudes and actions when required. Sales techniques, consumer buying habits, products are susceptible to change. Keep abreast of what's happening in your profession—in life—and adapt to it.

HARNESS YOUR ENERGY AND DIRECT IT IN THE RIGHT PLACE: mis-directed energy causes fatigue, ulcers, heart strain and accomplishes little of tangible value. Channel your energy into completing *one* task at a time. Confusion reigns when you attempt to take on too many assignments.

AVOID COMMUNICATION BREAKDOWNS: while you may have a pretty good idea as to the message you desire to impart to your salesmen, they might not fully understand your intenions. Get your message clear in your own mind before imparting it to others. Make sure they understand it. Question them on it. This will minimize wrong actions being taken.

DEVELOP A STRONG PERSONAL PHILOSOPHY: your beliefs and values are important. Construct a personal philosophy to live by. Adhere to ethical business practices.

BE AN ACTION TAKER: when decisions are to be made, make them. You are in a highly competitive field where fast and accurate decisions *must* be made. Don't keep your salesmen waiting for decisions that should and could be made quickly.

GET FIRM CONTROL OVER YOUR EMOTIONS: Uncontrolled behavior destroys self confidence. Learn to take charge of your thoughts and feelings and refrain from temper tantrums and shouting matches with subordinates. Calm down, relax and take problems as they come without emotionally falling apart. If you can change a situation, change it! If you can't, don't worry unnecessarily about it.

LOOK LIKE A SALES MANAGER: dress the part. Be well groomed at all times. Spend money on quality, well-cut clothes. Look like a successful person.

DEAL WITH STAFF COMPLAINTS AND SQUABBLES QUICKLY: get the facts that caused or led to the squabble or complaint. Don't allow personal clashes (of salesmen or office staff) to upset the team spirit. Be an impartial judge. Do not take sides unless one party is guilty of dishonesty or misconduct. In this instance fire the person concerned.

GIVE PRAISE WHERE PRAISE IS DUE: salesmen love to hear words of praise. Compliment the right action and hard work of those in your team. Salesmen are apt to display loyalty to a boss whom they know appreciates their worth and efforts.

CHECK THE MORALE OF YOUR TEAM: be concerned with the progress of each member of your team. Your success is determined by the results of your sales force. Show that you have confidence in their ability to get the job done and done well. Do not over-supervise them. Teach them to make decisions and to display initiative. Keep a close check on the morale of your team. Are they enjoying their work? Do they respect you as their leader? Are they satisfied with their work and salary conditions? Do they work as a team? Do they approve of company policies?

PROJECT EMPATHY: gain an understanding of people. Be sensitive to the needs of others. Become a *people conscious* sales manager.

KEEP YOUR DOOR OPEN TO STAFF: set aside time each day to discuss problems, reports, etc., with your salesmen. It is preferable to set specific appointments prior to 9 a.m. or after 5 p.m. Keep these meetings short.

DELEGATE AUTHORITY: delegation is more than allotting duties. It is giving authority, responsibility and encouragement to subordinates. Show them that you aren't afraid to let others assume responsibility. Recruit one or two efficient 'back-stops' capable of carrying out your tasks in the event of your illness or when you go on vacation.

MOTIVATE YOUR TEAM TO GREATER PRODUCTIVITY: apply the YOU FACTOR. Fulfill wants and needs and you will have little difficulty motivating your sales team to perform well. Support them in every way. Lead, direct, inspire and motivate a *team* spirit.

BE RELIABLE AND KEEP YOUR WORD: superiors and subordinates alike, must know that they can count on you. Never compromise your ideals. Keep to your word. See projects through to completion.

HANDLE CUSTOMER COMPLAINTS FAIRLY: get the facts and if necessary, visit the customer personally. Do everything in your power to uphold the image of your company. By all means protect company interests but be fair to customers.

KNOW YOUR COMPANY POLICY: a sales manager who does not know his company policy or the image his company wishes to build, is dodging his basic responsibility. Fully understand your company policy. Know its *real* function.

ESTABLISH AN EFFECTIVE ROUTINE: do not mistake excessive paper work for an efficient routine. Spend more time looking after orders than worrying about and looking after systems. They are important, yes, but must not dominate your work day. Develop an organizational chart which pin points lines of authority. If you are away from your office for any length of time it is important to have your understudy promptly process orders.

CHART YOUR CUSTOMERS: the life of an average customer is four to five years. With increasing competition, takeovers, liquidations, staff changes, this 'average' life is getting shorter. Appraise your customer list, discover the near-to-end customers and add at least one new account for every five on your list.

KNOW YOUR PRODUCT: how well do you know the plus and minus factors associated with your product or service? Research each product and become well informed on the items you are selling. What do they do? How do they work? Are they value for money?

KNOW YOUR COMPETITION: you cannot afford *not* to know what your competition is doing and the relative values of the goods or services offered by competitors. How do your sales compare with those of your competitors? Is your share of the market increasing at a faster rate than theirs? Who are their poor accounts—the slow or non-payers? Ask your salesmen to keep you informed (through field reports) on apparent changes and competitor activity. Better still, regularly check territories yourself.

CONSTANTLY IMPROVE YOUR PERFORMANCE: this is essential to long-term success. Monitor your own performance. Is it up to the level you would set for another person in a similar position? Pay careful attention to how you can program your career for future success. Develop your managerial knowledge and skills.

ACTIVITY REPORTS ARE ESSENTIAL: salesmen do not like filling out activity reports. However, they are necessary to a sales manager's success. When hiring salesmen, insist on their filing regular activity reports. They are an important management tool. They should warn of product failures and successes, of customer buying habits and market trends.

KEEP PROPER RECORDS: establish a card system on customers' buying habits, performance of your sales team, potential new business, results of advertising and special promotions. Set up an 'ideas file' and entice your salesmen to contribute to it. Analyze activity reports and type out a single page summation of the week's activities. These are quick reference guides to note sales trends and consumer buying habits.

289

DEVELOP PUBLIC SPEAKING ABILITY: enrol in a public speaking course or join a debating or public speaking group. Develop your ability to express ideas and motivate others to action. Effective oratory skill is a magnificent success tool.

SET OBJECTIVES: plan goals for your department and make sure that each team member knows what is expected of the department. Set short-term objectives (one year), medium term (five years), long term (10 years). Know where you are going and how you will achieve the aims and objectives you set.

HAVE REGULAR MEDICAL CHECK-UPS: many sales managers do not get sufficient sleep, exercise or adhere to a proper diet. There is a certain amount of strain at the top. Therefore, have your doctor check your blood pressure and general state of health every three months. You will work with greater ease if you know that you are in a good state of health.

KEEP YOUR EYE ON THE CONSUMER MARKET: disposable income is rising, education is widening, age distribution is shifting and social moves are broadening. Buying habits and tastes are changing. Study trends and adjust to them. Alfred C. Fuller, the world's first door-to-door salesman, is quoted as saying, 'the door is finally closing on door-to-door selling techniques'. Mr. Fuller started in 1906 in the US as a door-to-door salesman selling brushes. He built-up a $54 million business known as the Fuller Brush Company. Its image spread around the world and Fuller Brush became a household name. But alas, the market is changing. 'There has been a tremendous decline in door-to-door selling because of a great shortage of manpower and today's prosperity,' he says. As one market closes, another opens. The 'alert' sales manager is always seeking new methods and new markets to conquer.

HOW CUSTOMER RELATIONS CONSCIOUS ARE YOU?

Customer relations can make or break a company. Good customer relations can be established by sales staff and the sales manager by showing a genuine interest in the problems of the customer and by handling his objections and complaints quickly and fairly.

Product guarantees and salesmen's promises must be honored if harmony is to reign between company and customer. Regardless of the extra time it might take for a sales manager to personally deal with a customer complaint, it is advisable to do so. The customer will be flattered by the attention he receives.

An excellent example of good will being established is the letter sent to a client of Sun Electric Company. The sales manager, Barry Levy, personally worked on solving a problem until he was satisfied that the situation was satisfactory to the client. With his permission I include a copy of a letter he sent to his customer. It is an example of good letter writing, good follow-through and good customer relations building.

SUN ELECTRIC COMPANY PTY. LTD.

Manufacturers   Electrical Merchants   Importers

Also at
ADELAIDE
SYDNEY
BRISBANE
PERTH

Head Office: 28-56 QUEENSBRIDGE STREET, SOUTH MELBOURNE, 3205

Telephones 62 0691   Telegrams: Norlev   Box No. 181, South Melbourne, 3205

In reply please quote:
BKL:EB

Managing Director,
Briad Productions,
Suite 304, Newstead House,
229 Castlereagh Street,
SYDNEY. N.S.W. 2000

Dear Sir,

As I feel sure you have now learned, we have only just commenced selling Schick electrical products in Australia. It is our earnest desire that we give fast and efficient service at all times so as to promote customer good will.

Having only had the products on the market for the last four weeks we are naturally extremely desirous of detecting any problems so that they may be brought to light during the initial launch period, which will ensure that any small imperfections that may possibly crop up are found and eliminated without delay.

The writer would like to emphasise that Schick products will be serviced with as much enthusiasm as we have for the sale of the product itself, and that you would be helping us considerably if you can arrange to have your 336 Dryer returned "Post Collect" to the above address, and marked for the attention of the writer. We will then have the item inspected, serviced and returned to you the same day, at no charge.

Should the item, in the opinion of our National Service Manager, require replacement, we will not hesitate to provide you with a unit free of cost.

Yours faithfully,

Franks.

B.K. LEVY

BUSINESS LETTER WRITING

There is no such thing as a 'standard' sales letter—or any standard type of letter for that matter. Don't try to write the way you think someone else wants the letter written. Write it in your own style—as you would speak. Your letter writing can become distinctive if you allow your thoughts to follow an orderly sequence. If you write it as you would speak it and allow your personality to show through your writing. Use words your readers will understand. Don't worry too much about writing as text books would have you write. Five letter writing suggestions are:

1. Is grammar correct?
2. Is it reasonably and understandably punctuated?
3. Is spelling correct?
4. Are you conveying exactly what is in your mind?
5. Are words, sentences, easily understood?

These five principles will help you to establish the ground rules of good letter writing. Other suggestions are: write short sentences and to the point; be friendly and convey warmth; be descriptive (paint a picture in the mind of the reader); present ideas one at a time— separate them; eliminate too many bridging words: *and, if, but, also, however,* etc.

PUNCTUATION

When you come to the end of an idea (one complete thought) put down a *period* and begin a new sentence. Use *commas* for clarity in long sentences or to separate a series of words such as: My sales team includes: Australians, Canadians, Americans, Englishmen, Scotsmen, etc. Otherwise the comma can safely be omitted. The use of the *dash* is an effective way of adding an idea or pointing up a statement: Our new pump has done well—so well we are out of stock.

Punctuation devices should be used to clarify the meaning. Don't over-punctuate or be too concerned with exactness of punctuation. Remember, it's *clarity* you strive for, not a literary award.

LETTER WRITING POINTS TO FOLLOW

Do not use a constant flow of superlatives or you'll sow seeds of doubt in the mind of the reader. Eliminate cliches, unproved claims, flippancy, talking down or lengthy phrases. Get to the point early. Pose a question or make a positive statement as an opener. Offer some reward, fulfill a need or solve a problem. Clarity, simplicity, correct spelling and one idea to each paragraph are the rules of good letter writing.

DEVELOP A PERSONAL WRITING STYLE

Every sales manager should develop a personal letter writing style. This can be done by injecting ideas and expressions of speech which are peculiar to the writer. Style takes shape from an individual's attitude of mind. Style cannot be taught; it is the writer's personality, his character and his way of looking at things.

FOR REFERENCE AND ACCURACY IN WRITING

A good dictionary, such as *Webster's New World Dictionary* or *The Concise Oxford Dictionary* are strongly recommended. A *Roget's Thesaurus,* is a valuable aid to letter writing and *The New Dictionary of Thoughts,* a digest of thoughts from the great thinkers, is also worthy of purchase. Fowler's *Modern English Usage,* will prove to be a valuable addition to the sales manager's library. There are many books on letter writing and these can be researched and selected by the individual wishing to improve his writing ability.

LETTER FORMS

A business letter should create a favorable impression in the mind of the reader. The quality of paper, the artistic layout of the letter-head, the framing of the text are important to creating a good first impression.

The Simplified Form (NOMA) devised by the National Office Machines Organization, is a layout which cuts down on wasteful typing movements (constant shifts) and to my mind is the neatest looking of all the various forms of letter-text layout.

All text is typed at the left margin. The salutation and complimentary close are eliminated (considered meaningless) and in the place of the salutation the subject title of the letter is typed in capitals. (This can be modified by including the salutation and the complimentary close as shown in the 'Sample Letter'.)

ELIMINATE THESE BRIDGING CLICHES

- *acknowledge receipt of . . .*
- *anticipating your favor . . .*
- *at the present writing . . .*
- *in answer to same . . .*
- *pleasure of a reply . . .*
- *take the liberty of . . .*
- *your letter at hand . . .*
- *kindly confirm same . . .*
- *duly noted . . .*
- *for your information . . .*
- *in due course . . .*
- *hereby advise . . .*
- *in conclusion . . .*
- *beg to advise . . .*
- *concerning yours of . . .*
- *up to this writing . . .*
- *referring to yours of . . .*
- *pursuant to . . .*
- *due to the fact . . .*
- *hoping to hear . . .*
- *as noted per . . .*
- *I take the liberty of . . .*
- *this writer is of the opinion . . .*

LETTER LAYOUT—MODIFIED NOMA FORM

Mr. J. H. Hanson
General Manager
J. H. Hanson Associated Companies Ltd.
Suite 304 Bart House
231 Castlereagh Street
Sydney, N.S.W. 2000

Dear Mr. Hanson:

I have arranged for your shipment to Toronto to include the necessary spare parts you requested at our last meeting. I'm sure this will help to boost sales of the units for you.

Delivery will be approximately three weeks from the departure date indicated in our contract. I will have our Toronto office notify you immediately the shipment arrives for customs clearance.

As I am anxious to meet our obligations to you, please do not hesitate to contact me should you require further assistance.

Yours truly,

John G. Barry

John G. Barry
DIRECTOR OF MARKET EXPORT.
JGB:aw

THE PURPOSE OF SALES MEETINGS

The sales meeting is an important fact-finding source for the sales manager and an excellent opportunity for sales staff to air grievances, report customer complaints, plan future sales strategy, note sales trends and consumer buying habits, work out details of special promotions, solve territory problems, make suggestions relating to greater work efficiency, present activity reports, analyze new sales techniques and set sales objectives.

A sales meeting must have its own list of objectives. Calling regular meetings without a well-planned agenda, a clear purpose, is a waste of man hours. Many sales meetings I've attended as a spectator have succeeded in doing little more than bore the participants. In many instances, attendance of key sales staff was poor—the very people necessary to a successful meeting.

A well-planned agenda by the sales manager, printed and distributed to each member of his sales team with a polite but firm insistence that *all* members be present, is the first step in preparing a meeting of sales staff. Each salesman should be requested to file a field (activity) report and talk on his activities within his territory. The sales meeting should be planned in the following manner:

1. Prepare an agenda and distribute to all sales personnel.

2. Set a regular time and place for meetings and insist on all salesmen being in attendance. Limit the meetings to one or two hours.

3. Start on time.

4. Finish on time.

5. Chair the meeting with professional decorum. Do not allow it to get out of hand. Remain in firm control. Keep to the agenda.

6. Select a venue free from noise and interruptions. It must be well-lighted and properly ventilated or air conditioned.

7. Take a short break for coffee.

8. Do not allow smoking during the meeting.

9. Seek: information, opinions, solutions to problems. Set sales targets.

10. Inject a short motivation lecture to raise the morale of the group.

BEST TIMES AND VENUES FOR SALES MEETINGS

Hold sales meetings at reasonable times. If weekly meetings are advisable, 7.30 a.m. to 9 a.m. on Monday morning *or* Friday morning are the best times and days to hold them. Monday morning is preferable because everyone is fresh for the new week. Also, it gives the sales manager an opportunity to assess (over the weekend) the activity reports filed on the previous Friday.

Many companies prefer to hold sales meetings monthly and often select a hotel as a meeting place. If country sales staff are out on the road it is not always convenient to call them back each week. Times and places for meetings should be given careful study and once decided upon, remain unchanged.

Location of the meeting can be a problem if suitable facilities are not available within company premises. A quiet location where distractions and interruptions will be at a minimum, is essential. If a hotel or motel is selected, it should be close enough to the company's headquarters so that branch and head office personnel can be at the meeting without spending a great deal of time traveling. Parking is another consideration. The cost of hiring premises is also to be considered.

Natural daylight in the conference room is a decided advantage—particularly if the sessions are longer than an hour. Facilities for serving light refreshments are also advisable. A location can often make or break a sales meeting and for this reason due consideration should be given to its selection.

If possible, the following aids should be used:

1. Large blackboard.
2. Lectern.
3. Comfortable chairs with tablet arms for writing purposes (or conference tables).
4. Suitable writing materials for all present.
5. Projector for movie or slides (if necessary).

GUEST SPEAKERS

Outstanding sales meetings and conferences can be achieved by inviting professional guest speakers in addition to careful preparation of an interest-building agenda.

A variety of technical, general and motivational speakers should be rostered and well publicized to the sales team. A stimulating agenda, with all sales personnel participating, an enthusiastic, well-spoken guest speaker, a clean, light and well-ventilated function room will help to guarantee a successful sales meeting.

INVITING PARTICIPATION

Many people have a natural reluctance to get involved in group discussions. This is often due to lack of confidence, shyness and lack of emotional involvement with the subject under discussion.

Participation of *all* members of the meeting is advisable. This is best achieved by placing each member on the agenda to speak for two minutes on the 'activity' within his territory. The sales manager, as chairman, might consider having each salesman chair the meeting in turn. A question and answer period is another method of encouraging group activity. Without proper participation, sales meetings cannot reach their aims of successful fact-finding and problem solving.

THE THINK TANK

Informal brainstorming or *think tank* groups are a useful technique for solving complex problems. The entire sales team or selected key salesmen, join forces to 'think-out' solutions to problems, produce new ideas or judge new concepts presented by management.

Think tanks are a *team* effort. Each member exploits his own creative ability by projecting ideas which are taken up by the group and explored. No idea is discarded as impractical but analyzed for an opportunity to 'hitch-hike' on to a different approach. Think tank groups are now a formalized business tool and a practical and creative way to solve problems and generate new ideas.

Brainstorming sessions must not be dominated by any one person. No idea should be negated. At the beginning, any idea—regardless of how implausible it might sound—should be recorded and discussed. All comments must be in the affirmative and participants encouraged to stretch their imaginative powers and depart from conventional thinking patterns. The rule to follow at think tank meetings is: *never attempt to judge ideas while they are being generated and discussed.*

KEEP A RECORD OF THINK TANK SESSIONS

Listen and gather beneficial information and ideas which stem from think tank sessions. Be especially observant of facial expressions giving you an insight into participants' attitudes and responses.

Enlist the aid of an efficient shorthand-typist to take down the 'meat' of the session and prepare a precis for later analysis and or record the event on tape.

LIMIT THE SIZE OF THINK TANK GROUPS

The success or failure of a meeting is often the result of the *number* of participants involved. Three to 10 people can accomplish a great deal. Twenty or more, trying for a free-flowing exchange of ideas, are hampered by their numbers. It is difficult to (quickly) establish a suitable rapport among large numbers of people.

ESTABLISH A PRESSURE-FREE ENVIRONMENTAL CLIMATE

It is also important to free the atmosphere from the pressures of rank. Senior management must not stifle the creative mood of the group by its presence. If top-level management desires to participate, it must do so as equal members of the team.

The purpose of a think tank is to get each participant to experience *new* ways of solving problems; to make mental connections they wouldn't otherwise make and to get an insight into the relatedness of apparently unrelated things. When problems are approached from this viewpoint, the creative thinker sees things he wouldn't normally see. Therefore, it is imperative that a pressure-free atmosphere be established.

DEVELOP LATERAL THINKING HABITS

Lateral thinking consists of deliberately escaping repetitive thinking patterns, of rejecting the obvious ways of looking at any problem. *Conventional thinking* (vertical thinking) tends to mentally 'imprison' the person using this approach. (It reinforces previously recognized concepts leading the 'thinker' in circles.)

Conventional thinking excludes the irrelevant and always commences from the obvious and most reasonable approach. It uses logic to move from one point to the next and sometimes uses negatives to block certain pathways.

Lateral thinking, on the other hand, deliberately escapes repetitive thinking patterns and rejects the obvious ways of looking at any problem. Any number of ideas can be thrown into a 'mental pot' and then sorted out until a particular pattern of 'ideas' thinking emerges. Negatives are eliminated. All ideas or paths of action are studied, no matter how impractical they may seem.

Einstein was a lateral thinker. He put together new concepts and used the powers of disciplined imagination to arrive at workable theories. A great deal of an individual's potential is wasted through a failure to use his imagination. The imaginative processes must not be restricted but allowed free reign to create and expand and to take in the larger aspects of things. The imagination is a powerful force; if man can free himself from the barriers that limit human potential, he will leap across present mental and physical hurdles and experience life on a grander scale.

TRAINING IS IMPORTANT TO THE SUCCESS OF A SALES TEAM

Whether an internal staff training scheme is established or an outside group retained, is a matter for management to decide. The important thing is, that *all* companies employing salesmen should have some form of regular training. Basic to success at any level of selling is knowledge. Experience is not always the best teacher. A man can go on making mistakes, year-after-year, without knowing why. Formal course study in all aspects of selling and human relations can give him the *why* before he blunders into a valuable territory and destroys its potential.

It's difficult to understand the reasoning behind some company decisions to allow untrained sales staff to represent them in the field. To spend thousands of dollars in slick advertising campaigns to establish a prestige company and product image and then allow some half-baked, untrained, heavy-handed representative loose to undo the good created by advertising professionals is diabolical.

There are many companies utilizing training schemes that aren't worth the time and money expenditure. Training is an art, a science and a highly professional approach is essential to its success. A personnel manager who has read a few good books on selling, has an impressive scholastic background but never *experienced* a professional sales salesmen encounter, is no man to train salesmen. Yet, many managements have just such men heading their staff training departments. I've spent 15 years in the training, motivational research and metaphysical fields and I've encountered hundreds of ill-informed, incompetent trainers in the sales and human relations training areas. Academic qualifications do not necessarily guarantee good trainers any more than they guarantee good doctors, dentists, lawyers or ministers of religion.

LEAVE TRAINING TO THE PROFESSIONALS

Whatever the decision regarding a training scheme (internal or outside assistance), employ professional trainers to carry it out. Sales training is valueless unless the participants learn, absorb and *use* the knowledge gained—and use it quickly.

Training systems must be updated every year and new techniques incorporated and developed. I've worked with company training officers who taught from textbooks written over 40 years ago. I've monitored recognized training colleges and found some using methods and texts unsuitable to present-day conditions.

The rule, when selecting a training system, is to 'check-it-out' completely until satisfied that the system offered is suitable to your own particular conditions. Employ professional trainers—not amateurs 'filling-in' or individuals with academic qualifications but no actual experience in selling situations. And make sure that your trainers can effectively communicate and motivate. Poor speakers are a bore and do not deserve a place behind a rostrum.

SPECIAL SKILLS DEVELOPMENT

The sales manager, in order to be considered for promotion to a higher position, must develop his own skills through training. Special abilities necessary for success in management include organizational and administrative talents, good communication and motivation skills, the ability to set objectives, delegate authority and control activities. Leadership ability is a prerequisite. Analytical skills resulting in sound judgement are also vital to success in management.

All types of management knowledge can be gained through formal study. Colleges, universities, professional institutes and business organizations offer a variety of courses in management. The time and cost may be an extra burden, but the ambitious sales manager will be rewarded when the opportunity to move-up is presented.

EXPLORE NEW WAYS OF DOING THINGS ADVISES CANADIAN TRAINER

Henry Evering, of Evering Consultants in Toronto, is an exponent of *Biofeedback CreativityTraining* for salesmen and management personnel. 'People must learn to interact, to relate to each other,' he feels. 'A more meaningful relationship can be established between salesman and customer if the salesman learns to relate to his customers needs. Most of our daily encounters are external—fragmented, superficial and therefore frustrating,' Evering says.

He suggests sales managers encourage their salesmen to seek a higher state of consciousness. To learn to control or at least modify their attitudes and actions. 'It is essential to explore new ways of doing things—to reject the "cannot" attitude and supplant it with "I can and will" response,' he says.

FORMER INSURANCE SALESMAN EXPLORES NEW TEACHING METHODS

Frank Ogden, a former top Canadian insurance salesman and property manager, is now teaching art students in Toronto how to 'experience more life' and thus create with greater awareness, perception and sensitivity. He maintains that students of his 24-hour non-stop high-intensity courses are able to cope with most situations they are faced with in life.

The Ontario College of Art, where Ogden teaches first year students his unusual development methods, accepts the fact that a true artist must learn more than just technique. He has to learn the relationship that exists between everything in life. Although Ogden teaches at an art school he is not an artist. He's an ideas man, a person capable of looking at things and seeing *more* than the average person would. He teaches students to really *think, look, listen, touch, taste, smell.* He subjects them to a great many *experiences* so they can begin to see the relationships between things.

'As a salesman I became aware of the vast numbers of people who live within a very narrow cultural environment. This limits the individual tremendously, particularly his creative powers. I teach my students to experience as much as they can, to get excited about the different and endless varieties of life-experiences they can enjoy,' he told me. He calls his sessions 'survival training against future shock.' It's a way of teaching them how to become self-sufficient.

Ogden is Co-Chairman of International Synetics Foundation, Canada's first think-tank group. The organization is devoted to generating creative ideas and solving what some experts might call 'unsolvable' problems facing man.

Ogden feels sales managers should join forces (even from opposing companies) and pool their ideas to find better ways of marketing their products and services. 'Drop the false barriers to expansion and development and commit to a common aim: solving sales problems and bringing about better products at lower consumer prices,' this creative thinker suggests.

USE THE OGDEN FORMULAS FOR GREATER SUCCESS

There are values to be gained from Ogden's teaching methods. Particularly for sales managers conducting sales meetings and seminars. They are:

- Motivate salesmen to *experience more of life*: to become *more aware* of the varieties of life around them.
- Teach salesmen to become *self-sufficient* so they do not have to rely on others.
- *Work toward a common aim.* Employ the minds of friends and competitors in creative think-tank groups.

HOW TO HIRE SALES STAFF AND PROFIT BY IT

Asking the right questions is at the top of the list of suggestions for recruiting good sales personnel—interviewing requires expertise. A sales manager cannot afford to ask the wrong questions. If he does, he's going to wind up hiring the wrong candidates.

A candidate's qualifications must match the job requirements as closely as possible. Always relate questions to the needs of the job and look for behavior patterns in the candidate's answers and manner of answering. Study application form answers, aptitude test results, references and other details of an applicant's file.

The interview should be conducted in a quiet office free from interruptions. Greet the applicant warmly, smile and put him at ease. Describe the position, then mention the qualifications you seek. Invite the applicant to talk about himself. Judge him on:

- Dress and grooming.
- General manner: walk, posture, handshake, eye contact.
- Self confidence.
- Ability to communicate.
- Obvious preparation for the interview.
- Personal application file.
- Speech and vocabulary.
- Personality.
- Valuable qualifications: experience, training, education.

Begin with simple questions regarding the man's age, past experience, education and training. As the interview progresses, questions should become more probing. Take notes and score the applicant according to suitability. Do not eliminate a potentially good man who lacks actual sales experience if he is willing to train to become proficient in selling.

After you have interviewed all candidates, go back over the applications and your notes and narrow the field down to three potential candidates. Call them in for another interview and make your decision as quickly as possible. The longer you leave your decision, the greater the risk of losing the 'best' man to another employer.

Consider the use of a management consultant when sales staff are required. Professional staff consultants can save you a great deal of time and expense, particularly if you are looking for highly qualified people. And a word of warning: always check the credentials of the person you hire. A few discreet calls to past employers will help to verify the information supplied by an applicant.

INTERVIEW QUESTIONS WORTH ASKING

The following questions will help you to judge the suitability of an applicant:

1. Of all jobs held, which did you like least and which the best?
2. What plans have you made for your future?
3. Where do you expect to be in 10 years and what position do you hope to be in?
4. What are your strengths and weaknesses?
5. Why are you interested in working for this company and what do you feel you can accomplish for us if you are selected?

THE REASONS FOR HIGH STAFF TURNOVER

High turnover of sales staff is due to job dissatisfaction. While this is the major reason it is not the only reason. Job turnover is high when salesmen feel that their jobs have low social status, are monotonous or offer poor chances of promotion. Disinterest, difficult-to-sell products or services, continuous customer complaints, poor personal relationships with fellow employees, a feeling of not belonging, lack of confidence in coping with the job, are also reasons for staff leaving.

Money is not always at the root of staff turnover problems. Creative satisfaction, a promise of 'bigger things' in the future, appreciation of services rendered and pleasant working conditions are reasons why salesmen display company loyalty.

HOW TO SPOT TIME WASTERS

Time wasters have distinct characteristics. Some of these are:

- The job changer. He's a window shopper. Has a job but looking for a better one. He's had 6 jobs this year.

- Potential trouble maker. He has a chip on his shoulder and blames others for his mistakes. Seldom has a good word about anyone.

- The grouch. Negative to the core. Every day is a bad day. Always has an excuse why sales figures are down. He's a regular Mr. Doom.

- Big mouth. He'll tell you how to run your business and make no bones about it.

- The flatterer. He'll tell you your company is 'the greatest'. It's pure flattery and insincere flattery at that. Be wary of him. You'll never get a straight answer and he's likely to be a 'yes' man.

- The egomaniac. He's looking for flattery and isn't satisfied until he gets everyone telling him how great he is. He's always talking about himself.

- The name dropper. He knows everyone (of importance) from the President of the United States to the manager of that 'little store down the street.'

- The talker. You can't shut him up. Wind him up and he rattles on until he's out of breath. He never listens and loves the sound of his own voice.

- The story teller. Watch him. He's not to be trusted. He'll tell you what he thinks you *want* to hear. But alas, he lies.

- The dashing hero type. He's second cousin to Errol Flynn. He spends most of his time chatting-up pretty secretaries. He looks good, but you get little activity out of him—at least not the kind you'd like for the good of the company.

- The procrastinator. Don't waste time with this individual. He'll never come to a decision and he's hard to motivate.